THE SCIENCES OF LEARNING AND INSTRUCTIONAL DESIGN

There are two distinct professional communities that share an interest in using innovative approaches and emerging technologies to design and implement effective support for learning. This edited collection addresses the growing divide between the learning sciences community and the instructional design and technology community, bringing leading scholars from both fields together in one volume in an attempt to find productive middle ground. Chapters discuss the implications of not bridging this divide, propose possible resolutions, and go on to lay a foundation for continued discourse in this important area.

Lin Lin is Associate Professor of Learning Technologies at the University of North Texas, USA.

J. Michael Spector is Professor and former Chair of Learning Technologies at the University of North Texas, USA.

THE SCIENCES OF LEARNING AND INSTRUCTIONAL DESIGN

Constructive Articulation Between Communities

Edited by Lin Lin and J. Michael Spector

NEW YORK AND LONDON

First published 2018
by Routledge
711 Third Avenue, New York, NY 10017

and by Routledge
2 Park Square, Milton Park, Abingdon, Oxon, OX14 4RN

Routledge is an imprint of the Taylor & Francis Group, an informa business

© 2018 Taylor & Francis

The right of Lin Lin and J. Michael Spector to be identified as the authors of the editorial material, and of the authors for their individual chapters, has been asserted in accordance with sections 77 and 78 of the Copyright, Designs and Patents Act 1988.

All rights reserved. No part of this book may be reprinted or reproduced or utilized in any form or by any electronic, mechanical, or other means, now known or hereafter invented, including photocopying and recording, or in any information storage or retrieval system, without permission in writing from the publishers.

Trademark notice: Product or corporate names may be trademarks or registered trademarks, and are used only for identification and explanation without intent to infringe.

Library of Congress Cataloging-in-Publication Data
Names: Spector, J. Michael, editor. | Lin, Lin (Professor of learning technologies), editor.
Title: The sciences of learning and instructional design : constructive articulation between communities / edited by J. Michael Spector and Lin Lin.
Description: New York, NY : Routledge, 2017. | Includes bibliographical references.
Identifiers: LCCN 2016057295 (print) | LCCN 2017022002 (ebook) | ISBN 9781315684444 (e-book) | ISBN 9781138924314 (hbk) | ISBN 9781138924321 (pbk) | ISBN 9781315684444 (ebk)
Subjects: LCSH: Instructional systems—Design. | Educational technology. | Computer-assisted instruction. | Communication in education.
Classification: LCC LB1028.38 (ebook) | LCC LB1028.38 .C659 2017 (print) | DDC 371.33—dc23
LC record available at https://lccn.loc.gov/2016057295

ISBN: 978-1-138-92431-4 (hbk)
ISBN: 978-1-138-92432-1 (pbk)
ISBN: 978-1-315-68444-4 (ebk)

Typeset in Bembo
by diacriTech, Chennai

CONTENTS

1 Historical Introduction 1
  J. Michael Spector and Lin Lin

2 The Sciences of Learning 8
  Pablo N. Pirnay-Dummer and Norbert M. Seel

3 Finding a Middle Ground: Wars Never Settle Anything 36
  Paul A. Kirschner and Kristine Lund

4 Comparing the Goals and Methodologies of Learning
  Scientists and Educational Technology Researchers 51
  Thomas C. Reeves and Eunjung Grace Oh

5 Learning Sciences and Instructional Design: Big Challenges
  and Multi-field, Multidisciplinary Solutions 64
  Wellesley R. Foshay and Jeremy Roschelle

6 Implications: Cherishing the Middle Ground 79
  Jan Elen

7 Reconsidering Design and Evaluation 88
  Andrew S. Gibbons and David D. Williams

8 Learning Science Applications for Research in Medicine 108
  Susanne P. Lajoie

9	An Asian Perspective on the Divide *Allan H. K. Yuen*	119
10	The Collaboration Imperative *Ellen B. Meier*	131
11	Synthetic Environments for Skills Training and Practice *Robert Hubal and Thomas Parsons*	152
12	Instructional Design and Learning Design *Nancy Law*	186
13	Learning Analytics Design *Dirk Ifenthaler*	202
14	Continuing the Discourse *Lin Lin and J. Michael Spector*	212

List of Contributors *226*
Index *233*

1
HISTORICAL INTRODUCTION

J. Michael Spector and Lin Lin

Background and Terminology

The motivation for this volume is the existence of two professional communities (the sciences of learning, and instructional design and technology) that are largely aimed at similar goals (e.g., improving learning, making effective use of educational technologies) and that conduct related research. In some parts of the world, there is not a strong distinction between these two communities and academics involved in them commonly exist in the same academic department and often collaborate and conduct collaborative research. In other parts of the world, separate departments exist and scholars who associate with one or the other area only participate in conferences targeted to that professional community and typically only publish in a journal associated with that professional community. Some members of one or the other group tend to ignore and sometimes disparage the research methods and findings of the other group.

Given common goals (improve learning) and limited resources and funding support from local, state, national, and non-profit organizations, it would seem reasonable for the two groups to be more collaborative and engage in more synergistic research and development. Several attempts have occurred in recent years to bring about increased collaboration and articulation among these communities. For example, a book series edited by Spector and Lajoie entitled "Explorations in the Learning Sciences, Instructional Systems, and Performance Technologies" published by Springer attempted to create meaningful dialogue and collaboration among these communities (see www.springer.com/series/8640). While that series generated six high quality volumes and is still open for new submissions, none of the published volumes included the kinds of collaboration that the series editors sought.

As a result, one of those series editors organized a multidisciplinary panel at the annual meeting of the Association for Educational Communications and Technology (AECT) in 2014 that addressed the title of this volume. A recording of that session is available from AECT (see http://aect.site-ym.com/news/news.asp?id=209885&hhSearchTerms=%22recorded+and+sessions%22). That session was designed to have established scholars from both disciplines. Immediately following the session, a senior editor from Routledge approach the session facilitator and asked if an edited volume based on that session could be developed for publication. This volume is a direct result of that 2014 AECT Presidential Panel on this topic.

The thread that runs throughout this volume is that the barriers that apparently separate the two communities are somewhat arbitrary and inhibit constructive articulation and the progressive development of the sciences of learning and instruction. The bridges that can be constructed to promote dialogue and collaboration include (a) interpersonal involvement (as best exemplified by our departed colleague, David H. Jonassen), (b) sharing research tools and instruments (see, for example, http://stelar.edc.org/ and www.teleurope.eu/pg/front page), (c) joint publications (as exemplified by this volume), (d) framing or establishing research projects in a way that requires the participation of both communities, which has also been done by some authors in this volume, and (e) simple recognition that each professional community has much to offer that can serve to improve learning, teaching, and instruction. That is our hope. As a first step, a brief overview of each approach is provided next, followed by a review of the challenges to collaboration which we hope will be addressed by researchers in both communities.

Historical Overview of the Sciences of Learning

The learning sciences (LS) community is relatively young dating back to the early 1990s. LS evolved as cognitive science and technologies such as the Internet, intelligent tutors, and simulations were gaining prominence in the broad area of educational technology. Contributing disciplines to the emergence of LS included cognitive psychology, computer science, educational technology, anthropology, and applied linguistics, resulting in a professional community that is interdisciplinary and interested in designing and implementing innovative technology-facilitated solutions aimed at improving life-long learning and both formal and non-formal instruction.

The academic home for the learning sciences professional community is the International Society of the Learning Sciences (ISLS; see www.isls.org/). ISLS sponsors two journals—the *Journal of the Learning Sciences* (JLS, first published in 1991) and the *International Journal of Computer Support for Collaborative Learning* (ijCSCL, first published in 2006). ISLS also sponsors two conferences—the International Conference of the Learning Sciences (ILS, which was first held in 1992) and the International Conference on Computer Supported Collaborative Learning (CSCL, which was first held in 1995).

The most prominent publication to date is the seven-volume *Encyclopedia of the Sciences of Learning* (Seel, 2012; see www.springer.com/us/book/9781441914279#aboutBook). A second prominent journal is *Instructional Science: An International Journal of the Learning Sciences*, also published by Springer (see http://link.springer.com/journal/11251). It is worth noting that contributors to these two publications also contribute to publications associated with the much older instructional design and technology professional community.

Historical Overview of Instructional Design and Technology

What is currently considered the instructional design and technology (IDT) community can be dated back to the early decades of the 20th century with the interests of prominent behavioral psychologists such as John Watson and Ivan Pavlov in explaining learning and emerging audio and visual technologies. One outcome of that synergy was the formation of the Division of Visual Instruction (DVI) by the National Education Association in 1923. As the IDT community has a much longer history, this section is an attempt to present an overview of that history.

Many date the origins of the instructional design community to World War II when there was a requirement to develop effective and efficient instruction on a large scale (Reiser, 1987, 2001a, 2001b; Spector & Ren, 2015). In the postwar era, DVI became the Department of Audio-Visual Instruction (DAVI) and eventually emerged as an independent professional association called the Association for Educational Communications and Technology (AECT) in 1969.

The postwar period witnessed the first edition of Gagné's (1965) influential *Conditions of Learning and Theory of Instruction*. That volume was strongly influenced by behaviorial learning theory and experimental psychology. By the publication of the fourth edition in 1985, cognitive learning theory was Gagné's dominant perspective informing that and subsequent works. The seminal work by Reigeluth (1983; see www.indiana.edu/~idtheory/green1_toc.html) reviewing instructional design theories and models has a very strong cognitive perspective and includes chapters on technology applications and research approaches as well as collaboration and a perspective that is now regarded as socio-constructivist.

Primary journals associated with instructional design and technology are *Educational Technology Research & Development* (ETR&D; see www.springer.com/education+%26+language/learning+%26+instruction/journal/11423), the *British Journal of Educational Technology* (BJET; see, http://onlinelibrary.wiley.com/journal/10.1111/(ISSN)1467-8535), *Educational Technology* (see www.asianvu.com/bookstoread/etp/), and the *Journal of Research on Technology in Education* (JRTE; see www.iste.org/getinvolved/ed-tech-research). ETR&D dates back to 1953. It is sponsored by the Association for Educational Communications and Technology (AECT; see http://aect.site-ym.com/) and represents the merger of two journals—*Educational Technology Research* and the *Journal of Instructional Development* (archived at AECT.org). BJET is sponsored by the British Educational Research Association (BERA) and dates back to 1970. *Educational Technology* is a magazine published by Educational Technology Publications that dates back to the 1960s and covers both research and practice. The *Journal of Research on Technology in Education* is sponsored by the International Society for Technology in Education (ISTE; see www.iste.org/).

There are many other relevant journals that support both communities. AECT has a tenure and promotion guide (see http://c.ymcdn.com/sites/aect.site-ym.com/resource/collection/AD6CAA0B-8342-40E4-AB23-641A7078802B/The_AECT_Tenure_and_Promotion_Guide-v12.pdf) that contains a list of many journals. Trey Martindale maintains a list of lists for journals in instructional design and technology (see http://treymartindale.com/journals/). Gloria Natividad's (2016) dissertation examined what was being published, where, and by whom in ten top journals in the last 20 years, and that study has been submitted for publication in Springer's Lecture Notes in Educational Technology (see www.springer.com/series/11777).

AECT is the leading professional association for the international instructional design and technology community. Other associations related to this professional community include BERA, ISTE, and SITE (Society of Information Technology and Teacher Education) along with a number of associations around the world affiliated with AECT (see http://aect.site-ym.com/?page=affiliates_left_rai).

Challenges to Collaboration

The previous historical overviews are far from exhaustive and present only a small glimpse of the richness of both communities. A superficial view of that history suggests that many things are held in common—namely, a dedication to the goal of improving learning and instruction, especially through innovative and effective uses of technology, and a deep understanding of the variety of learning environments, situations, tasks, and technologies. Many of the same questions are investigated—for example, which pedagogical approaches, learning activities, instructional designs, and uses of technology work in different contexts and circumstances. Both communities are (a) firmly grounded in cognitive psychology, (b) share a strong interest in socio-constructivist and collaborative approaches, (c) recognize the role of non-cognitive factors, (d) emphasize life-long learning and both formal and informal learning, (e) draw on multiple disciplines, and (f) stress the importance of ongoing professional development, especially for teachers.

The common interest in collaboration is worth highlighting. Within the LS community, when a collaborative approach to learning is studied, the tendency is to emphasize specific aspects and particular examples, as if to say "look at what happens when these learners start to collaborate." Within the IDT community, with regard to the same collaborative approach, there is a tendency to look for a principle that might generalize to other situations, as if to say "here is what we can learn from this situation."

Given that there is so much in common, it seems odd that more cross-fertilization has not occurred between these two communities. There are, of course, differences as well as lingering biases. Learning scientists tend to consider each case investigated as somewhat unique and place particular emphasis on the design of learning activities and generally perceived outcomes. The LS community is actively multidisciplinary and strongly focused on learning and that which enables and facilitates learning in various situations. One result of that orientation is a tendency to resist claims about generalizing findings across multiple contexts or drawing conclusions about principles related to instructional design, which is often perceived as overly formulaic.

The IDT community is also an interdisciplinary enterprise. However, many IDT researchers focus on outcomes and solutions that are scalable, broadly effective, and affordable. While the IDT community does place emphasis on learning outcomes, there is also strong emphasis on instructional design principles and models (for example, see Reigeluth, 1983). Some IDT researchers build on case findings in LS research, use those findings to construct models, and then test those models in controlled studies, which are rarely found in the LS literature.

These and other differences, however, are not good reasons to ignore or denigrate the other community. Both have much to offer to improve learning and instruction, and both could benefit from more collaboration and articulation across the artificial boundaries between the communities. Assuming that to be the case, what then are specific challenges to address and overcome, and what specific steps might be taken to increase collaboration and articulation?

Challenges

One challenge is to have those involved recognize the biases they might have concerning those in the other community. Making biases explicit might be one way to overcome those biases. For example, some are inclined to believe that IDT research is based on a narrow behaviorist view of learning, and that instructional design models are formulaic and inflexible. If such a bias is put forward explicitly, then there are ways to determine if what IDT professionals are doing support such a bias. For example, a dominant theme of the 2016 AECT conference involved creativity, with a number of invited and keynote speakers addressing that theme, including a presentation by Cirque du Soleil on how technology, human performance, and art can be interwoven in creative ways. There was also a keynote address on play and creativity in classrooms and another one on visual understanding. These presentations involved professionals outside the normal IDT community who could have easily presented at an LS conference.

Likewise, some might be inclined to believe that LS researchers are only interested in case studies. However, if one looks at a recent issue of *The Journal of the Learning Sciences*, one will find studies that lead to instructional principles, such as fading concreteness in algebra instruction or using dialogue rather than monologue in video instruction. In other words, LS researchers do have interest in instructional design principles. Keynote speakers at the 2015 International Conference on Computer Supported Collaborative Learning included a computer scientist addressing face-to-face and virtual collaborations, another computer scientist who stressed support for discovery learning, and a third speaker addressing *neuromarketing* and a need to understand how ordinary objects affect our lives. These talks would of course have been of interest to many in the IDT community as well.

Another challenge involves the common language use in these communities. There are many of the same words in use but they tend to have a different meaning. For example, for some in the LS community, "learning" is characterized by engagement and persistent interest on the part of an individual learner or small group of learners. Within the IDT community, "learning" is viewed as a stable and persistent change in what a person or group of people know and can do (Spector, 2015). These views are not incompatible, but they suggest an interest in observing different aspects of a learning experience or environment. Likewise, the word "instruction" has different connotations in the two communities. For some in the LS community, instruction is associated with a highly structured, didactic approach to learning, whereas many in the IDT community view instruction as that which is designed or intended to support learning (Gagné & Merrill, 1990).

With regard to language and bias considered together, one might suggest to LS professionals that "instruction" is not a bad word and to IDT researchers that cases are the building blocks of understanding. Such advice points to potential differences in perspectives—specifically differences in world views and scientific perspectives. As it happens, differences in perspectives, as well as other differences, can be found within each community. However, some in the LS community believe that those in the IDT community tend to believe in objective realities, causal explanations of phenomena, and a positivist approach to science. On the other hand, some in the IDT community are inclined to view many in the LS community as overly focused on subjective interpretations of phenomena and a post-modern, non-determinist understanding of reality. Such overgeneralizations all too easily become exercises in brow and breast beating and do little to push forward our understanding of how to improve learning and instruction—the common goal of nearly all those involved in education.

Next Steps

Some of the differences and barriers to cross-collaboration should be addressed. What can be done to improve collaboration and articulation? Those responsible for organizing conferences can invite representatives of the other community as keynote speakers. Editors responsible for the various journals can elicit invited contributions from those who typically publish in the other community's journals. One such publication in ETR&D is now in process by a distinguished LS researcher.

Beyond those relatively simple steps, graduate curricula in various programs can actively include courses and activities usually associated with the other community. There is a tendency in the opposite direction in the USA, however, so curricula restructuring is not a simple or easy step to take.

Funding agencies could require proposals involving learning and instruction include researchers from both communities. Such a strategy is likely to result in broader dissemination of findings, which is valued highly by funding agencies.

Finally, we can all admit that it would be a remarkable coincidence if the world happened to conform to our imaginations and biases. To adopt a phrase currently in use in American politics, we are stronger together. We hope this volume takes a small step in that direction and perhaps leads to subsequent volumes and joint publications.

References

Gagné, R. M. (1965). *The conditions of learning and theory of instruction* (1st ed.). New York: Holt Rinehart & Winston.

Gagné, R. M. (1985). *The conditions of learning and theory of instruction* (4th ed.). New York: Holt Rinehart & Winston.

Gagné, R. M., & Merrill, M. D. (1990). Integrative goals for instructional design. *Educational Technology Research and Development, 38*(1), 23–30.

Natividad Beltrán del Río, G. (2016). An analysis of educational technology publications: Who, what and where in the last 20 years (Unpublished doctoral dissertation). University of North Texas, Denton, TX.

Reigeluth, C. M. (Ed.) (1983). *Instructional-design theories and models: An overview of their current states*. Hillsdale, NJ: Erlbaum.

Reiser, R. A. (1987). Instructional technology: A history. In R. M. Gagné (Ed.). *Instructional technology: Foundations*. Hillsdale, NJ: Erlbaum.

Reiser, R. A. (2001a). A history of instructional design and technology: Part I: A history of instructional media. *Educational Technology Research & Development, 49*(1), 53–64.

Reiser, R. A. (2001b). A history of instructional design and technology: Part II: A history of instructional design. *Educational Technology Research & Development, 49*(2), 57–67.

Seel, N. M. (Ed.) (2012). *Encyclopedia of the sciences of learning*. New York: Springer.

Spector, J. M. (2015). *Foundations of educational technology: Integrative approaches and integrative perspectives* (2nd ed.). New York: Routledge.

Spector, J. M., & Ren, Y. (2015). History of educational technology. In J. M. Spector (Ed.). *The SAGE encyclopedia of educational technology*. Thousand Oaks, CA: Sage Publications.

2
THE SCIENCES OF LEARNING

Pablo N. Pirnay-Dummer and Norbert M. Seel

Introduction

A long time ago, the German educator Willmann (1889) defined "teaching as the making of learning" and decades later Skinner (1954) distinguished between "the science of learning and the art of teaching." Both authors postulated a close relation between learning and teaching: when you want to teach people you must know how people learn (cf. Bransford et al., 2000). Herbart (1806) already stated that the mere "jog trot" of just case-to-case practicing must be freed from its arbitrariness, and he proposes a link between theory and practice, which he called "tact." *Tact*, in Herbart's sense, means understanding the art of learning and teaching as a particular and unique form of education. However, learning is an extremely broad concept and there are many things to be learned: small children learn to avoid dangerous objects, to use a knife and fork, to dress themselves, to follow certain rules of behavior with adults and peers, to write their name, and so on. Later, children learn reading, writing, mathematics, physics, and chemistry at school; they also learn about history and politics in addition to learning social skills and attitudes. The list of examples could be extended because learning happens all the time and everywhere: at home, on the street, in front of the television, on the farm, at the office, in the lab, on the playground, in the clinic, and, of course, especially at school—guided by instruction!

Clearly, the basic understanding of learning has a practical core because it refers primarily to a constant change in that which one knows or can do on the basis of experiences. This practical understanding of learning as "knowing or being able to do something better than before" also forms the basis of the psychological concept of learning that, however, encompasses a multitude of processes—from changes in behavior and knowledge brought about by everyday experiences up to changes in value positions and ideologies mediated by media. Basically, most psychologists and educators agree on the point that learning has taken place when a certain mode of behavior appears more often than it did before. According to this view, learning changes the probability distribution of behavior. Alternatively and in contrast to behaviorism, Lewin (1942) distinguished between learning as a change of cognitive structures, as a change in motivations, and as a change in social values. Summarizing the various views on learning Roth (1963) distinguished eight variants of human learning:

1. Learning in which the emergence of an *ability* is the main goal as well as the automation of abilities to form motor and mental skills.
2. Learning centered on *problem solving* (thinking, understanding, "insight").
3. Learning which aims at *construction, retention, and remembrance of knowledge*.
4. Learning in which the main goal is to *learn a procedure* (learning to learn, learning to work, learning to do research, learning to look things up, etc.).
5. Learning in which *transferal to other domains* is the main point, i.e., the heightening of abilities and efforts (learning Latin as an aid for learning other Romanic languages).
6. Learning in which the main goal is to *develop one's social positions, value positions, and attitudes*.
7. Learning in which the main goal is to *gain an increasing and heightened interest in a topic* (differentiation of motives and interests).
8. Learning in which the goal is a *change in behavior*.

This distinction is based on the assumption that humans (and other animals) are capable of adapting promptly and sensitively to changes in their physical and social environments: they do this either through *habituation*, i.e., by modifying their patterns of behavior to fit the requirements of their environment, or by means of *learning*. Both kinds of adaptations to the environment result in significant changes of dispositions that go back either to biological maturation or learning. The important point is that the biological maturation can be accelerated significantly through learning, which can be considered as the central means of intelligence. A major characteristic of intelligence is associated with the ability of species to adapt to specific socio-cultural conditions generated by dynamic changes in the environment and to influence these conditions to suit the specific needs of humans (and other animals). According to Rumelhart et al. (1986) three capabilities are essential for intelligent behavior. First, humans are very good at pattern matching. That is, they are obviously able to quickly "settle" on an interpretation of any input pattern. This ability is central to perceiving, remembering, and comprehending. It is probably **the** essential component to most cognitive behavior, which is organized by *schemas*. Secondly, humans are very good at modeling their world. That is, they are good at anticipating the new state of affairs resulting from actions or from an event they might observe. This *ability to build up expectations based on former experiences* is crucial to learning, and it is closely related to the construction and use of mental models. Thirdly, humans are very good at manipulating their environments. This is a version of man-the-tool-user that is perhaps the crucial skill, which allows humans to think logically, to do mathematics and science, and in general, to build a culture. The ability to manipulate the environment results in the creation of artifacts and "artificial realities" (such as the classroom or a museum as particular learning environments).

Based on these capabilities, intelligence is closely connected with the ability to operate successfully with *new* problems. According to Sternberg (1985), this presupposes:

- *Knowledge-acquisition components*, which are tuned to use all available information resources to create new knowledge. Besides the experiences stored in one's memory, a useful resource is the information available in the given environment.
- Specific *thinking abilities*, such as deductive and inductive reasoning as well as productive and critical thinking.
- *Metacomponents*, which are used to plan, evaluate, and control how we think when we solve certain problems. The assumption here is that intelligent actors are conscious of their learning and thought processes and implement them methodically and strategically to master new problems.
- Connected to these "metacognitive" strategies is another component of intelligent behavior which Sternberg refers to as the *use and transfer of what one has learned* and sees as a fundamental criterion of successful learning as well as the precondition for problem solving.

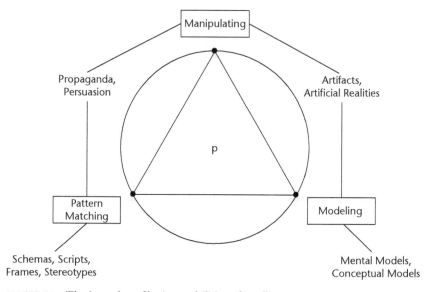

FIGURE 2.1 The interplay of basic capabilities of intelligence

Each of these components can be improved systematically through practice and training. Furthermore, Sternberg argues that there is an unbreakable relationship between learning and thinking. Thinking creates new knowledge on the basis of pre-existing knowledge so that it is not necessary for an individual to fall back on additional information from the environment to learn something (Seel, 2012a). Thinking forms the basis of a kind of learning, which transcends immediate experiences. This point of view has been specified by the German philosopher Heidegger (1968) with the phrase *thinking is learning to think*.

Contemporary research on learning is diverse, but it always has been diverse. Learning is existential, and so its study must be complex and interdisciplinary. Over the past centuries, many theories have been posited in various disciplines to explain how humans and other animals learn. Thus, the following section will sketch out the history of the science(s) of learning.

Historical Review

A genuine interest in learning can be traced back to roots in ancient Greek philosophy where an early epistemological use of the term "learning" can be found in the fragments of the pre-Socratics. For them, learning denotes acts of knowledge that are understood as receptive acknowledgments with a focus on theoretical content, such as the beliefs of mortals. Whereas the pre-Socratic and sophistic tradition defined *learning as the adoption of external knowledge*, Plato developed a theory of learning as *reminiscence* in which learning is conceived as recollection of already completed cognition. This concept of learning is closely related to the acquisition of findings and corresponds to "pure reminiscence." For Aristotle, the other great Greek philosopher, a "prescience" was as a major constituent of learning, too. Interestingly, Aristotle considered *reasoning as part of learning* and argued that the process of learning has to start with the *essence of sensual things* and to progress to more general and abstract concepts. These ideas represented by Plato and Aristotle influenced the philosophical thinking for centuries.

> Above all, the memory of children should be trained and exercised: for this is, as it were, a storehouse of learning; and it is for this reason that the mythologists have made Memory the mother of the Muses, thereby intimating by an allegory that there is nothing in this world like memory for creating and fostering. (Plutarch, *Education of Children*, §13)

More than 2,000 years later, Koffka (1925, p. 115) concluded that "all of our learning is founded on the fact that we have a memory." For Koffka, *learning is not possible without retention*. Actually, the early conceptions of learning of ancient philosophy constitute the archetype of the understanding of learning over more than two thousand years. Plato and Aristotle influenced not only the concepts of learning in the Middle Ages and the Renaissance but until modern times of philosophy. In medieval times St. Augustine referred to Plato as well as Albertus Magnus and other medieval philosophers. However, there was no specific theory of learning before Thomas Aquinas, who discussed the problem of knowledge acquisition by referring to Aristotle, and thus focusing on the interplay between learning and thinking. In the aftermath of medieval scholasticism, the Renaissance marks the transition to modern times. Attracted by the values and rhetorical eloquence of ancient writers, Renaissance humanists, such as Desiderius Erasmus, rejected medieval scholasticism and its concept of learning but continued to refer to either Plato or Aristotle.

Following the Renaissance the period of *Enlightenment* initiated the advancement of learning within the realm of science. Generally, this period can be characterized through the concurrence between *empiricism* and *rationalism*. Advocates of empiricism, such as Hobbes, Locke, Hume, Mill, and Comte denied the existence of concepts prior to experience. For them, all *knowledge is a product of human learning* based on perception. In contrast to empiricism, the *rationalism* represented by Spinoza, Leibniz, and Reid argued that there are innate ideas, which cannot be found in experience. These ideas exist independently of any experience humans ever may have. They may be derived from the structure of the human mind or may exist independently of the mind. Additionally, rationalists focused on the role of emotions and faculties of the mind. It was Kant who worked out a synthesis of empiricism and rationalism, inasmuch as he relied on both sensory experience and innate faculties in areas such as perception, language, intellectual development, and problem solving. Kant argued that people certainly do have knowledge that is prior to experience and is not devoid of cognitive significance.

Parallel to the synthesis of empiricism and rationalism reached by Kant, romanticism and existentialism emerged as important movements in the early 19th century. However, romanticism has its origins in the 18th century because Jean-Jacques Rousseau is widely considered as its originator. What he had to say about learning can be found in his *Emile*, i.e., a comprehensive novel of *natural* and experiential *learning*. In contrast to the romantic view on learning by experience, proponents of existentialism, such as Schopenhauer, Kierkegaard, and Nietzsche, focused on the thinking based on learning: "We can think over only what we know, and so we should learn something; but we know only what we have thought out" (Schopenhauer, 1851, §257). In a similar vein, Nietzsche (e.g., 1888/2001) called for a "learning to think."

Although the 19th century saw numerous paradigms of epistemology concerned with learning, the rise of *experimental psychology* deserves particular attention. Whereas Wundt, who is considered as one of the founders of experimental psychology, did research on nearly every subject of psychology, but not on learning, Ebbinghaus (1885) focused his systematic research on learning and memory. His monograph, *On Memory: An Investigation in Experimental Psychology* (1885), marked a turning point in psychology, being the first time that the processes of learning and memory had been studied *as* they occur rather than after they had occurred (as investigated by means of introspection). In its original form the psychology of learning consisted of experimental memory psychology.

Parallel with the movement of experimental psychology, the *paradigm of functionalism* emerged in the United States of America strongly influenced by William James. He especially focused on instinctive behavior, which he considered as modifiable by learning experiences. According to James, new instinct-like patterns of behavior develop within the lifetime of an organism. James called these learned patterns of behavior *habits*, which result from continuous repetition of a particular activity. Other proponents of American functionalism were Dewey, Cattell, and especially Thorndike, who did pioneering work in research on learning and was one of the first to use nonhuman subjects for experimental research. On the basis of numerous puzzle-box experiments with animals, Thorndike concluded that *learning is incremental* and occurs automatically (i.e., it is not mediated by thinking). Furthermore, he concluded that the same principles of learning apply to all mammals, i.e., humans learn in the same manner as all other mammals, and that there was, therefore, no longer a need for introspection.

Thorndike's seminal work represents the transition from the 19th to the 20th century with newly emerging approaches to research on learning and thinking. Maybe the most influential movement on research on learning was *associative psychology*, which adopted the concept of the *association of ideas* that was first advanced by Aristotle and then raised to the principle of mental life by Hume. At the center of this theory are the so-called *laws of association*, the most well-known of which are the law of resemblance, according to which ideas may be associated with other ideas with similar content, the law of contrast, which states that ideas may be associated with other ideas with contrasting content, the law of spatial and temporal congruity, which states that ideas may be associated with other ideas which originated at the same time or in the same place, and the law of causality, which states that ideas may be associated with other ideas with the same relationship between cause and effect.

However, the associative approach was not only the fundamental basis of Thorndike's associative psychology but was also reflected in Russian reflexology by Bechterev and Pavlov. At the beginning of the 20th century, associative psychology and reflexology gave rise to *connectionism* and the idea of *learning by trial and error*. Connectionism combined the paradigm of association from associative psychology, the idea of reducing behavior to a stimulus-response schema from reflexology, and the methodical principle of limiting its scope to observable behavior and not attempting qualitative interpretations. The method of connectionism is referred to as "instrumental conditioning," to differentiate it from "classical conditioning" and is founded on experiments with animals (cats, dogs, fish, and monkeys). The most important findings of connectionism can be summed up in three laws: the laws of success, willingness, and practice (Hilgard & Bower,

1971). *Learning by trial and error* is based on these laws and occurs when one associates a stimulus situation with a behavioral pattern, which arose by chance in this situation and led to a successful conclusion. It has thus also been referred to as learning from success. Skinner's *model of operant conditioning* constitutes an extension of the stimulus–response (S–R) conception of learning in that it creates a mode of behavior, which is no longer expressed spontaneously but rather affects the environment to bring about consequences (Skinner, 1951). Skinner's theoretical model found a practical pedagogical application in programmed instruction and in behavior modification.

The psychological understanding of learning that was developed within the realm of associative psychology and behaviorism was connected exclusively with changes of observable *behavior*. Learning processes only take place when a specific stimulus situation triggers a correspondingly specific behavioral reaction in the subject that was not observable before. According to this conception, it can only be ascertained whether learning has taken place if there are observable changes in the subject's behavior. The processes that take place within the subject—in a black box so to say—have no place in this theoretical approach because they are not observable.

In a sharp contrast to behaviorism, Gestalt psychology argued that humans do experience the physical and social world in meaningful, intact configurations, which are called *Gestalt* (i.e., "configuration," "form," or "whole"). Usually, the trio of Wertheimer, Koffka, and Köhler is associated with Gestalt psychology. They emphasized a kind of *cognitive trial-and-error learning* and they believed that brain activity tends toward a balance, or equilibrium (in accordance with the *law of Prägnanz*). This tendency toward equilibrium continues naturally, unless it is somehow interrupted, for example, by a problem, which evokes a state of disequilibrium. Because a state of disequilibrium is unnatural, it creates a tension with motivational properties that keeps the organism active until the problem is solved. Based on the conception of cognitive trial and error, Gestalt psychologists developed the theories of *insightful learning* (Köhler, 1969) and *productive thinking* (Wertheimer, 1959). Learning is conceived as a process in which experiences are reorganized and it is not complete until the moment of insight, when the field of experience is visible in its entirety and the solution to the problem becomes apparent.

Gestalt psychology marks not only a turning point in research on human learning but also on animal learning. Many naturalists had studied aspects of animal behavior. The physiologist Pavlov's experiment with a dog can be considered as the beginning of systematic laboratory research on animal learning. This kind of research became the standard in connectionism and behaviorism. For instance, among Thorndike's most famous investigations was his research on how cats learn to escape from puzzle boxes, which led him to formulate the law of effect. Inspired by this research, Skinner used a particular research tool, the so-called Skinner box, in order to investigate operant conditions of rats and pigeons. However, systematic research on animal learning was popular in Gestalt psychology, too, as the example of Köhler's research on the mentality of apes may illustrate. In this experimental field research, Köhler observed the manner in which chimpanzees solve problems by insight. This kind of comparative psychology with regard to animal learning and behavior was to a great extent influenced by the evolutionary theory of Charles Darwin and is still practiced today.

When psychology became a science, it was, first of all, a science of conscious experience; only later did it become a science of behavior. How, then, could a psychology emerge that emphasized the unconscious mind at all? This question concerns the rise of *psychoanalysis*, founded by Sigmund Freud. In Freud's theory of personality there are numerous implications for human learning. Personality contains three major faculties: *id, ego, and superego*. The *id* (German "Es" meaning "the it") is the driving force of the personality. It contains all instincts ("drives" or "forces"), such as hunger, thirst, and sex, all of which are innate. The *id* is completely unconscious and regulated by the *pleasure principle*. That is, when a need arises, the *id* wants immediate gratification of that need. The collective energy associated with the instincts is called *libido* (the Latin word for "lust"), and libidinal energy accounts for most human behavior. The activities in the *id* occur independently of personal experience. Because they provide the foundation for the entire personality, Freud called them *primary processes* and considered them irrational and determined by a person's need states. The *ego* (German "Ich") is aware of the needs of both the *id* and the physical world, and thus is concerned with coordinating these needs. The ego is determined by the *reality principle* because the produced results must fit with the environment. When the ego finds an object in the environment that will satisfy a need, it invests libidinal energy into the thought of that object, thus creating a *cathexis* (from the Greek κατηεξο, which means "to occupy") between the need and the object. The activities of the ego are called *secondary processes*. Finally, the *superego* (from the German "Überich") can be considered the moral part of personality. It has two divisions. The *conscience* consists of the internalized (learned) experiences for which the child has been consistently punished. Any engagement in or even thinking about engaging in such activities makes the child feel guilty. The second division, the *ego ideal*, consists of the internalized (learned) experiences for which the child has been rewarded. It is associated with good feelings. Once the superego is developed, the child's behavior and thoughts are governed by internalized values, usually those of its parents, and the child is said to be socialized. Although not mentioned by Freud explicitly, learning takes place in the development of both the ego and superego. Furthermore, learning plays an important role in psychoanalysis as an educational process in which unconscious conflicts are consciously confronted and mastered. Cognitive learning was important in Freud's work, and insight into one's unconscious processes is vital for regulating one's own behavior. Freud's orthodoxy, which has been widely described in the literature, provoked the development of alternative approaches of psychoanalysis. For example, regarding the field of learning, Jung emphasized two major orientations, or attitudes, that people cultivate when interacting with the external world. One is called introversion, the other extraversion. Both constitute the fundamental basis of the Jungian learning styles.

To complete the picture of learning research in the 20th century, it is important to refer also to the rise of phenomenology and the related field of existential psychology. The leading figure of this school was Martin Heidegger, but generally learning did not play a significant role in the philosophical work of the existentialists.

This also holds true with regard to the emerging developmental psychology in the beginning of the 20th century that is closely related to the names of Jean Piaget and Lev Vygotsky. Piaget was highly interested in psychoanalysis and deeply influenced by Binet. Later, Piaget became one of the most influential developmental psychologists and a representative of *constructivist evolutionism*. Clearly, Piaget was not a learning theorist and he understood learning as a mere secondary process of the development of intellect. According to this view, the possibility, range, and quality of learning are determined by the level of cognitive development a learner has reached. In accordance with the Gestalt principle of equilibration, Piaget argues that cognitive development results from the individual's efforts to attain a state of equilibrium with the demands of the environment (Piaget, 1985). Learning was considered either as acquisition of facts or the result of the interplay between assimilation and accommodation to reach a state of equilibrium. Although Piaget was not a learning theorist he had a strong influence on the emergence of cognitive psychology and its understanding of human learning.

Parallel with Piaget and familiar with his early work, Lev Vygotsky also focused on developmental psychology but with a special emphasis on social processes. Moreover, Vygotsky was influenced by Marxist theory and Pavlov's reflexology as well as Gestalt psychology and social anthropology. Vygotsky discussed the cognitive role of tools of cultural mediation and internalization (sometimes defined as a kind of "knowing how"). As an innovative metaphor for describing the potentials of cognitive development, he introduced the notion of *zone of proximal development* but evidently his most important contribution concerns the relationship between language development and thinking discussed in terms of inner speech (Vygotsky & Kozulin 1997). Vygotsky's work not only focused on the development of mental concepts and cognitive awareness, but also on the development of higher mental functions as well as on the relation between learning and human development, concept formation, play as a psychological phenomenon, the study of learning disabilities, and abnormal human development.

Gestalt psychology and constructivist evolutionism established the fundamental basis for the emergence of *cognitive psychology* that some authors (e.g., Shuell, 1986) date back to the appearance of the book *Cognitive Psychology* by Neisser (1967). However, at about the same time, Aebli, Ausubel, Bruner, and Wittrock introduced their pedagogically influential approaches to cognitive learning. Cognitive theories link learning to all processes involved in taking in information, in its further processing and storage in memory, and in its use in specific problem situations. In contrast to learning theories from behavioral psychology, those from cognitive psychology attempt to explain the processes that take place within learners as they process information. Two important explaining models have been developed for this purpose, each of which operates with a metaphor. The first metaphor to gain acceptance was that of "learning as information processing," which likened human learning to the functioning of a computer (see Lachman et al., 1979). Later, the metaphor of "learning as knowledge construction" gained prevalence and molded the current understanding of learning in cognitive psychology (see Mayer 1996; Seel, 2003a).

No one has yet succeeded in observing whether and how a person learns, but we believe that it is possible to find clues in the behavior or verbal expressions of a person having learned something. We assume for instance that a person has learned something if he or she is able to solve certain types of problems as effectively or even more effectively the second time around, a "problem" being understood in this case as any demand made on the learner by the world of experience. Accordingly, cognitive psychologists apply the term learning not only to refer to the acquisition of knowledge but also to describe every component of information processing—including the gradual increase of certainty in behavior as well as the development of anxiety, interests, and inclinations, the ability to act and solve problems methodically, the acquisition of social and moral competence, the development of habits, and the gradual refinement of motor skills. The various cognitive conceptions of human learning agree on the point that human learning is dependent on the individual cognitive dispositions (e.g., the ability to remember and retain information) of the learners, their state of intellectual development, their motivational and affective dispositions, and the social conditions of the learning situation.

In the 1980s, a new discipline—called *machine learning*—became a promising field of the sciences of learning. However, machine learning is only a particular area of the broader field of *informatics*, which also contains the areas of artificial intelligence, knowledge engineering, robot learning, intelligent tutorial systems, etc. One challenge for machine learning is to determine opportunities for applying theories of information processing and learning in artificial systems to natural systems and vice versa. Although informatics is also concerned with learning in natural systems, its particular emphasis is on *artificial learning*. An artificial system learns whenever it changes its structure, program, or data (based on its input or in response to external information) in such a manner that its expected future performance will improve. Artificial learning usually refers to the changes in artificial systems that perform complex tasks associated with *artificial intelligence* (AI) and its various applications.

From ancient times until today, many theories and approaches to research on learning have been developed—in fact in such a big number that it is not possible here to give justice to them. Therefore, we conclude the historical review with a reference to the *Encyclopedia of the Sciences of Learning* (Seel, 2012b) as the most comprehensive overall view on animal, human, and machine learning.

Contemporary Research on Learning

Contemporary research on learning is diverse, but it always has been. In its long history, there has never been a time when all scientists agreed on a single paradigm. Even at the point of its culmination, behaviorist approaches on learning were contrasted by approaches from the area of Gestalt psychology and social learning theory that focused on cognitive processes involved in learning. This can be demonstrated by referring to Tolman (1932) who was interested in purposive behavior and in consequence used the terms purpose and cognition to explain learning. And even when programmed learning and instruction was mainstream in education there were alternative conceptions that focused on meaningful verbal learning and discovery learning and problem solving. This can be illustrated by referring to Gagné's (1965) seminal work on the conditions of learning that are considered as highly influential in the area of instructional design and technology. Gagné spanned the scope of learning from basic stimulus-response learning up to higher-order learning processes, such as concept learning and problem solving.

The parallelism of paradigms can also be seen in the contemporary research on learning. Although cognitive theories of human learning and artificial learning currently constitute the predominant areas in the science of learning there is a continuation of traditional research on animal learning aimed at the identification of biological constraints of learning (Domjan, 2012). However, as far as learning is connected to teaching and instruction most theorists agree on the point that human learning is determined by cognitive, motivational, affective, and socio-cultural conditions. Cognitive processes—conceived as learning—result in changes in cognitive structures, in motivational states, and in social values and attitudes (Lewin, 1942). Cognitive theories of learning operate on the basis of several characteristics. First, they apply the ability to learn to every component of information processing and define learning as a change in psychological dispositions in relation to (1) information processing in the sense of *constructing knowledge* or developing cognitive skills and abilities, (2) the production of new knowledge by way of inferential thinking, and (3) the application and transfer of knowledge and skills to new situations. Secondly, they attribute *previous knowledge* a decisive role in information processing and the construction of new knowledge. And finally, (3) they assume that learning is closely related to thinking as a process in which individuals operate with symbols that enable them to represent subjective experiences, ideas, thoughts, and feelings. Although several formats have been proposed for these operations, the format most commonly advanced is representation through concepts expressed by means of language. Thus, to a large extent, cognitive theories on learning are concerned with concept learning as a kind of meaningful verbal learning.

A Cognitive Architecture of Learning

Rumelhart et al. (1986) divide the cognitive system into two functional modules. One module—called an *interpretation network*—is concerned with producing appropriate responses to any input from the external world, while the other module is concerned with constructing a *model of the world*. Its main function is to simulate possible changes to the world in dependence on operating on a mental representation of something. There are two basic mechanisms of cognition that support information processing: schemas and mental models. From a psychological point of view, it can be argued that the *interpretation network* operates with *schemas*, which help the learner to assimilate new information into cognitive structures. In accordance with the early conceptions of Selz (1913) and Piaget (1936), schemas can be characterized as slot-filler structures used to organize concepts, relations between them, and operations with them. Schemas are implicit in people's knowledge and are triggered by the events that they have to interpret. They can be understood as recognition devices aimed at the evaluation of their goodness-of-fit to the data being processed. Complementarily, mental models (as models of the world) aim at the interpretation of what will happen when actions are performed. Accordingly, the function of the mental model is to simulate actions in the mind, to assess their consequences, to interpret them, and to use these interpretations for making inferences.

According to Seel (1991), this cognitive architecture corresponds to Piaget's (1970) idea that cognition results from the interaction between assimilation and accommodation in order to adjust the mind to meet the necessities of operating successfully in the physical and social world. Assimilation occurs as an activation of cognitive schemas and serves central cognitive functions, such as integrating new information into cognitive structures, regulating attention, making inferences in the process of acquiring knowledge, and reconstructing it from memory. As soon as learners have consolidated schemas to a sufficient extent as a result of maturation and learning, they provide them with the cognitive framework for "matching" information from the external world with content from memory. Anderson (1984, p. 5) captures the essence of the functions of schemas when he remarks: "Without a schema to which an event can be assimilated, learning is slow and uncertain." Schemas represent the *generic* knowledge a person has acquired in the course of numerous individual experiences with objects, people, situations, and actions. As soon as a schema can be activated, it is automatically "played" and regulates the assimilation of new information in a "top-down" procedure. This allows information to be processed very quickly, a function that is vital for humans as it enables them to adapt to their environment more quickly.

Assimilation is a basic form of cognitive processing, but certainly not the only one. Another basic form consists of *accommodation*, aimed at restructuring knowledge. Accommodation aims, first of all, at a modification of a schema by means of accretion, tuning, or the reorganization of its structure and content (Rumelhart & Norman, 1978). This kind of accommodation presupposes an adjustment of existing schemas to new but familiar input information. However, if this adjustment of a schema is not possible, i.e., if the accretion, tuning, and/or reorganization of a schema fails—or if there is no schema to be activated at all—the learner either can abandon the cognitive processing or invest mental effort to develop a mental model as an elaborated form of accommodation. As central means of accommodation, mental models aim at adjustments of cognitive structures to the environment whenever the subject is not able to activate and modify an appropriate schema (Seel, 1991, 2006). In contrast to schemas, mental models operate from the "bottom up" under the continuous control of consciousness. Mental models may serve as models for reasoning (Johnson-Laird, 1983) or as models for understanding (Mayer, 1989). They are constructed to meet the specific requirements of situations and tasks the subject is faced with for which the activation and/or modification of a schema fails (Seel et al., 2008). In other words, as long as new information can be assimilated promptly into cognitive structures and as long as new information can be in some way embedded into existing schemas and explained by them, there is no need to construct a mental model.

Figure 2.2 shows the theoretical framework that is synthesized from the cognitive activation approach discussed above (Seel et al., 2008) and from the framework of model-centered learning and learning environments (Seel, 2003b, Pirnay-Dummer et al., 2012). A task or problem state presents itself to the learner,

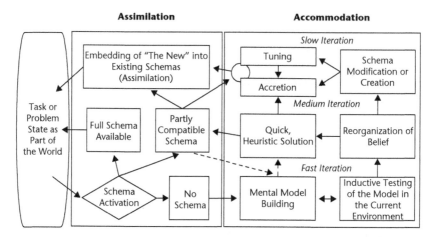

FIGURE 2.2 Schemas and mental models as a means of assimilation and accommodation

and once it is recognized as something worth spending attention and effort on, the learner iteratively interacts with the environment that contains the task or problem until either some solution can be created or the model building process is halted for various possible reasons (e.g., inability to solve the problem, frustration, distraction, any volitional or motivational interruption). If the cognitive system is focused and within its boundaries to solve the problem or task, it will first search automatically whether there are any schemas available to solve it. If there is a full and suitable schema available, the task will be solved and nothing will be learned apart from maybe a good and plausible feeling towards the topic. If schemas are partly available, the system will first try to fill in the blanks (embedding, see Figure 2.2), and then try to accrete and tune them, which is at least in part accommodation. If no schema is available, a cognitive conflict will lead to a mental model building process and thus either to a quick, heuristic solution (Johnson-Laird, 1981, 1983) or to an inductive testing of the model in the current environment (Seel, 2003b; Pirnay-Dummer et al., 2012). If enough time and a scaffold (Azevedo & Hadwin, 2005; Vye et al., 1998; Wood, 1976) are available, a reorganization of belief can either improve the heuristic or even lead to the creation of a schema from the mental model or to a deep schema modification. The latter would also involve a dismantling of existing parts and a complete change in the corresponding belief (knowledge) within the schema. Slower iteration (see Figure 2.2) may be expected to lead to more accommodation resistance. Accommodation resistance is the tendency of a system to reject new knowledge or information if it opposes the current world view. The different levels do not depend only on the learners' traits and information processing capabilities and their dedication but in large parts also on the adequacy of the learning environment and the levels of interaction and involvement it allows for a specific group of learners. Feedback, scaffolds, attention, verbalization, de-contextualization opportunities, and different surfaces and formats—in short, all kinds of other supports—must be addressed to allow a working interaction between the learner and the learning environment (Pirnay-Dummer et al., 2012).

In accordance with this theoretical conception we distinguish between two basic forms of cognitive learning: schema-based learning and model-based learning.

Schema-Based Learning

Schema-based learning builds on the schema theory (Eckblad, 1981). According to this theory, schemas regulate the assimilation of information to be processed into pre-existing knowledge structures. However, it is not enough to have a collection of schemas to be activated but rather an individual must also know how to apply them. Bransford (1984) points out that while it is possible to activate existing schemas with a given topic, this does *not* necessarily mean that a learner can apply this activated knowledge to develop new knowledge and skills.

In consequence, Bransford stresses the importance of helping learners to "activate various pre-existing 'packets' of knowledge" and to "reassemble and construct this knowledge into an integrated new schema" (Bransford 1984, p. 264).

A couple of years before, Pascual-Leone and Goodman (1979) distinguished several operators that are involved in the construction of new knowledge based on the activation and application of schemas. Gestalt *field forces*, such as field dependence, that drive the individual to perceive and represent environmental stimuli as integral wholes compete with "silent operators" to determine which of the many available schemas will be activated to regulate the processing of new information. During the course of information processing, the activated schemas are enriched or restructured by internal operators. Pascual-Leone and Goodman distinguish between L-operators representing former learning experiences, A-operators representing emotional and affective side effects of information processing, and B-operators that represent stable personality traits. Finally, they add an M-operator, a moderator for using information processing capacity gained during biological development. This comprehensive approach to schema-based learning can be applied to the gradual development of contents and structures of declarative and procedural knowledge as well as to emotional and social learning.

Schema-based learning is not limited to the development of knowledge, because assimilation resistance is connected also with emotional effects that drive the process of equilibration (see, for more details: Eckblad, 1981; Kuhl, 1983). Whenever assimilation in a schema fails, this schema enters a state of disequilibrium, which in turn evokes emotional arousal. The term "motive" can be used to denote the presence of disequilibrium—whenever an attempt at assimilation fails and corrective attempts are not immediately successful, a motive for creating equilibrium will be originated (Berlyne, 1971). Consequently, psychological theories on emotion operate to a large extent with the concept of *emotional schemas*. Especially in the area of clinical psychology, the roles of maladaptive schemas are considered as decisive for the emergence of phobias and anxiety disorders (Beck, Emery & Greenberg, 1985).

Since Bartlett (1932) applied an early version of schema theory on language processing it has become evident that social attitudes have strong influences on the reproduction of knowledge. Bartlett's pioneering work in schema theory aimed at exploring cultural differences in the interpretation of stories shows that schemas incorporate evaluative beliefs. As a central component of attitudes, evaluative beliefs provide the information "needed to assess the (inter)subjective position of social members" towards social behaviors (van Dijk, 1987, p. 187). Evaluative beliefs make up attitudes, which are associated with emotive aspects. According to van Dijk, attitudes containing "general, context-free information" are organized in schematic clusters of the memory. Attitudes can be understood as social categories that organize the perception of persons and formation of impressions. In his research on *communicating racism* van Dijk has used the term "prejudice schemas" to represent tools of prejudice in discourse and talk.

This term corresponds to some extent with Allport's (1954) idea of social stereotyping, which is category based. According to Fiske et al. (1987), social categorization presumably invokes schemas from memory, and when categorizing people, these schemas often are stereotypes (i.e., a set of rigid beliefs about a social group and its members). An alternative approach considers *cultural schemas* as constituents for social interactions between individuals in a cultural environment (Nishida, 1999). In accordance with Bartlett, cultural schemas can be defined as structures of the mind that extend into the social and cultural world; they "explain the constitutive role of culturally organized experience in individual sense making" (McVee, Dunsmore, & Gavelek, 2005, p. 535).

In general, schema theory has been applied to a wide range of cognitive processes involved in learning: from knowledge acquisition and application up to learning-dependent development of social values and attitudes—but not in the field of educational/instructional psychology where the focus has been on assimilative processes within the realm of concept learning and mastery of cognitive learning tasks. This can be demonstrated by referring to Ausubel's theory of meaningful verbal learning and the approach of cognitive load.

Ausubel's theory of meaningful learning (1968) is meant to help students activate their pre-existing knowledge so that new verbal information can be assimilated, tuned, and restructured into new schemas. Hence, Ausubel introduced the theory of "advance organizers" to support the learner's pre-existing knowledge. Advance organizers can help learners to activate schemas more effectively and allow them to use their pre-existing knowledge in a more effective manner. However, Bransford (1984) argues that advance organizers should be written differently depending on whether they are to be used for schema activation or schema construction. He states that an advance organizer can be effective if the learner has already acquired the necessary schemas for the given problem. However, it will not be of much help for schema construction. Similarly, *cognitive load theory* assumes that learning consists primarily of the activation and application of schemas to master cognitive tasks. Sweller (1988) understands schemas as cognitive structures that compose an individual's knowledge and can be activated to solve learning tasks. The cognitive load approach is grounded on the assumption of a limited processing capacity of the working memory as introduced by Miller (1956). Accordingly, the central argument of cognitive load theory is that an overload can result if learning tasks are too complex. Cognitive load may be affected by the mental effort necessary to process new information (intrinsic cognitive load), the manner in which the material to be learned is presented (extraneous cognitive load), or the effort needed for activating schemas (germane cognitive load). Earlier, Berlyne (1971) had already introduced the idea of information overload and suggested that the more elements a pattern contained, the more complex that pattern would be. The cognitive load approach deals with complexity using a single construct: element interactivity. If many elements interact, element interactivity is high; if few interact, element interactivity is low.

To bypass the limitations of working memory, cognitive load theory stresses the activation of cognitive schemas that may encapsulate numerous elements of information in a single chunk. The activation of schemas allows automatic processing and thus minimizes the load of working memory. This is how performance can progress from slow and difficult (novice-like) to smooth, fast, and effortless automation (expert-like). If no schema is available, instructional techniques, such as worked-out examples, are needed that take the optimal level of cognitive load into account and do not interfere with schema acquisition, which is a slow process (Sweller, 1988). As Ausubel's advance organizers worked-out, examples aim at clarifying, step by step, the procedures required to solve cognitive tasks (Sweller, 1988). Studying worked examples may impose a low level of cognitive load but it does not contribute to higher levels of cognitive learning, such as problem solving (Seel, 2008).

From our point of view, the idea that the activation of a cognitive schema contributes essentially to problem solving indicates a substantial misunderstanding of the characteristics of problem solving. In cognitive psychology, a problem is characterized by three components: (1) a given initial state s_α, (2) a desired final state s_ω, and (3) a barrier between s_α and s_ω. A problem occurs if a person does not know how to proceed from s_α to s_ω. In other words, if a person knows the necessary steps to achieve the desired final state then there is no problem, but rather a task to be accomplished. More specifically, if a person can activate a schema for mastering a given task then this task clearly does not constitute a problem to be solved. It may be easy and successful to provide a learner a worked-out example or an advance organizer, but this would be counterproductive when learners should learn how to solve problems by themselves. According to Bruner (1966), problem solving by means of productive (or creative) thinking requires discovery learning as an active process, in which learners construct new ideas or concepts based on their existing knowledge. That means the learner does not apply an existing schema but actively selects and transforms information, constructs hypotheses, and makes decisions based on cognitive structures that may be organized as schemas. Bruner asserts that the cognitive structure supports the learner, actively generates meaning for real-world experiences, and allows the individual to process information in a meaningful way. Bruner's argumentation corresponds to a large extent with the idea of model-based learning and cognitive performance.

Model-Based Learning

The idea of model-based learning and performance has a long past, but short history. Schichl (2004) and Johnson-Laird (2004) have traced the roots of mental modeling back to the cultures of the Ancient Near East (Babylon, Egypt) and Ancient Greek philosophy. These authors delineate two major lines of argumentation. Schichl focuses on the use of mathematical models to represent the real world through mathematical objects (or a formalized mathematical language), whereas Johnson-Laird emphasizes the concept of *internal models* as a particular format of mental representation. A couple of decades before, information science considered learning as a complex procedure of information processing initiated by the "reaction" of a learning system on the basis of the information exchange and communication with the environment (which can be "natural" or designed). Pioneers of information science, such as Chapanis (1961), Steinbuch (1961), and Weltner (1970), defined the totality of learning processes as the construction of internal models of the environment.

In the 1980s, the theory of mental models struck a chord and became one of the most prosperous fields of research in cognitive science. Due to the particular emphasis on language and reasoning in Johnson-Laird's (1983) seminal textbook, the theory of mental models and related research focused on text and discourse processing (Rickheit & Habel, 1999) and deductive reasoning (Evans & Over, 1996) for over two decades. Furthermore, the theory of mental models became prominent in the areas of human–computer interaction, system dynamics and simulation, spatial cognition, developmental and cultural psychology, and educational psychology. Reconsidering the research on mental models, we can distinguish several core areas, such as understanding and explaining complex phenomena by means of models, deductive and inductive reasoning, decision making, and the use of models for creative inventions. Whereas in cognitive science the focus has been on the role of mental models in reasoning, in educational psychology *models for understanding* have attracted researchers.

Models for understanding that are necessary for problem solving have their starting point in the tentative integration of relevant simple structures or even single bits of domain-specific knowledge into the coherent design of a "working" model in order to meet the requirements of the problem to be solved. Johnson-Laird (1983) considers this process of a stepwise enrichment of a model with more and more information units as a process of "fleshing out." Models for understanding *represent the structure of world knowledge* because they are generated to structure it and not to reproduce or copy a given external structure. Nevertheless, models for understanding can be externalized by means of particular symbol systems (e.g., mind tools) and generate subjective plausibility with regard to complex phenomena to be understood and explained. It is noteworthy that models for understanding are cognitive artifacts which correspond only more or less to the external world, since people can also construct pure thought models which bear no direct correspondence to the external world, but rather only to world knowledge. This corresponds to the idea of *coherence epistemology* (Seel, 1991) as described in detail by Al-Diban (2002, 2012). In general, models for understanding share the following characteristics: (1) they are incomplete and constantly evolving; (2) they are usually not an accurate representation of a phenomenon but typically may contain errors and contradictions; (3) they are parsimonious and provide simplified explanations of complex phenomena; and (4) they often contain measures of uncertainty about their validity that allow them to be used even if incorrect (see, for more details, Pirnay-Dummer et al., 2012). Within the realm of problem solving, a mental model simulates specific transformations of a problem representation as a kind of *thought experiment* to produce qualitative inferences with respect to the problem to be solved. According to Johnson-Laird (1983):

> mental models play a central and unifying role in representing objects, states of affairs, sequences of events, the way the world is. ... They enable individuals to make inferences and predictions, to understand phenomena, to decide what action to take and to control its execution, and, above all, to experience events by proxy. (Johnson-Laird, 1983, p. 397)

In consequence, mental models are indispensible with regard to problem solving in general and to creative invention in particular. It is generally assumed that creative problem solvers, such as inventors or catastrophe managers, use mental models as sets of heuristics to develop their ideas and inventions. Accordingly, a mental model can also be defined as the ideas and concepts an inventor has about an invention. Mental models are dynamic prototypes an inventor can run in the mind's eye. Their decisive advantage is that they allow an inventor to radically reconstruct previous knowledge about various domains to help solve a complex problem. In other words, mental models for invention often are based on analogies between different domains. This can be illustrated with the example of inventing the telephone. Its inventor, Alexander Bell, had an expertise in human anatomy that he used in developing a mental model of the telephone (Gorman & Carlson, 1990). Innovation and creative inventions are inherently very complex phenomena and subject to manifold cognitive and social requirements. As the evidence grows for the close link between invention and mental models (and its basic functions), there is no doubting the need for theoretical and practical advances in the understanding of how mental models work at creative problem solving (Seel, 2013).

Instruction for model-based learning has a strong focus on the environment that initially fosters a productive kind of misunderstanding, an irritation that will lead to an internal, cognitive acceptance by the learner to change his or her belief to the point of giving up something that had value to him or her until now. It is the learning environment—and more specifically the instructional process—that needs to address this aspect carefully, as opposed to a naively constructed environment that would just state "Sorry, you're wrong!" or induce a series of experiences of failure. On the contrary, any induced failure of cognitive concept by the learner must feel like an immediate success to the learner. Otherwise the change and thus the learning will not be sustainable. Working with curiosity (Loewenstein, 1994) and even awe toward the wonders and complexities of the world—ontological experiences (Fink, 1977)—is an important part of successful model-based learning environments. Seven core instructional principles are also important for the design of such environments.

Because of the nature of irritation and initial misunderstanding, it is quite easy for the learners to get lost in model-based learning environments. Thus, it is even more important to have a very proper basis for the topic. The two core principles for addressing this problem are analytic and epistemic access. *Analytic access* (1) requires a stable, proper, and well laid-out expertise to base the environment on. *Epistemic access* (2) requires a deep understanding of the kinds of beliefs the learners have, including but not limited to significant aspects of their prior knowledge. Only with analytic access will designers and teachers be able to expect at least some of the effects that will be induced in the learners by the learning environment. Another principle is cognitive *conflict and puzzlement* (3), the key factor for inducing model building in the first place. An environment must convey tasks or problems that are truly suitable for inducing the conflict within the learner. Otherwise no mental models can be constructed. Since what allows for inductive construction and testing is a sequence of single experiences, the change is prone to all kinds of overgeneralization. This happens, for instance, when the learner regards circumstantial information within the environment as important and factors it into his or her understanding of the situation. It is thus important to provide a *diversity of surfaces* (4). Over time, the learners will be able to distinguish between the key concepts and the circumstantial ones. For the same reason and to support transfer, the instruction must include *de-contextualization* (5), where the important practical and narrative context of a task or problem is carefully faded to allow a more general transfer. If schemas are constructed over time and stabilized by the learners, they will be more likely to have properties that can be transferred to other kinds of tasks and problems. Equally important is the explorative nature of model-based learning environments. To construct models, one needs to follow a diverse set of possible paths. After all, the models cannot be constructed outside of the learner. Thus, model-based instruction will need to provide a *multiplicity of goals and performance evaluations* (6). Allowing and encouraging more goals over single-goal environments will support the intermediate and slow iteration processes (see Figure 2.2) and slow down quick and heuristic solutions. If the evaluation of the learning process does not only depend on a single output variable, but, is, at best, even compensatory, richly evaluated, then it will encourage individual involvement and create a pull towards more diverse problem solving—one of the strengths of model-based instruction. For example, a student would be encouraged not only to change his or her model of anatomic models for successful plastic surgery—where every case can be completely different—but also to decide where to operate on the basis of the models and at the same time become able to offer more options to patients after an accident. Thus, in model-based instruction it is even more important to have *diagnostic access to the learning process* (7)—because the outcome does not describe important parts of the quality of the learning. If there were only information on the outcome, teachers, designers, and all the decision makers for the learning environment would not be able to reconstruct where in the learning process a misconception was built. Knowledge of as many aspects of the learning process itself as possible facilitates both the evaluation and, even more importantly, the important feedback.

Learning and Language

Regardless of whether learning theories are founded on behavioral, gestalt, or cognitive psychology, they all regard learning, thinking, and motivation as theoretical constructs that need to be made accessible through appropriate methods of observation and experimentation. No one has yet succeeded in observing whether and how a person learns, but we believe that it is possible to find clues in the behavior or verbal expressions of persons that they have learned something. In the end, even the smallest learning experiences are—no matter how they were conceived—encoded in language. Of course, we can have a concept of a chair without knowing the word "chair." And most of the time we do have a concept before the word. Although spoken language uses words and syntax, concepts still need some sort of internal language, thus linking meaning to objects and then meaning of objects to words or signs (Vygotsky, 1987). Teaching by using language is at first nothing more than throwing words at the learners. However, a meaning must pre-exist within the learner and it cannot be a definition. A definition does not contain meaning per se but references meaning to other meaning. It can only be a reminder of concepts that are already there but cannot really help to create new concepts. Receiving a word within a specific pragmatic set (a speech act, see Austin, 1962; Searle, 1969; Searle & Grewendorf 2002) is a schema activation and model construction in itself: even a simple sentence like "Peter, please do the dishes" will need a schema of what this means in general and of the fact that Peter has to get up and use water and the dishwasher to clean the dishes. But is also has a model component: Peter has to know which dishes to clean and the sentence means something completely different depending on whether Peter's dad says it at home, or whether it is said at a friend's house or at a hotel. Depending on the place, Peter also needs to know or guess where to put away the dishes afterwards and maybe specifics for each context on how the dishes are expected to be cleaned. The sentence does not mean anything without a reference to a schema (even if the words are known) and it cannot have a meaning within a certain situation if a model is not constructed around it. A schema for a concept will only be created if the person constructing it encounters a problem (Aebli, 1981). Moreover, there will be no two persons who inherit the same meaning or concept—maybe the same object, but this is also rare. Thus, any reflective part of learning—and these are the ones that are needed for every transfer and generalization of fact—needs to use language, at least internally. It is thus not surprising that language has so many meta-functions in learning and instruction, among the most common of which are write to learn, read to learn, write to teach, read to teach, speak to teach, listen to learn, listen to teach, and many more. In every situation where we cannot relive all experiences necessary for understanding, knowing, or being able, specific uses of language rearrange the world within in our knowledge. But this also means, there always has to be a concept first. Very few people went through the process of inventing the steam machine, but significantly more know its basic functions, and even more know its purpose. Hence, language is not only an internal part of knowledge but also a medium, a part of the object world, which learners rearrange to build their understanding on. But nevertheless, language is never a simple medium where one transmits and another receives: within the object world there are only words (signs), and they don't mean anything without the concepts, which again are always individually constructed. When we use language to teach, we do not connect to the same concepts. This is particularly important when the expertise is different, which is again the main reason to teach in the first place. In learning, the use of language is special: it systematically connects different epistemes between those who learn and those who teach—which of course is not necessarily static and includes peer tutoring, for example. But this is also one of the reasons why peer tutoring usually has higher levels of plausibility for the learners: the epistemes of peers might be more alike (as they are still non-experts), and their patience to acquire a more diverse view of the matter may still be higher, but they will at the same time also need more guidance for the interaction (King, 1990; Roscoe & Chi 2007).

Figure 2.3 summarizes the different uses of language in the learning processes. First, there is no learning and instruction without the use of some kind of language. A communication of some kind needs to be established, and this communication must at least allow those engaged in it to refer to objects and to connect objects

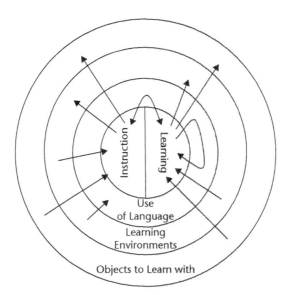

FIGURE 2.3 Basic model of the use of language and learning

to objects (proposition)—this can essentially also be pointing. If there is cognitive change, there is a use of language. And even in the case of reflection within the individual learner, things and kinds of things (Bach, 1989; Montague, 1974) will be referenced to each other as entities that are not the objects themselves. The learning environments—if at all successful—will establish concepts (Aebli, 1981) within the learners and help or guide them to bind them to each other in numerous ways. And if further objects in the learning environment are used for a change in the individual cognition, then they too must be encoded in concepts and references with words and referenced to each other in easy and complex relations to each other. Not only are the associations and relations properties of the objects that translate into relations between concepts, but the associations can also be loose, flexible enough to allow things and kinds of things to be placed in a functional or probabilistic relation with each other. For example, a throne will be expected at a castle. But a throne says something beyond the properties of the room, the function of the room, or the kind of chair if a story puts it into the mayor's office. Of course, we would need a concept of a throne first to understand why a satirist puts it into the mayor's office. Satire works like this, and it illustrates wonderfully how it is also very well possible through cognitive means to *learn* something from satire. Of course, the model would be completely different if we were to put the throne into the repository of a theater, a place where we expect a throne for an entirely different reason. The example is of course a bit oversimplified. But it works at an even more complex level when teachers and their students handle concepts as references to objects and their relations by words and syntax. From the very basic reflection process to the understanding and classification of objects, language is an integral part of all cognitive learning processes within which teachers and students try to navigate the existing meaning of things and kinds of things towards the goal of a meaningful change in someone else's imagination, thought, belief, and knowledge. What they utilize to steer these complex waters is their own understanding and their own concepts—and be it a concept they believe the other person to have. What they effect however, is changes in the other person's concepts, and this is not independent of what that person expects and thinks of the particular learning situation. This is already complex with two persons in the room, even if those two persons have a common use of concepts—see any marriage counselor for plenty of examples. But within the epistemic differences, with the particular and fast goals of cognitive understanding in learning environments, or with a whole group of individual students and not just one, the interaction becomes even more complex. Without informed meta-cognition, the use of language for instruction is almost impossible (Winter, 1992). The more complex the model building and schematization processes within the learners need to be, the more carefully language needs to be implemented, for example for feedback, for discourse, for asking questions, for moderation, for evaluation, and very importantly also for grading.

Conclusion

The more we know about learning and teaching, the easier learning should get. But this depends on how well teaching—instruction in general—is carried out. While teaching initially gets more complex the more we know, contemporary efforts in research on learning and instruction have also embarked on the quest to make teaching simpler—despite the complexity of the multitude of interactions and situations that learning and instruction evoke. Of course, from a professional standpoint, teachers will always have to grasp a significant part of the complexity of their field. Many decisions are dependent on a real-time modeling of the situation in which learning takes place. Thus, individual learners have numerous factors that are important for their learning, such as parts of their personality traits and their current states as well as contextual factors. And as if that were not enough to interact with, learners usually come in groups, which makes teaching all the more complex. And teachers obviously come with a whole set of important internal and external factors too, which means that there are many different ways to teach successfully (or unsuccessfully). The success of teaching thus does not depend solely on the outlook of a particular method but also on an interaction between the person and the method. And this in turn always calls for a complex expertise to accompany the teaching. Naïve teaching has too many blind spots. It may still look successful—especially with "you-cannot-reach-everybody" beliefs, but it may even do harm or at least discriminate against those who happen not to fit the methods although they have the potential. It should go without saying that both learning and teaching will always make use of technology that helps to reduce the complexity of the process. However, technologies always need to adapt to the core process of learning and teaching, and rarely will it work out if it is done the other way around. But technologies can only adapt to this process if their creators have an in-depth understanding of the processes of learning and instruction. In sum, no one who works in teaching or instructional technology can afford to not have in-depth knowledge on learning and teaching: how they take place, how they are influenced, on what they depend, how goals are reached, and how change takes place within and between the individuals who are learning and teaching. These questions have been, are, and will continue to be answered by the interdisciplinary sciences of learning.

References

Aebli, H. (1981). *Denken: Das Ordnen des Tuns. Denkprozesse.* (Vol. 2) [Thinking: The order of doing]. Stuttgart: Klett-Cotta.

Al-Diban, S. (2002). *Diagnose mentaler Modelle* [Assessment of mental models]. Hamburg: Kovac.

Al-Diban, S. (2012). Mental models. In N. M. Seel (Ed.), *Encyclopedia of the sciences of learning* (Vol. 5, pp. 2200–2204). New York: Springer.

Allport, G.W. (1954). *The nature of prejudice*. Reading, MA: Addison-Wesley.
Anderson, R. C. (1984). Some reflections on the acquisition of knowledge. *Educational Researcher, 13*(9), 5–10.
Austin, J. L. (1962). *How to do things with words*. Oxford: Clarendon Press
Ausubel, D. P. (1968). *Educational psychology. A cognitive view*. New York: Holt, Rinehart, Winston.
Azevedo, R., & Hadwin, A. F. (2005). Scaffolding self-regulated learning and metacognition – Implications for the design of computer-based scaffolds. *Instructional Science, 33*(5–6), 367–379. doi: 10.1007/s11251-005-1272-9
Bach, E. (1989). *Informal lectures on formal semantics*. New York: State University of New York Press.
Bartlett, F. C. (1932). *Remembering: A study in experimental and social psychology*. Cambridge: Cambridge University Press.
Beck, A. T., Emery, G., & Greenberg, R. L. (1985). *Anxiety disorders and phobias: A cognitive perspective*. New York: Basic Books.
Berlyne, D. E. (1971). *Aesthetics and psychobiology*. New York: Appleton.
Bransford, J. D. (1984). Schema activation versus schema acquisition. In J. O. Anderson & R. Tierney (Eds.), *Learning to read in American schools: Basal readers and content text* (pp. 259–272). Hillsdale, NJ: Lawrence Erlbaum Associates.
Bransford, J. D., Brown, A. L., & Cocking, R. R. (Eds.) (2000). *How people learn: Brain, mind, experience, and school*. Washington, DC: National Academy of Sciences.
Bruner, J. S. (1966). *Toward a theory of instruction*. Cambridge, MA: Harvard University Press.
Chapanis, A. (1961). Men, machines, and models. *American Psychologist, 16*, 113–131.
Domjan, M. (2012). Biological or evolutionary constraints on learning. In N. M. Seel (Ed.). *Encyclopedia of the sciences of learning* (Vol. 1, pp. 461–463). New York: Springer.
Eckblad, G. (1981). *Scheme theory. A conceptual framework for cognitive-motivational processes*. London: Academic Press.
Ebbinghaus, H. (1885). *Über das Gedächtnis: Untersuchungen zur experimentellen Psychologie* [About memory: Studies from experimental psychology]. Darmstadt.
Evans, J. S. B. T., & Over, D. E. (1996). *Rationality and reasoning*. Hove, East Sussex, UK: Psychology Press.
Fink, E. (1977). *Sein und Mensch. Vom Wesen der ontologischen Erfahrung*. Freiburg: Alber.
Fiske, S. T., Neuberg, S. L., Beatty, A. E., & Milberg, S. J. (1987). Category-based and attribute-based reactions to others: Some informational conditions of stereotyping and individuating processes. *Journal of Experimental Social Psychology, 23*, 399–427.
Gagné, R. M. (1965). *The conditions of learning*. New York: Holt, Rinehart and Winston.
Gorman, M. E., & Carlson, W. B. (1990). Interpreting invention as a cognitive process: The case of Alexander Graham Bell, Thomas Edison, and the telephone. *Science, Technology, and Human Values, 14*, 131–164.
Heidegger, M. (1968). *What is called thinking?* New York: Harper & Row.
Herbart, J. F. (1806). *Allgemeine Pädagogik aus dem Zweck der Erziehung abgeleitet* [Common paedagogy derived from the purpose of education]. Göttingen: Röwer.
Hilgard, E. R., & Bower, G. H. (1971). *Theorien des Lernens* (2nd ed.). Stuttgart: Klett.
Johnson-Laird, P. N. (1981). Mental models in cognitive science. In D. A. Norman (Ed.), *Perspectives on cognitive science* (pp. 147–191). Hillsdale, NJ: Erlbaum.
Johnson-Laird, P. N. (1983). *Mental models: Toward a cognitive science of language, inference and language*. Cambridge: Cambridge University Press.

Johnson-Laird, P. N. (2004). The history of mental models. In K. Manktelow & M. C. Chung (Eds.), *Psychology of reasoning: Theoretical and historical perspectives* (pp. 179–212). New York: Psychology Press.

King, A. (1990). Enhancing peer interaction and learning in the classroom through reciprocal questioning. *American Educational Research Journal, 27*(4), 664–687.

Koffka, K. (1925). *The growth of the mind: an introduction to child-psychology*. New York: Harcourt Brace.

Köhler, W. (1969). *The task of Gestalt psychology*. Princeton, NJ: Princeton University Press

Kuhl, J. (1983). Emotion, Kognition und Motivation. I: Auf dem Wege zu einer systemtheoretischen Betrachtung der Emotionsgenese. *Sprache & Kognition, 2*, 1–27.

Lachman, R., Lachman, J. L., & Butterfield, E. C. (1979). *Cognitive psychology and information processing: An introduction*. Hillsdale, NJ: Erlbaum.

Lewin, K. (1942). Field theory and learning. In D. Cartwright (Ed.), *Field theory and social science. Selected theoretical papers by Kurt Lewin* (pp. 60–86). New York: Harper & Row.

Loewenstein, G. (1994). The psychology of curiosity – a review and reinterpretation. *Psychological Bulletin, 116*(1), 75–98.

Mayer, R. E. (1989). Models for understanding. *Review of Educational Research, 59* (1), 43–64.

Mayer, R. E. (1996). Learners as information processors: Legacies and limitations of educational psychology's second metaphor. *Educational Psychologist, 31*, 151–161.

McVee, M. B., Dunsmore, K., & Gavelek, J. R. (2005). Schema theory revisited. *Review of Educational Research, 75*(4), 531–566.

Miller, G. A. (1956). The magical number seven, plus or minus two: Some limits on our capacity for processing information. *Psychological Review, 63*, 81–97.

Montague, R. (1974). *Formal philosophy: Selected papers of Richard Montague*. New Haven: Yale University Press.

Neisser, U. (1967). *Cognitive psychology*. New York: Meredith.

Nietzsche, F. (1888/2001). *The gay science*. New York: Cambridge University Press.

Nishida, H. (1999). Cultural schema theory: In W.B. Gudykunst (Ed.), *Theorizing about intercultural communication* (pp. 401–418). Thousand Oaks, CA: Sage.

Pascual-Leone, J., & Goodman, D. (1979). Intelligence and experience: A neo-Piagetian approach. *Instructional Science, 8*, 301–367.

Piaget, J. (1936). *La naissance de l'intelligence chez l'enfant*. Neuchâtel: Delachaux et Niestlé.

Piaget, J. (1970). *L'épistémologie génétique*. Paris: PUF

Piaget, J. (1985). *The equilibration of cognitive structures: The central problem of intellectual development*. Chicago: University of Chicago Press.

Pirnay-Dummer, P., Ifenthaler, D., & Seel, N. M. (2012). Designing model-based learning environments to support mental models for learning. In D. H. Jonassen & S. M. Land (Eds.), *Theoretical foundations of learning environments* (pp. 55–90). New York: Routledge.

Plutarch (110 CE/1927). *Moralia, Volume 1*. Loeb Classical Library 197 (translated by F.C. Babbitt). Cambridge, MA: Harvard University Press

Rickheit, G., & Habel, C. (1999). *Mental models in discourse processing and reasoning*. Amsterdam: North-Holland.

Roscoe, R. D., & Chi, M. T. H. (2007). Understanding tutor learning: Knowledge-building and knowledge-telling in peer tutors' explanations and questions. *Review of Educational Research, 77*(4), 534–574.

Roth, H. (1963). *Pädagogische Psychologie des Lehrens und Lernens* (7th ed.) [Educational psychology of learning and instruction]. Hannover: Schroedel.

Rumelhart, D. & Norman, D. (1978). Accretion, tuning and restructuring: Three modes of learning. In. J. W. Cotton & R. Klatzky (Eds.), *Semantic Factors in Cognition* (pp. 37–53). Hillsdale, NJ: Erlbaum.

Rumelhart, D. E., Smolenksy, P., McClelland, J. L., & Hinton, G. E. (1986). Schemata and sequential thought processes in PDP models. In D. E. Rumelhart, J. L. McClelland & T.P.R. Group (Eds.), *Parallel distributed processing. Explorations in the microstructure of cognition.* (Vol. 2: Psychological and biological models, pp. 7–57). Cambridge, MA: MIT Press.

Schichl, H. (2004). Models and history of modeling. In J. Kallhrath (Ed.), *Modeling languages in mathematical optimization* (pp. 25–36). Dordrecht, NL: Kluwer Academic Publishers.

Schopenhauer, A. (1851). *Parerga und Paralipomena II*. Berlin: A. W. Hayn. [Translated from German by E. F. J. Payne, Oxford: Clarendon Press, 1974].

Searle, J. (1969). *Speech acts. An essay in the philosophy of language*. Cambridge: Cambridge University Press.

Searle, J., & Grewendorf, G. (2002). *Speech acts, mind, and social reality*. Dordrecht: Kluwer Academic Publishers.

Seel, N. M. (1991) *Weltwissen und mentale Modelle*. Göttingen: Hogrefe.

Seel, N. M. (2003a). *Psychologie des Lernens. Lehrbuch für Pädagogen und Psychologen* [Psychology of learning. A textbook for paedagogues and psychologists] (2nd ed.). München/Basel: Reinhardt.

Seel, N. M. (2003b). Model centered learning and instruction. *Technology, Instruction, Cognition and Learning, 1*(1), 59–85.

Seel, N. M. (2006). Mental models in learning situations. In C. Held, M. Knauff & G. Vosgerau (Eds.), *Mental Models & the Mind* (pp. 77–101). Amsterdam: Elsevier.

Seel, N. M. (2008). Empirical perspectives on memory and motivation. In J. M. Spector, M. P. Driscoll, M. D. Merill & J. van Merrienboer (Eds.), *Handbook of Research on Educational Communications and Technology* (3rd ed., pp. 39–54). Mahwah, NJ: Erlbaum.

Seel, N. M. (2012a). Learning and thinking. In N. M. Seel (Ed.), *Encylopedia of the sciences of learning* (Vol. 4, pp. 1797–1799). New York: Springer.

Seel, N. M. (Ed.) (2012b). *Encyclopedia of the sciences of learning* (7 volumes). New York: Springer.

Seel, N. M. (2013). Mental models and creative invention. In E. G. Carayannis et al. (Eds.), *Encyclopedia on creativity, invention, innovation, and entrepreneurship* (Vol. 3, pp. 1244–1251). New York: Springer.

Seel, N. M., Ifenthaler, D., & Pirnay-Dummer, P. N. (2008). Mental models and problem solving: Technological solutions for measurement and assessment of the development of expertise. In P. Blumschein, W. Hung & D. Jonassen & J. Strobel (Eds.), *Model-based approaches to learning: Using systems models and simulations to improve understanding and problem solving in complex domains* (pp. 17–40). Rotterdam, The Netherlands: Sense Publ.

Selz, O. (1913). *Über die Gesetze des geordneten Denkverlaufs. Eine experimentelle Untersuchung. Erster Teil*. Stuttgart: W. Spemann.

Shuell, T. J. (1986). Cognitive conceptions of learning. *Review of Educational Research, 56*, 411–436.

Skinner, C. E. (1951). *Educational psychology* (3rd ed.). New York: Prentice Hall.

Skinner, B. F. (1954). The science of learning and the art of teaching. *The Harvard Educational Review, 24*(2), 86–97.

Steinbuch, K. (1961). *Automat und Mensch. Über menschliche und maschinelle Intelligenz*. Heidelberg: Springer.

Sternberg, R. J. (1985). *Beyond IQ: A triarchic theory of human intelligence*. New York: Cambridge University Press.

Sweller, J. (1988). Cognitive load during problem solving: Effects on learning. *Cognitive Science, 12,* 257–285.

Tolman, E. C. (1932). *Purposive behavior in animals and men*. New York: The Century Co.

van Dijk, T. A. (1987). *Communicating racism. Ethnic prejudice in thought and talk*. Newbury Park, CA: Sage.

Vye, N., Schwartz, D., Bransford, J., Barron, B., Zech, L., & CTGV. (1998). SMART environments that support monitoring, reflection, and revision. In D. Hacker, J. Dunlosky & A. C. Graesser (Eds.), *Metacognition in Educational Theory and Practice* (pp. 305–346). Mahwah, NJ: Erlbaum.

Vygotsky, L. S. (1987). Thinking and speech (N. Minick, Trans.). (Orig. 1934) In R. W. Rieber & A.S. Carton (Eds.), *The collected works of L. S. Vygotsky. Volume 1: Problems of general psychology* (pp. 37–285). New York: Plenum Press.

Vygotsky, L. S., & Kozulin, A. (1997). *Thought and language* (10th ed.). Cambridge, MA: MIT Press.

Weltner, K. (1970). *Informationstheorie und Erziehungswissenschaft*. Quickborn: Schnelle.

Wertheimer, M. (1959). *Productive thinking*. New York: Harper & Row.

Willmann O. (1889) *Didaktik als Bildungslehre nach ihren Beziehungen zur Socialforschung und zur Geschichte der Bildung* [Didactics as educational teachings after its relation to social research and the history of education], Vol 2. Braunschweig: Vieweg,

Winter, A. (1992). *Metakognition beim Textproduzieren*. Tübingen: Gunter Narr.

Wood, D., Bruner, J., & Ross, G. (1976). The role of tutoring in problem solving. *Journal of Child Psychology and Psychiatry and Allied Disciplines, 17,* 89–100.

3

FINDING A MIDDLE GROUND

Wars Never Settle Anything

Paul A. Kirschner and Kristine Lund

> War is what happens when language fails.
> Margaret Atwood

Swords into Ploughshares

Researchers and other academics working in the educational and the learning sciences seem to be perpetually caught up in paradigm wars. Recently one of the authors wrote an editorial for the *Journal of Computer Assisted Learning* (Kirschner, 2014) on how paradigms mutate into *paradogmas*. It was triggered by an email from an American PhD student whose manuscript was rejected by a well-known and respected journal as being out of its scope because it dared take a direct instruction stance on learning in STEM (Science, Technology, Engineering, Mathematics)! Though it is our hope and assumption that this is an outlier, we see the fights that lie at the basis of such behavior almost daily. Constructivists are at war with instructivists and/or cognitivists (depending on whether you are talking about an educational/learning approach or the paradigm on which it depends), proponents of traditional mathematics at all educational levels are at war with the proselytizers for real or reform mathematics as both a philosophy and a curriculum approach (actually known as the "math wars"; see http://en.wikipedia.org/wiki/Math_wars), phonics advocates are at war with the whole language advocates about how best to teach/learn reading, and so forth. These wars have an adverse effect on the sciences themselves, on education in general, and on the use of technologies to foster effective, efficient, and enjoyable education and learning.

This is strange since, for example, the natural sciences seem to have fewer problems in this respect. In physics, for example, quantum theory lives in harmony with classical Newtonian physics (the former for atomic and sub-atomic particles, the latter for the macro world) and it is accepted by all physicists that light can act as/be both a wave and a particle. The fact of the matter is that the world is not so simple that "one paradigm fits all." Maybe the time has come to take a hint from the hard sciences, beat our pens (or word processors) into ploughshares, and attempt to look at education and learning as a whole: from the neuronal and synaptic level to the governmental policy level. We need to look at learning, teaching, and education (and the sciences that try to describe and even predict them) as ecological systems wherein certain paradigms work at different levels for different things.

Behaviorism

In the first half of the 20th century, the basic paradigm guiding learning and instruction was behaviorism. Behaviorism was proposed by John Watson (1913) as an alternative to the then prevailing view of psychology where phenomena of consciousness were the focus. Instead of using methods such as introspection to study the relation between complex mental processes and their constituents, Watson suggested turning psychology into a "purely objective experimental branch of natural science" (op. cit., p. 158) where "[I]ts theoretical goal was the prediction and control of behavior" (op. cit., p. 158). He thus eliminated the obligation of evaluating the observation of behavior upon the extent to which it succeeds in yielding results that are interpretable only in the realm of human consciousness. Indeed, Watson argued that if states of consciousness were eliminated as objects of investigation from psychology, then no barriers would exist anymore between psychology and the other sciences: "[T]he findings of psychology become the functional correlates of structure and lend themselves to explanation in physico-chemical terms" (Watson, 1913, p. 177).

Based upon this new behaviorist paradigm, design models emphasized the success of the instructor/teacher instead of the learner, in that given a certain stimuli, a particular response can be predicted. B. F. Skinner (1935) took this a step further and tried to explain almost every type of human behavior in terms of stimulus-response chains. The learner was passive, yet responsive; (s)he was acted upon, rewarded (i.e., positively reinforced), or punished (i.e., negatively reinforced), and thus acquired what was meant to be acquired.

Cognitivism

Cognitive psychology's reaction to the inability of behaviorism to account for much human activity (e.g., the acquisition and development of a natural language) arose mainly from a concern that the link between a stimulus and a response was not straightforward; that there were mechanisms that intervened to reduce the predictability of a response to a given stimulus; and that stimulus-response accounts of complex behavior, such as the acquisition and use of language, were extremely complex and contrived (Winn & Snyder, 1996).

In 1960, the Center for Cognitive Studies was founded by Jerome Bruner and George Miller (Chamak, 1999; Gardner, 1985). The use of the term "cognitive" was a break from the then-dominant school of behaviorism, which considered cognition not fit for scientific study. Miller considered knowledge to be the manipulation of symbols and thus found the computer to be a good model for the human mind. In this paradigm, cognitivists reinstated the study of mental states—relegated to a *black box* by the behaviorists—and sought to construct formal models of cognitive processes that were going on in the learner's head. The learner was no longer seen as someone who was acted upon; rather the learner played an active role in the acquisition of knowledge. Instrumental here was Robert Gagné (1985), who in the fourth edition of his landmark book *The Conditions of Learning* described learning as a change in the cognitive structures in the mind of the learner. In his earlier work (even the first three editions of the book) Gagné was more of a behaviorist. Influenced by the information-processing view of learning and memory he then moved towards a synthesis of the two schools of research on learning, identifying internal (e.g., prior knowledge of the learner) and external (e.g., stimuli presented to the learner) conditions of learning. These changes may be supposed by a change in behavior, or by a more direct measure of cognition such as learner-created representations of concepts and their mutual relations. The learner, thus, became an information processor, taking in information from her/his environment and processing it in the brain, thereby changing her/his schemata. In this case, instruction assumes that a subject matter domain can be described in terms of both learning goals and changes of schemata. In addition, the optimal conditions for learning depend on the goal of the learning process and the abstract computer-based model that described how the change in schemata could come about.

Constructivism: Cognitive and Social

Constructivism (also known by some as cognitive constructivism) is a theory of cognitive development and a philosophy of learning founded on the idea that the learner constructs knowledge in action, based on his/her pre-existing mental structures and mental activity (e.g., Piaget & Inhelder, 1991). According to Spiro, Feltovich, Jacobson, and Coulson (1995), the view of Piagetian constructivism that had dominated cognitive and educational psychology since the early 1970s was that when a learner was confronted with information to be understood or a problem to be solved, (s)he would retrieve organized packets of knowledge or *schemas* from memory (e.g., prior knowledge) that the learner would then actively combine with the presented information in order to construct meaning (i.e., *assimilation*, integrating new information into existing schemas). In this view, it is thought that better learning will not arise from better teaching, but rather from giving the learner better opportunities to construct knowledge.

Although Piaget did not focus on how social interaction was supposed to work and concentrated rather on the logical structures by means of which the developing child organizes the world (s)he experiences, he still wrote that the most important occasions for *accommodation* (i.e., adaptation of a schema based upon new information that does not really fit into existing schemas) arose in social interaction (von Glasersfeld, 1988). That said, the father of social constructivism is Lev Vygotsky (1978); it was founded on his approach to cultural development in the early part of the 20th century:

> Any function in the child's cultural development appears twice, or on two planes. First it appears on the social plane, and then on the psychological plane. First it appears between people as an interpsychological category, and then within the child as an intrapsychological category. ... [I]t goes without saying that internalization transforms the process itself and changes its structure and functions. Social relations or relations amongst people genetically underlie all higher functions and their relationships. (Vygotsky, 1981, p. 143)

In this view, learning was not simply individuals assimilating new knowledge into existing knowledge or accommodating their schemata based upon conflicting knowledge, but it was also about the individual becoming part of a community. The cognitive focus of learning as an intra-individual cognitive process shifted towards viewing learning as a predominantly social process whereby knowledge doesn't exist, but is collectively constructed as a shared interpretation of the world around us (Linden et al., 2001). Indeed, Vygotsky rejected Piaget's attempt to use individualistic and biological reductionism to explain the genesis and the functioning of the human mind, preferring to argue that psychological development originates in a specific set of social interactions (Ageyev, 2003). From this point of view, an educational learning situation is seen as a community of learners where learners learn to take part in interactions in sub-communities of co-learners, practitioners, and professionals (Kirschner et al., 2004; Prudhomme et al., 2007; Scardamalia et al., 1994). Discussion, argumentation, and presentation are important processes here, as are planning, organizing, and carrying out communal activities. Sharing knowledge and information and negotiating meaning and position are the constructive activities that determine learning as a social process.

Social constructivism, as it has evolved, emphasizes the importance of culture and context (e.g., historical, social, vocational) in understanding what occurs in society and work and in constructing knowledge and developing competent professional behavior based on this understanding (Derry, 1999). It contends that categories of knowledge and reality are actively created by social relationships and interactions. These interactions also alter the way that scientific categories are created and scientific objects are perceived.

Other -isms

Examples of other -isms in the fields of education and learning are connectionism (Hebb, 1949), connectivism (Siemens, 2005), constructionism (Papert, 1990), pragmatism (Dewey, 1938), essentialism (Bagley, 1938), naturalism (Comenius, 1623), idealism (Kerns, 2009) and more. Adherence to any one of these -isms creates what philosophers call "false dichotomies" (also called false dilemmas). Such false dichotomies occur when an argument presents two—often oppositional—options and ignores, either purposefully or out of ignorance, other alternatives and gives the impression that the options are mutually exclusive (i.e., if you're not with us, you're against us) and that one of them is true. Spector wrote (2006, p. 1) that "these dichotomies are not really genuine in the sense of describing exclusive but all-inclusive categories of things and situations in the world, reminiscent of Peter Goodyear's (2000) description of false dichotomies in his article *Environments for Lifelong Learning: Ergonomics, Architecture and Educational Design*" (see Table 3.1 from Spector & Wang, 2002).

Many Roads Lead to Rome

What does all of this mean? Simply stated, the key point is that there is neither one single way nor one best way to design optimal learning experiences for any one learner nor all learners. For example, automatizing (e.g., learning addition tables) can best be achieved through drill-and-practice, a pure behaviorist approach even when it is masked in a so-called game. Constructing cognitive schemas via induction and elaboration as well as schema automation via knowledge compilation and strengthening are best achieved (i.e., effectively and efficiently) through a cognitivist approach to learning. Arriving at a shared

TABLE 3.1 False Dichotomies (see Goodyear, 2000)

Knowledge	*Versus*	*Skill*
Knowing That		Knowing How
Understanding		Doing
Academic Knowledge		Practical Knowledge
Declarative Knowledge		Procedural Knowledge
Explicit (articulate) Knowledge		Tacit Knowledge
Discursive Consciousness		Practical Consciousness
Theory	**Versus**	**Practice**

understanding of a task, problem, or field requires a constructivist approach where learners with different skills and backgrounds should collaborate on carrying out tasks and solving problems, while arguing and discussing together. Educators, instructional designers, and researchers can best make use of a well thought out combination of these approaches to create effective, efficient, and enjoyable learning experiences.

The Ecology of Education

Education and educational processes are determined by the interactions that take place between learners (i.e., their own individual cognitions, motivation, and regulation plus the social interactions between individuals), educators (i.e., teachers, tutors, and mentors and their personal professional theories, methods, and development), technologies and media (i.e., the tools that support and enable both learners and educators to optimally learn and instruct), and the environment (i.e., the external conditions and constraints that need to be taken into account). We can call this the ecology of education.

Learners

The word "learner" allows non-differentiation between learner age (i.e., child, adolescent, young adult, adult, senior), level (i.e., preschool, elementary, secondary, tertiary, post-tertiary, lifelong), or type (i.e., formal, non-formal, or informal (Van Merriënboer et al., 2009). As all learners enter into a learning situation with prior experiences, biases, habits, and beliefs, the following elements are taken into account: learner knowledge and skills, learner attitudes and dispositions (e.g., motivation, determination), learner meta-cognitive knowledge and skills (e.g., self-regulation), and the biological/environmental factors that can affect the learner and learning.

Educators

Numerous studies have demonstrated that the quality of the education depends greatly on the quality of the teacher (Hattie, 2003, 2008; McKinsey & Company, 2007). Teachers are vital not only to the quality of education; they are also responsible for the success or failure of educational innovation in the classroom. In the (near) future a development is foreseen in which this vital role of teacher transforms into a role of arranger/orchestrator. Teachers become more and more the ones who arrange or orchestrate the learning experience. With the emergence of seamless education it is likely that other players will be more directly employed in the learning experience, for instance coaches, parents, subject matter specialists, and so forth.

Technology and Media

In recent years learning environments have been used in multiple facets and increasingly stand for a blend of digital tools, virtual environments, and physical spaces. Recent research stresses linking the design of physical spaces, the special affordances of specific environments and objects in a physical environment, and the services and digital information to be used for learning and problem solving within these environments. Research is also stressing the seamless and ambient integration of technologies in physical environments in the sense of Weiser's notion of ubiquitous computing (Weiser, 1991).

Environment

The aforementioned elements do not interact in a vacuum. Each, separately or jointly, is influenced by entities outside of their span of control which, in turn, interact with each other. Examples are governments and policy makers at all levels (i.e., international, national, regional, local), political parties, commercial companies who both supply the three elements and hire their graduates, controlling organs such as inspectorates of education, teacher unions and student groups, the economy, etc.

As in all ecologies, education is a system and is systemic. As a *system*, it is a complex whole made up of many elements that work together as parts of an interconnecting network. Though bounded and separate from its environment, the educational system composed of educators, learners, and technologies/media is surrounded and influenced by that environment (e.g., all levels of government policy, politics, companies, controlling organs, teacher and student unions, the economy…). This environment is dynamic and in continual change, affecting the educational system's structure, purpose, and functioning.

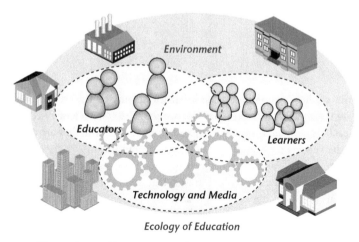

FIGURE 3.1 The ecology of learning and education

As *systemic*, any change or changes made in any part of the educational system will affect not only that part, but also all the rest of the system. According to Capra (1982):

> [T]he activity of systems involves a process known as transaction—the simultaneous and mutually interdependent interaction between multiple components. ... Systemic properties are destroyed when a system is dissected, either physically or theoretically, into isolated elements. Although we can discern individual parts in any system, the nature of the whole is always different from the mere sum of its parts. (p. 267)

As such, while in the course of studying parts of this ecosystem, the other parts need to be considered and studied. For example, we should not simply implement the results of a study on the relationship between effective collaboration and the complexity of the task or problem without also studying and then implementing changes in the actions of the instructor with respect to what the task complexity is and how complex tasks for collaborative learning should be designed and developed. And here we need to take into account both the characteristics of the technology and media for carrying out the task (e.g., does the physical or electronic environment allow for the necessary collaboration?) as well as the school's requirements for grading (e.g., does it allow the transformation of a group grade to individual grades?). As Greeno (1998) stated:

> Without analyzing the larger systems thoroughly, we risk arriving at conclusions that depend on specific features of activities that occur in the special circumstances that we arrange, and that these specific features will prevent generalization to the domains of activity that we hope to understand. (p. 7)

The goal of this ecosystem is the achievement of seamless learning (Looi et al., 2010), which can be defined as learning which "bridges private and public learning spaces where learning happens as both individual and collective efforts and across different contexts (such as in-school versus after-school, formal versus informal)" (p. 156).

How Can This Goal Be Achieved?

Those doing research should integrate the different perspectives in carrying out theoretically sound scientific research of complex, practice-relevant issues in the ecology of education. This research should deliver ecologically valid and high-quality results through an integrated approach to issues that draw upon theories of learning and cognition, technology, new media, and educators' practices and behavior (i.e., pedagogy, pedagogical content knowledge, technological pedagogical content knowledge). The research should improve the quality of

Describe, Explain, and Predict or Shed Light Upon

Carrying out theoretically sound research depends on the definition given to "theory." If theory is a general proposition or logically connected system of general propositions which establish a relationship between two or more variables (Abend, 2008), then a phenomenon P of interest is the value of a variable y which may be described in relation to other variables as a function $y = F(x_1, x_2,...x_n)$. In this case, good research in the educational sciences and/or the learning sciences should describe, explain, and predict.

First, it should *describe* phenomena that can and do affect learning and teaching. These phenomena run the gamut from cognitive psychological and biological/neuronal influences on learning (e.g., executive functioning, cognitive load, motivation and/or determination, personality and lifestyle factors, disabilities) through material influences on the learner, teacher, and environment (e.g., influence of the situation and its achievement via mobile devices) up to and including social and ecological influences on the teaching/learning process (e.g., teacher–learner relationship, classroom climate).

Second, it should *explain* the phenomena with emphasis on how they can be affected by the learning environment (e.g., materials, pedagogy, tools, peers, teachers, tutors, etc.). After observing and describing a phenomenon, the next step within this view of the theory is to explain how the observational data can be expressed in terms of a hypothesis or built into a model such that predictions can be made and tested.

Finally, it should attempt to *predict* the effects of interventions in the learning and teaching process in a way that the interventions will lead to evidence-informed implementation in education. The theory should be testable; that is, it is capable of (1) predicting future occurrences or observations of the same kind though not yet observed, and (2) being tested through experiment or otherwise falsified through empirical observation. In other words, it leads to theories and models that can be empirically tested and that are falsifiable.

Another way of carrying out theoretically sound research relies on a different definition for theory. Like the version above, its goal is to say something about empirical phenomena in the social world, but the question is not "What x causes y?" Rather researchers take a more *hermeneutical* approach and ask for a given phenomenon P (or relation or process): "How can we make sense of or shed light on P?" (Abend, 2008). If theory is used in this way, then good research in the educational and learning sciences will shed new light on an empirical problem or help us to understand a social process.

What good research should define, explain, and predict or otherwise shed light upon is how to learn and teach (i.e., design education and learning experiences) both domain-specific knowledge, skills, and attitudes and higher-order knowledge, skills, and attitudes.

Constructive Research Alignment

How should this be done? Educational research requires integrating the full scale of qualitative and quantitative methods used in the different fields of the Educational and Learning Sciences as well as those used in Human–Computer Interaction and Informatics Research. In other words, it requires mixed methods research, research that makes use of "research designs using qualitative and quantitative data collection and analysis techniques in either parallel or sequential phases" (Teddlie & Tashakkori, 2003, p. 11). Such a multi-method, pragmatic approach (Creswell et al., 2003) takes into account development and implementation in the complex Ecological Edu-niche, while also being strongly embedded in robust educational science. Since there is not one "super theory" of education, a well-organized selection of state-of-the-art theoretical perspectives has to be made from the wide variety available. Most important is an approach similar to Biggs's *Constructive Alignment* (1996, 2014). According to Biggs, for optimal learning, all components—curriculum, teaching methods used, and intended outcomes/assessments—are aligned to each other.

In the same way as instruction, constructive research alignment requires that the research question studied and/or the hypothesis to be tested, the empirical method employed, the analytical (i.e., quantitative, qualitative) techniques used, and the conclusions that the researcher can draw/decisions that can be made based upon the research results are properly aligned.

Although it seems simple, in every research situation there needs to be an alignment between the four relevant elements. Based upon the research question being studied/asked, an empirical method that fits the question needs to be chosen (i.e., a method that is suited to answering the question being asked). In the following section, a small collection of methods is given. Once the method has been chosen, the data need to be gathered and analysis techniques that suit the method need to be employed. This means, for example, if the method that is chosen is empirical and quantitative, then there should be no parametric testing of nominal

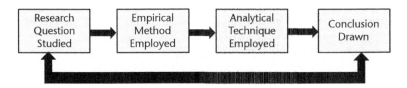

FIGURE 3.2 Constructive research alignment

scales (e.g., testing means and standard deviations of 5-point Likert scales that are then compared via *t*-tests) and there should be no analyses of variances when there are interdependencies between variables (e.g., as is the case when looking at how a person interacts with others and with the task at hand in a team as her/his type and degree of interaction is dependent on how the other members of a team interact with each other and with the task). The next step is drawing valid and reliable conclusions based upon the results. This means not deriving causality out of correlations based upon structural equation modeling (i.e., what Reinhart et al. (2013) called squeezing causality and recommendations for practice out of correlational data) or the same based on case studies where the results are already known and 20/20 hindsight can be used to explain it. Finally, the conclusions drawn need to be well aligned with the original question.

As is the case with Biggs's constructive alignment (1996, 2014), it really does not matter what question is being asked (from eye movements while studying hypertext to the effects of argumentation), what method is used (from small scale laboratory interventions to large scale observational studies), what analytical technique is being applied, and what conclusions are being drawn. What matters is that they are properly aligned!

Methods

While not even pretending to be complete, here are some of the most used research methods and their roles:

- *Observational studies* to draw inferences about the possible effect of a treatment in situations where assignment of participants into a treated or a control group is outside the control of the researcher.
- *Descriptive research* to describe a population or a phenomenon being studied to answer the *what* question and not questions about how something happens, when it happens or will happen, or why something happens.
- *In-depth studies of particular settings* to provide accounts of causal relationships and processes. In such work, direct perception of causal relationships is viewed as possible rather than causal inference requiring some sort of systematic comparison of situations in which the presumed causal factor is present or absent, or varies in strength (Maxwell, 2004).
- *Design research* to study designing, developing, and evaluating educational interventions as solutions to complex educational problems, while advancing knowledge of the characteristics of the interventions and the processes of designing and developing them (Plomp & Nieveen, 2009).
- *Controlled laboratory experiments*—not necessarily a laboratory—where it is possible to control external influences and make accurate measurements. The gold standard here is random allocation of participants to each independent variable group.

- *Quasi-experimental field experiments* carried out in everyday educational/learning environments (i.e., real life), but where the scale and design is such that the experimenter has the possibility of manipulating the independent variable. As there are often no real control conditions here, there are specific designs that alleviate this problem (see Campbell & Stanley, 1963).
- *Uncontrolled real-world experiments* are conducted in the everyday educational or learning environment (i.e., real life) of the participants. Here, the experimenter often has little to no control over the independent variable as it occurs naturally in real life. However, these experiments are ecologically more valid.
- Other research approaches that are used are survey research in order to develop research questions, literature research in order to motivate research questions or ground hypotheses, secondary analyses in order to repurpose existing datasets, retrospective studies in order to examine exposures to suspected risk or protection factors in relation to an outcome that is pre-established, meta reviews in order to better evaluate research results, etc.

Closing

Education is, thus, an integrated system. It requires an integrated approach to perform research on and in it as well as to apply methods within it and to it. Research questions relating to education accordingly need to be seen as embedded in a complex system in which different perspectives and subsystems work together. This means that the research carried out needs to:

- Span the laboratory situation, small-scale learning environments and ecologically valid educational settings
- Integrate all of the components of the educational ecosystem
- Involve relevant stakeholders at all levels in the research process

Educational science and the learning sciences, along with their subgroups, need to stop turning their paradigms into paradogmas (Kirschner, 2014) and lay down their weapons and work together (cf. Greeno, 1998 for one example of an integrative approach). In the words of Lennon and Marx:

> War is over ... If you want it.
>
> *John Lennon*
>
> Those are my principles, and if you don't like them ... well, I have others.
>
> *Groucho Marx*

References

Abend, G. (2008). The meaning of 'theory'. *Sociological Theory, 26*(2), 173–199.
Ageyev, V. S. (2003). Vygotsky in the mirror. In A. Kozulin, B. Gindis, V. S. Ageyev, & S. M. Miller (Eds.), *Vygotsky's Educational Theory in Cultural Context* (pp. 432–449). New York: Cambridge University Press.

Bagley, W. C. (1938). An essentialist's platform for the advancement of American education. *Education Digest* 4(2), 1–5.
Biggs, J. (1996). Enhancing teaching through constructive alignment. *Higher Education, 32*, 347–364.
Biggs, J. (2014). Constructive alignment in university teaching. *HERDSA Review of Higher Education, 1*, 5–22.
Campbell, D. T., & Stanley, J. C. (1963). Experimental and quasi-experimental designs for research on teaching. In N. L. Gage (Ed.), *Handbook of research on teaching* (pp. 171–246). Chicago, IL: Rand McNally.
Capra, F. (1982). *The turning point: Science, society and the rising culture*. New York: Simon and Schuster.
Chamak, B. (1999). The emergence of cognitive science in France: A comparison with the USA. *Social Studies of Science, 29*(5), 643–684.
Comenius, J. A. (Jan Amos Komensky) (1623). *The great didactic*. In *Classics in education* (no. 33). New York: Teachers College Press, 1967.
Creswell, J. W., Plano Clark, V. L., Gutmann, M. L., & Hanson, W. E. (2003). Advanced mixed methods research designs. *Handbook of mixed methods in social and behavioral research* (pp. 209–240). Thousand Oaks, CA: SAGE Publications, Inc.
Derry, S. (1999). A fish called peer learning: Searching for common themes. In A. O'Donnell & A. King (Eds.), *Cognitive perspectives on peer learning* (pp. 197–211). Mahwah, NJ: Lawrence Erlbaum Associates.
Dewey, J. (1938). *Logic: The theory of inquiry*. New York, NY: Holt, Rinehart, and Winston.
Gagné, R. M. (1985). *The conditions of learning* (4th ed.). New York: Holt, Rinehart & Winston.
Gardner, H. (1985). *The mind's new science: A history of the cognitive revolution* New York: Basic Books.
Greeno, J. G. (1998). The situativity of knowing, learning, and research. *American Psychologist, 53*, 5–17.
Goodyear, P. (2000). Environments for lifelong learning. Ergonomics, architecture and educational design. In J. M. Spector & T. M. Anderson (Eds.), *Integrated and holistic perspectives on learning, instruction and technology: Understanding complexity* (pp. 1–18). Dordrecht, The Netherlands: Kluwer.
Hattie, J. (2003). *Teachers make a difference: What is the research evidence?* Paper presented at the Australian Council for Educational Research Annual Conference on Building Teacher Quality, Melbourne.
Hattie, J. (2008). *Visible learning: A synthesis of over 800 meta-analyses relating to achievement*. New York, NY: Routledge.
Hebb, D. O. (1949). *The organization of behavior*. New York, NY: Wiley.
Kerns, J. D. (2009). *Shaping an "idea without hands": Bronson Alcott's educational theory brought to life in Little Women* (Unpublished master's thesis). Iowa State University, Ames, Iowa. Available at http://lib.dr.iastate.edu/etd/10082/
Kirschner, P. A. (2014). When a paradigm becomes a paradogma. *Journal of Computer Assisted Learning, 30*, 297–299.
Kirschner, P. A., Martens, R. L., & Strijbos, J. -W. (2004). CSCL in higher education? A framework for designing multiple collaborative environments. In P. Dillenbourg (Series Ed.) and J. -W. Strijbos, P. A. Kirschner, & R. L. Martens (Vol. Eds.), *Computer-supported collaborative learning: Vol 3. What we know about CSCL … and implementing it in higher education* (pp. 3–30). Boston, MA: Kluwer Academic Publishers.
Linden, J. L. van der, Erkens, G., Schmidt, H., & Renshaw, P. (2001). Collaborative learning. In P. R. J. Simons, J. L. van der Linden, & T. M. Duffy (Eds.), *New learning* (pp. 37–54). Dordrecht, The Netherlands: Kluwer Academic Publishers.

Looi, C.-K., Seow, P., Zhang, B, So, H. -J., Chen W., & Wong, L. -H. (2010). Leveraging mobile technology for sustainable seamless learning: A research agenda. *British Journal of Educational Technology, 41*(2), 154–169.

Maxwell, J. A. (2004). Causal explanation, qualitative research, and scientific inquiry in education. *Educational Researcher, 33*(2), 3–11.

McKinsey & Company (2007). *How the world's best-performing school systems come out on top.* Amsterdam, The Netherlands: McKinsey & Company.

Papert, S. (1990). Introduction. In I. Harel (Ed.), *Constructionist learning* (pp. 1–8). Cambridge, MA: A Media Laboratory Publication.

Piaget, J., & Inhelder, B. (1991). *The child's conception of space.* New York: Norton.

Plomp, T., & Nieveen, N. (Eds.). (2009). *An introduction to educational design research.* Enschede, the Netherlands: SLO.

Prudhomme, G., Pourroy, F., & Lund, K. (2007). An empirical study of engineering knowledge dynamics in a design situation. *Journal of Design Research, 6*(3), 333–358.

Reinhart, A. L., Haring, S. H., Levin, J. R., Patall, E. A., & Robinson, D. H. (2013). Models of not-so-good behavior: Yet another way to squeeze causality and recommendations for practice out of correlational data. *Journal of Educational Psychology, 105*(1), 241–247.

Scardamalia, M., Bereiter C., & Lamon, M. (1994). The CSILE project: Trying to bring the classroom into world 3. In K. McGilly (Ed.), *Classroom lessons: Integrating cognitive theory and classroom practice* (pp. 201–229). Cambridge, MA: The MIT Press.

Siemens, G. (2005). Connectivism: A learning theory for the digital age. *International Journal of Instructional Technology and Distance Learning, 2*(1). Retrieved May 1, 2015 from www.itdl.org/Journal/Jan_05/article01.htm

Skinner, B. F. (1935). The generic nature of the concepts of stimulus and response. *Journal of General Psychology, 12*, 40–65.

Spector, J. M. (2006, March 22). Challenging dichotomies – Inspired by Paul Kirschner's inaugural address at Utrecht University. Retrieved February 24, 2016 from www.learndev.org/dl/BtSM2007/MichaelSpector-Challenging_dichotomies.pdf

Spector, J. M., & Wang, X. (2002). Integrating technology into learning and working: Promising opportunities and problematic issues. *Educational Technology & Society, 5*(1), 1–7.

Spiro, R. J., Feltovich, P. J., Jacobson, M. I., & Coulson, R. L. (1995). Cognitive flexibility, constructivism, and hypertext: Random access instruction for advanced knowledge acquisition in ill-structured domains. In L. P. Steffe & J. E. Gale (Eds.), *Constructivism in education* (pp. 85–107). Mahwah, NJ: Lawrence Erlbaum Associates.

Teddlie, C., & Tashakkori, A. (2003). Major issues and controveries in the use of mixed methods in the social and behvioral sciences. In Tashakkori, A., & C. Teddlie (Eds.), *Handbook of mixed methods in social and behavioral research* (pp. 3–50). Thousand Oaks, CA: Sage Publications, Inc.

Van Merriënboer, J., Kirschner, P. A., Paas, F., Sloep, P. B., & Caniels, M. (2009). Towards an integrated approach for research on lifelong learning. *Educational Technology Magazine: The Magazine for Managers of Change in Education, 49*, 3–15.

von Glasersfeld, E. (1988). *Cognition, construction of knowledge and teaching* (Eric Document Reproduction Service No. ED 294 754).

Vygotsky, L. (1978). Interaction between learning and development. *Readings on the development of children, 23*(3), 34–41.

Vygotsky, L. S. (1981). The instrumental method in psychology. *The concept of activity in Soviet psychology* (pp. 135–143). Armonk, NY: Sharpe.

Watson, J. B. (1913). Psychology as the behaviorist views it. *Psychological Review, 20*(2), 158–177.

Weiser, M. (1991). The computer for the 21st century. *Scientific American, 265*(3), 94–104. http://wiki.daimi.au.dk/pca/_files/weiser-orig.pdf

Winn, W., & Snyder, D. (1996). Cognitive perspectives in psychology. D. H. Jonassen (Ed.), *Handbook of research for educational communications and technology: A project of the Association for Educational Communications and Technology* (pp. 79–112). Bloomington, IN: The Association for Educational Communications and Technology.

4

COMPARING THE GOALS AND METHODOLOGIES OF LEARNING SCIENTISTS AND EDUCATIONAL TECHNOLOGY RESEARCHERS

Thomas C. Reeves and Eunjung Grace Oh

Introduction

Although not every one agrees, an argument can be made that the learning sciences and educational technology are distinct fields of inquiry and practice. Educational technology has been defined as "the study and ethical practice of facilitating learning and improving performance by creating, using and managing appropriate technological processes and resources" (Januszewski & Molenda, 2008, p. 1). The learning sciences is commonly referred to as an interdisciplinary field focused on furthering scientific understanding of learning as well as enabling the design and implementation of effective learning innovations (Sawyer, 2005). These definitions suggest that educational technology has a stronger applied science orientation with an emphasis on improving learning and performance whereas the learning sciences has a stronger basic science orientation with an emphasis on understanding the nature of learning as well as enabling the development of more effective innovations.

Saettler (2004) traces the origins of the educational technology field in the USA back at least 90 years when first visual instruction and later audio-visual instruction became the focus of interest within the National Education Association (NEA). Scholarly work related to educational technology increased rapidly during and after World War II, especially as related to the use of films and other audio-visual aides to meet the enormous demand for military training at the time (Giordano, 2004). Recommendations for new directions of educational technology research were published as early as the 1960s. Published critiques of educational technology research include those by Mielke (1968), Clark (1983), Salomon (1991), and Reeves (1995). A common theme across these critical analyses was a call for enhanced research approaches.

According to Sawyer (2005), the learning sciences as a distinct field has its origins in the 1970s "based in research emerging from psychology, computer sciences, philosophy, sociology and other scientific disciplines" (p. 2). Over the past quarter century, the learning sciences have flourished as its proponents have snared the lion's share of the research funding in the USA from groups such as the National Science Foundation (NSF) and the Institute of Education Sciences (IES) of the U.S. Department of Education (DOE). Recommendations for redirecting learning sciences research also exist, albeit in limited numbers (Hammer & Berland, 2014; Rourke & Friesen, 2006). These critiques include questioning whether education can even be studied in ways that approximate the quantitative methods used in traditional scientific domains such as physics and chemistry.

The book in which this chapter appears is intended to bridge a troublesome gap between those who identify themselves as learning scientists and those who identify as educational technology researchers. Throughout this volume, interesting strategies for bridging the generally weak collaboration between scholars and practitioners in these two educational research communities are described. The intention of this specific chapter is to present a comparison of the research papers published in two reputable journals: one, the *Journal of the Learning Sciences* (JLS), strongly associated with the learning sciences field, and the other, *Educational Technology Research and Development* (ETRD), strongly identified with the field of educational technology. Specifically, the goals and methodologies of the research studies published in JLS and ETRD are compared over a six-year period from 2009–2014. Having a better understanding of the differences and similarities between these two journals may provide insights into why there is insufficient cross-fertilization between learning scientists and educational technology researchers and enable this lamentable situation to be improved.

Research Goals and Methodologies

Educational research studies can be categorized according to their goals and methodologies (Reeves, 1995). Six categories of educational research goals include the following:

- Studies with Theory Development/Synthesis goals focus on explaining how education works through the logical analysis and synthesis of theoretical knowledge and principles related to teaching, learning, and performance as well as the results of research with other types of goals.
- Studies with Exploratory/Hypothesis-Testing goals focus on discovering or specifying how education works by testing hypotheses related to theories and models of teaching, learning, and performance.
- Studies with Descriptive/Interpretivist goals focus on portraying how education works by describing and interpreting phenomena related to teaching, learning, and performance. Some research in this category may be more

descriptive whereas other studies may be more interpretive, including efforts to derive theoretical principles.
- Studies with Critical/Postmodern goals focus on examining the assumptions underlying education and its effects on teaching, learning, and performance with the ultimate goal of revealing hidden agendas and empowering disenfranchised minorities.
- Studies with Design/Development goals focus on the creation and improvement of effective solutions to education problems as well as identification of reusable design principles related to teaching, learning, and performance. Educational researchers conduct design research in close collaboration with practitioners.
- Studies with Action/Evaluation goals focus on a particular program, product, or method, usually in an applied setting, for the purpose of describing, improving, or estimating its effectiveness and worth. These goals differ from design/development goals in that researchers with action/evaluation goals do not usually seek to identify new theoretical knowledge, but are more interested in solving local problems.

There are many different research methodologies used by educational and other social sciences researchers. Reeves (1995) identified five broadly defined types of research methodologies commonly found in educational research studies:

- Quantitative methodologies include experimental, quasi-experimental, correlational, and other methods that primarily involve the collection of quantitative data and its analysis using descriptive and/or inferential statistics.
- Qualitative methodologies include observation, case studies, diaries, interviews, and other methods that primarily involve the collection of qualitative data and its analysis using grounded theory and ethnographic approaches.
- Critical Theory methodologies include the deconstruction of "texts" and the technologies that deliver them through the search for binary oppositions, hidden agendas, and the disenfranchisement of minorities.
- Literature Review methodologies include various forms of research synthesis that primarily involve the analysis and integration of research reports conducted using other research methods. Frequency counts, logical analysis, and meta-analyses may be encompassed in this methodology.
- Mixed Methods methodologies include research studies that combine a mixture of methods, usually quantitative and qualitative, to triangulate findings.

The Journals

According to the Taylor & Francis website, the *Journal of the Learning Sciences* (JLS)

> provides a multidisciplinary forum for research on education and learning as theoretical and design sciences. It publishes research that elucidates

processes of learning, and the ways in which technologies, instructional practices, and learning environments can be designed to support learning in different contexts.

JLS has been published since 1991 as an official periodical of the International Society of the Learning Sciences (ISLS), and it currently publishes four issues per year. According to its website, the "2014 Thomson Reuters, Journal Citation Reports ® for 2013 ranks *Journal of the Learning Sciences* 9 out of 219 in Education & Educational Research and 6 out of 53 in Psychology, Educational," with a 5-Year Impact Factor of 3.26. According to the SCImago Journal & Country Rank portal, JLS is ranked number 13 of 914 education journals.

According to the Springer website for the *Educational Technology Research and Development* (ETRD) journal, it is the "only scholarly journal for the field focusing entirely on research and development in educational technology." (The editors of refereed publications such as the *British Journal of Educational Technology*, the *Australasian Journal of Educational Technology*, or other similar journals might take issue with this statement.) ETRD has been published since 1953, although it did not adopt its current title until 1989. It was previously published under two other titles, specifically *Audio-Visual Communication Review* (AVCR) (1953–1977) and *Educational Communication and Technology Journal* (ECTJ) (1978–1988). It is now issued bi-monthly as an official publication of the Association for Educational Communications and Technology (AECT). According to ETRD's website, it has an impact factor of 1.420 according to the 2014 Thomson Reuters, Journal Citation Reports ® for 2013. The SCImago Journal & Country Rank portal ranks ETRD number 43 of 914 education journals.

In its current format, ETRD has two distinct sections, which according to the journal description on the Springer website are the following:

- A Research Section featuring well-documented articles on the practical aspects of research as well as applied theory in educational practice, a comprehensive source of current research information in instructional technology
- A Development Section publishing articles concerned with the design and development of learning systems and educational technology applications

For the purposes of this study, only the papers in the Research Section were analyzed.

Since 2011, Rick West and his graduate students at Brigham Young University have published a series of articles in *Educational Technology* magazine that analyze educational technology-related research journals. Of particular relevance to this chapter, Zaugg, Amado, Small, and West (2011) analyzed the contents of ETRD from 2001–2010 and Randall, Bishop, Alexander, and West (2011) analyzed the contents of JLS for the same decade. West and Borup (2014) provided an overview of the processes used in the analyses of ten such journals from 2001–2010.

The articles by West and his students provide useful insights into the nature of ETRD (Zaugg et al., 2011) and JLS (Randall et al., 2011). According to West and Borup's (2014) analysis of both journals across a decade, JLS primarily published math- and science-related studies and ETRD included numerous papers related to problem-based learning (PBL) and learning environment design. However, a significant weakness of the analyses by Zaugg et al. (2011) and Randall et al. (2011) is that their analytical schemes conflate educational research goals and methods. West and his graduate students do not specifically address the goals of researchers in their reviews, but instead focus on methods using these seven categories in the instance of their review of ETRD (Zaugg et al., 2011):

- Developmental/design based
- Survey
- Quantitative
- Qualitative
- Theoretical/philosophical
- Content/discourse
- Combined methods (p. 44)

Rather than utilize the same categories, Randall et al. (2011) reduced the number to five in their review of the methods used in studies reported in JLS:

- Statistical/quantitative
- Qualitative/interpretive
- Theoretical/philosophical (including reviews of literature)
- Combined methods
- Commentaries (p. 48)

We posit that it is essential to distinguish between the goals pursued by educational researchers and the methods employed within a specific study. We view it as legitimate for someone to self-identify as a design researcher or as an interpretivist, but it is somewhat dubious when a person describes him or herself as a qualitative or a quantitative researcher. The latter is akin to claiming to be a "hammer carpenter" or a "saw carpenter." After all, methods are tools and they only have meaning in the context of a particular job. Individual researchers may certainly have preferences for one method over another and there is often some degree of alignment between certain goals and specific methods, but the final choice of method is a secondary decision dependent on the nature of the researcher's goals and specific research questions as well as on factors such as budget and feasibility.

The Comparison

After agreeing upon the research goals and methodological categories described above, the authors reviewed papers published in ETRD and JLS over a six-year span from 2009–2014. The first author reviewed all the papers in both journals to code the research goals and methods, and the second author reviewed a representative sample of papers from each journal to provide the basis for a reliability check of the categorization process. For example, using a random sample of 34 articles from ETRD, an interrater reliability (Cohen's Kappa) was calculated as 0.91 for research goals and as .83 for research methods. These results are considered as indicative of very good strength of agreement by Landis and Koch (1977). Subsequently, the two researchers conferred concerning the categorizations upon which they initially differed and attained an agreement about the final coding.

Table 4.1 presents the classification of 95 research papers appearing in JLS from 2009–2014. Papers excluded from the analysis included brief articles introducing special issues, *In Memoriam* pieces, and other non-research paper contributions.

Table 4.2 presents the classification of 102 research papers appearing in the ETRD from 2009–2014. Papers excluded from the analysis included brief articles introducing special issues and other non-research paper contributions.

Comparing Tables 4.1 and 4.2 illustrates interesting differences between JLS and ETRD. With respect to Research Goals, 19% of the research papers in JLS

TABLE 4.1 Classification of JLS articles (2009–2014)

	Quantitative	*Qualitative*	*Critical Theory*	*Literature Review*	*Mixed Methods*	*Total*
Theory Development/ Synthesis				14	4	18 19%
Exploratory/ Hypothesis-Testing	15				12	27 28%
Descriptive/ Interpretivist		30			7	37 39%
Critical/ Postmodern						
Design/ Development		1			12	13 14%
Action/ Evaluation						
Total	15 16%	31 32%		14 15%	35 37%	95 100%

TABLE 4.2 Classification of ETRD articles (2009–2014)*

	Quantitative	Qualitative	Critical Theory	Literature Review	Mixed Methods	Total
Theory Development/ Synthesis				8	2	10 / 10%
Exploratory/ Hypothesis-Testing	52				17	69 / 68%
Descriptive/ Interpretivist		11			5	16 / 16%
Critical/ Postmodern						0 / 0%
Design/ Development	1				4	5 / 5%
Action/ Evaluation					2	2 / 2%
Total	53 / 52%	11 / 11%	0 / 0%	8 / 8%	30 / 29%	102 / 100%

*Note: Also in Reeves & Oh (2016).

have Theory Development/Synthesis Goals whereas only 10% of the research papers in ETRD have Theory Development/Synthesis Goals. Interestingly, Reeves (1995) reported that 33% of the research papers published in ETRD from 1989–1994 had Theory Development/Synthesis Goals. This finding indicates that there has been a major decrease in the percentage of papers in ETRD over a 20-year period that are written to explain how education works through the logical analysis and synthesis of theoretical knowledge and principles related to teaching, learning, and performance as well as the results of research with other types of goals. It is unknown why there has been a reduction in papers with Theory Development/Synthesis Goals in ETRD or why JLS has almost twice as high of percentage of such papers as ETRD. Interestingly, West and Borup (2014) reported that the most cited paper in ETRD from 2001 to 2009 was Merrill's (2002) paper on First Principles of Instruction published in ETRD, which has Theory Development/Synthesis Goals and has been cited 775 times. Likewise, seven out of the nine most-cited papers from the selected ten Educational Technology journals described by West and Borup (2014) were theoretical or literature-based synthesis papers.

A much higher percentage of papers in ETRD have Exploratory/Hypothesis-Testing Goals (68%) than in JLS (28%), and a corresponding lower percentage of papers with Descriptive/Interpretivist Goals can be found in ETRD (16%) than in JLS (39%). With respect to Research Goals, these are dramatic differences. Randall et al. (2011) noted the high percentage of papers they categorized as "Qualitative/interpretive" and surmised "JLS's liberal policy of not imposing page limits allows for qualitative work to be better reported" (p. 49). To be sure, JLS has higher word limits on submissions than ETRD. The JLS website states that regular submissions to the journal will be "10,000–15,000 words" whereas the ETRD website states that papers over 8,000 words in length are unlikely to be published. Our word count for the articles published in these two journals from 2009–2014 found that JLS papers averaged 15,516 words while ETRD papers averaged 10,117 words.

But it is doubtful that word limits alone explain these large differences in research goals between JLS and ETRD. It may well be that these variances relate to the establishment and maintenance of a long-term design research agenda being more prevalent among learning scientists than among educational technology researchers. There are a higher percentage of papers with Design/Development Goals in JLS (14%) than in ETRD (5%). In addition, it may be that many papers among the 39% in JLS categorized as having Descriptive/Interpretivist Goals are also part of a longer-term design research agenda, but this was not explicitly stated in these papers.

It is evident that many of the researchers publishing in JLS have strong identities within the design-based research movement that has been expanding over the past two decades since the publication of seminal papers by Brown (1992) and Collins (1992). For example, Randall et al. (2011) listed Sasha Barab, Paul Cobb, Daniel Edelson, and Kurt Squire, all strongly associated with design-based research, as among the top ten researchers publishing multiple papers in JLS between 2001 and 2010. In fact, Barab and Squire (2004) published the most frequently cited paper about design-based research (1,435 citations reported by Google Scholar in March 2016). According to Zaugg et al. (2011), the most frequently published scholars in ETRD from 2001 included Howard Sullivan, Michael Hannafin, Jeroen Merrienboer, Paul Kirschner, and David Jonassen, all excellent educational technology researchers, but their work is not strongly associated with design-based research per se except for Wang and Hannafin's (2005) paper on design-based research, which is the second most frequently cited paper about design-based research (960 citations, according to Google Scholar in March 2016).

Whereas ETRD published 2% of its papers with Action/Evaluation Goals, JLS had none during this time period. Indeed, the JLS website explicitly states that it "generally does not publish manuscripts that primarily report the results of an evaluation of a program, curriculum or innovation." On ETRD's website, nothing is stated about Action/Evaluation goals on the Research side of the journal, but "empirically-based formative evaluations" appear to be welcomed on the Development side.

Finally, neither journal published any papers with Critical/Postmodern Goals during the six years from 2009–2014. In the pages of ETRD, a quarter century ago, Solomon (2000) called for a postmodern research agenda in the field of educational technology, but except for a critique of the postmodern agenda by Evans (2011), there has been almost no research published with these goals in ETRD. Interestingly, in an essay describing the Learning Sciences, Nathan and Alibali (2010) claimed that the learning sciences "reflect both Modern and Postmodern views of human behavior" (p. 330). However, in the same essay, they wrote that:

> Postmodern views argue against the existence of a knowable universe and acknowledge—even embrace, at times—skepticism and the subjective nature of knowledge. A central aspect of Postmodernism is "critical theory," where the objective is to critique and change society, rather than explain it. (p. 330)

Both Nathan and Alibali have published in JLS (Alibali & Nathan, 2012), but their paper did not have Critical/Postmodern Goals. Searches in multiple databases for papers by Learning Scientists espousing Critical/Postmodern Goals or applying critical theory methods such as deconstruction were unfruitful.

With respect to Methodology, the results vary widely across the two journals. Quantitative Methods were solely employed in more than half (52%) of the papers published in ETRD whereas in JLS they were used exclusively in only 16% of the studies. Qualitative Methods were used in only 11% of the ETRD papers whereas nearly a third (32%) of the papers in JLS used Qualitative Methods alone. Mixed Methods were adopted in 29% of the ETRD papers and 37% of the JLS papers, a finding that certainly reflects the much wider acceptance of Mixed Methods across the educational research spectrum. In comparison, Reeves (1995) found that only 12% of the papers published in ETRD from 1989–1994 used Mixed Methods. Literature Review was the method of choice in 8% of the papers published in ETRD during from 2009–2014 whereas 15% of the papers employed literature review as the sole methodology in JLS papers during this time. No papers in either journal reported using Critical Theory methods (Lather, 1992).

There is, of course, a strong correlation between research goals and methods. Researchers with Theory Development/Synthesis Goals tend to rely upon Literature Review as the preferred method; those with Exploratory/Hypothesis-Testing Goals more often apply some type of Quantitative Method, especially those of experimental or quasi-experimental design, in their studies, and those with Descriptive/Interpretivist Goals frequently use Qualitative Methods, especially case studies. Almost all researchers with Design/Development Goals employed Mixed Methods in the studies published in both journals during this time period.

Implications

Our analyses found major differences in both the goals and methodologies between research papers published in JLS and ETRD. First, over two-thirds of the research published in ETRD had Exploratory/Hypothesis-Testing Goals (68%) compared to less than a third (28%) in JLS. Second, over half (53%) of the papers in JLS espouse Descriptive/Interpretivist Goals or Design/Development Goals whereas the percentage of papers in these categories in ETRD was only 21%. Third, with respect to methodologies, over half (52%) of the papers in ETRD used Quantitative Methods exclusively whereas only 16% of the papers in JLS used these methods alone.

If it is desirable that there be greater articulation between learning scientists and educational technology researchers (and we think it is), then we recommend that representatives from these two groups come together and discuss these differences, and identify steps toward a more robust shared research agenda for the benefit of the field of education. Such an exchange could be held at the annual meeting of the American Educational Research Association and hosted by the editors of JLS and ETRD (Iris Tabak of Ben Gurion University of the Negev and Joshua Radinsky from the University of Illinois at Chicago for JLS and Mike Spector from the University of North Texas and Tristan Johnson from Northeastern University for ETRD). Alternatively, a separate meeting or conference could be held, with funding for such an exchange being obtained from agencies such as the Spencer Foundation, NSF, IES, or other organizations.

Our personal bias would be that both groups coalesce around an educational design or design-based research agenda (McKenney & Reeves, 2012; Oh & Reeves, 2010). Educational research has long been criticized for its lack of relevance for practitioners such as teachers (cf. Kaestle, 1992; Kane, 2016; Kennedy, 1997). The reasons for this problem are too complex to be discussed in this paper, but educational design research tackles this issue directly. McKenney and Reeves (2012) wrote that "the educational design research process advances both theory and practice simultaneously, even synergistically" (p. 19). Further, they argue that during the early stages of substantive design research initiatives, educational researchers should "respectfully and critically engage with practitioners in search of problems that: (a) they perceive and care enough about to bother solving; and (b) which also fall within the researcher's area of expertise" (p. 89).

Our call for a collaborative research agenda with Design/Development Goals is not intended to disparage researchers with other goals. However, in light of the findings of our analyses that there is a complete absence of papers published in JLS and ETRD with Critical/Postmodern Goals, we especially want to encourage the editors of these leading journals to seek out contributions with these goals. Perhaps a collaborative special issue with articles shared in both journals could be commissioned that would invite scholars with a critical and/or postmodern perspective to turn their deconstruction lenses to the core nature of the learning sciences and educational technology. Such a contribution would enrich the current scholarship and future practice by broadening our perspectives through insightful discovery and deeper reflection on education, learning, and technology.

In addressing the question "What counts as education research?" Lee (2010) quoted the British Philosopher of Education, Wilfred Carr, as follows:

> [E]ducational research now embraces so many traditions, paradigms, theoretical perspectives, methodological frameworks and academic disciplines that it cannot claim to meet even the most minimal criteria of homogeneity that any notion of a "research community" presupposes and requires. It is thus unsurprising that any identity educational research may have stems more from its institutional embodiment in conferences, research journals and learned societies than from any internal intellectual coherence. (p. 3)

The quotation from Carr illuminates the dilemma that educational researchers of all kinds must confront. They know in their hearts that their inquiry will be more socially responsible and have more impact if they pursue their research agendas as collaboratively as possible with fellow researchers, practitioners, and other stakeholders, but there are enormous pressures inherent in the tenure and promotion reward system for distinguishing themselves as independent researchers who present at highly selective conferences, publish in just the right journals, and receive funding from the most prestigious sources. Those of us involved in maintaining this antiquated reward system must try to loosen its grip on the future of scholarship in the learning sciences and educational technology, and seek to establish more collaborative research agendas that are both rigorous and relevant (Reeves, 2011). If these two research communities can unite, they may provide the catalyst and model for systemic reform throughout the educational research enterprise.

References

Alibali, M. W., & Nathan, M. J. (2012). Embodiment in mathematics teaching and learning: Evidence from learners' and teachers' gestures. *Journal of the Learning Sciences, 21*(2), 247–286.

Barab, S., & Squire, K. (2004). Design-based research: Putting a stake in the ground. *Journal of the Learning Sciences, 13*(1), 1–14.

Brown, A. L. (1992). Design experiments: Theoretical and methodological challenges in creating complex interventions in classroom settings. *Journal of the Learning Sciences, 2*(2), 141–178.

Clark, R. E. (1983). Reconsidering research on learning from media. *Review of Educational Research, 53*(4), 445–459.

Collins, A. (1992). Toward a design science of education. In E. Scanlon & T. O'Shea (Eds.), *New directions in educational technology* (pp. 15–22). Berlin, Germany: Springer-Verlag.

Evans, M. A. (2011). A critical-realist response to the postmodern agenda in instructional design and technology: A way forward. *Educational Technology Research and Development, 59*(6), 799–815.

Giordano, G. (2004). *Wartime schools: How World War II changed American education.* New York: Peter Lang.

Hammer, D., & Berland, L. K. (2014). Confusing claims for data: A critique of common practices for presenting qualitative research on learning. *Journal of the Learning Sciences, 23*(1), 37–46.

Januszewski, A., & Molenda, M. (Eds.). (2008). *Educational technology: A definition with commentary.* New York: Routledge.

Kaestle, C. F. (1993). The awful reputation of education research. *Educational Researcher, 22*(1), 23–31.

Kane, T. J. (2016). Connecting to practice: How we can put educational research to work. *Education Next, 16*(2), 80–87.

Kennedy, M. M. (1997). The connection between research and practice. *Educational Researcher, 26*(7), 4–12.

Landis, J., & Koch, G. (1977). The measurement of observer agreement for categorical data. *Biometrics, 33*(1), 159–174.

Lather, P. (1992). Critical frames in educational research: Feminist and poststructural perspectives. *Theory into Practice, 31*(2), 87–99.

Lee, A. (2010). What counts as educational research? Spaces, boundaries and alliances. *The Australian Educational Researcher, 37*(4), 63–78.

McKenney, S. E., & Reeves, T. C. (2012). *Conducting educational design research.* New York: Routledge.

Merrill, M. D. (2002). First principles of instruction. *Educational Technology Research and Development, 50*(3), 43–59.

Mielke, K. W. (1968). Asking the right ETV research questions. *Educational Broadcasting Review, 2*(6), 54–61

Nathan, M. J., & Alibali, M. W. (2010). Learning sciences. *Wiley Interdisciplinary Reviews: Cognitive Science, 1*(3), 329–345.

Oh, E., & Reeves, T. C. (2010). The implications of the differences between design research and instructional systems design for educational technology researchers and practitioners. *Educational Media International, 47*(4), 263–275.

Randall, D. L., Bishop, M. A., Alexander, J. A., & West, R. E. (2011). Educational technology research journals: *The Journal of the Learning Sciences*, 2001–2010. *Educational Technology, 51*(6), 47.

Reeves, T. C. (2011). Can educational research be both rigorous and relevant? *Educational Designer: Journal of the International Society for Design and Development in Education, 1*(4). Retrieved online at: www.educationaldesigner.org/ed/volume1/issue4/article13/

Reeves, T. C. (1995). Questioning the questions of instructional technology research. In M. R. Simonson & M. Anderson (Eds.), *Proceedings of the Annual Conference of the Association for Educational Communications and Technology, Research and Theory Division* (pp. 459–470), Anaheim, CA.

Reeves, T. C., & Oh, E. G. (2016). The goals and methods of educational technology research over a quarter century (1989–2014). *Education Tech Research Dev.* doi: 10.1007/s11423-016-9474-1.

Rourke, L., & Friesen, N. (2006). The learning sciences: The very idea. *Educational Media International, 43*(4), 271–284.

Saettler, P. (2004). *The evolution of American educational technology.* Charlotte, NC: Information Age Publishing.

Salomon, G. (1991). Transcending the qualitative-quantitative debate: The analytic and systemic approaches to educational research. *Educational Researcher, 20*(6), 10–18.

Sawyer, R. K. (Ed.). (2005). *The Cambridge handbook of the learning sciences.* New York: Cambridge University Press.

Solomon, D. L. (2000). Toward a post-modern agenda in instructional technology. *Educational Technology Research and Development, 48*(4), 5–20.

Wang, F., & Hannafin, M. J. (2005). Design-based research and technology-enhanced learning environments. *Educational Technology Research and Development, 53*(4), 5–23.

West, R. E., & Borup, J. (2014). An analysis of a decade of research in 10 instructional design and technology journals. *British Journal of Educational Technology, 45*(4), 545–556.

Zaugg, H., Amado, M., Small, T. R., & West, R. E. (2011). Educational technology research journals: *Educational Technology Research and Development*, 2001–2010. *Educational Technology, 51*(5), 43–47.

5

LEARNING SCIENCES AND INSTRUCTIONAL DESIGN

Big Challenges and Multi-field, Multidisciplinary Solutions

Wellesley R. Foshay and Jeremy Roschelle

In approaching a challenging learning design project, we start from a simple premise: we need all the help we can get. From our diversity of experience and research interests, we have come to realize that many of the important, complex problems of understanding and creating teaching, learning, and assessment (whether delivered online, in the classroom or workplace, formally or informally, for the purposes of education or training) exceed the scope of any single field, such as Learning Science (LS) or Instructional Design (ID). To effectively advance the state of the art, these complex problems require close collaboration among team members with a broad range of perspectives.

This chapter emerges from a continuously running discussion between the authors, who worked together across a variety of projects over the past decade, addressing issues such as the challenges of adaptive learning. We both view ourselves as scholar-practitioners. In our collaborations, we often found the need to pragmatically examine knotty problems of theory and practice from each of our perspectives. Our goal has always been to achieve a deeper understanding of the problem at hand; neither of us has any use for academic turf wars.

We should start by defining our perspectives:

One of us (Foshay) has over 40 years of experience in a range of instructional design work and teaching at the K-12 and post-secondary levels, including professional education, technical, and management training at every level. The majority of work contexts have included commercial educational technology companies and consulting in the private sector. His perspective is grounded in the fields of Instructional Design (ID) and Human Performance Improvement (HPI), as well as a background in educational psychology and learning theory (both behaviorist and cognitive), organizational development, and performance-based assessment.

The other of us (Roschelle) directs the Center for Technology in Learning at SRI International, which primarily conducts research and evaluation projects for government and philanthropies. However, Roschelle has also expanded the team and projects to scale up research-based designs from proof of concept prototypes to implementation in hundreds of schools simultaneously—and also expanded SRI's business from its base in government research to work on design improvement with technology companies and publishers. His perspective is grounded in cognitive science and the learning sciences, with a specialization in technology for mathematics learning and assessment.

LS and ID: Cousins, but Not Twins

We have found it helpful to think of LS and ID not as competing disciplines, but as neighboring fields of applied science in the sense of *Pasteur's Quadrant* (Stokes, 1997). Both fields are defined first by the problems they address, and they pragmatically meld partial theories from a variety of sources and epistemologies in order to tackle those problems. By contrast, a discipline is devoted to development of a single body of theory, using a defined scope of inquiry and evidence. As applied fields, we find that LS and ID share a number of defining characteristics:

- Both draw on cognitive learning theory (Donovan et al., 1999).
- Both are evidence-based and design-oriented.
- To varying degrees, both fields draw from computer science and information science, design theory, systems theory, measurement theory, economics, project management, and engineering.

There is something noteworthy in each of the names of the two fields. ID is about designing instruction; the main focus is on making design decisions with the goal of building learning environments using replicable and generalizable methods. LS focuses on the science of learning. In LS, designs are proposed in order to shed light on a research question about how people could learn difficult subject matter more easily or deeply; researchers are willing to make strong assumptions to remove from consideration aspects of the problem that are not important to the scientific interest, so that the specific research question can be investigated. Thus, while both fields are applied, there is a qualitative difference: the defining focus of ID is the process of designing, while the defining focus of LS is the process of research in designed settings.

In our view, this distinction helps explain why the two fields provide complementary perspectives on applied problems. The field of ID emerged in the 1960s and had a major influence on bringing to scale the adoption of instructional design standards and practices, especially in the military, government, and in private sector training, including the use of (then-new) e-learning technologies.

A considerable body of knowledge on learning environment design practices has been systematized and continues to grow rapidly. Systematic design, which started by conflating project management, analysis, and design, has more recently separated these foci and developed each separately. By contrast, LS emerged from the Cognitive Science revolution of the 1980s. The field has had a major impact on how we talk about learning: we now recognize the importance of misconceptions and can articulate a nuanced view of why they are instructionally complex to deal with. The field has also clarified issues of representation and cognition; learning is seen as social and constructive. More recently, metacognition and self-regulation are on the table for both fields. Importantly, both LS and ID see learning as trajectories of participation and not just acquisition of knowledge and skills.

An example of the complementarity of the two fields may be seen in the role each field may be playing in a practical challenge such as implementation of the next generation of national curriculum standards. The general curriculum standards are shifting from a primary emphasis on facts and routine problem solving to also emphasize disciplinary practices and understanding the big ideas that generate coherence across a discipline. This is highly evident, for example, in the Next Generation Science Standards (NGSS). The NGSS framework (NRC, 2013) has three dimensions:

1. Practices: how scientists do science
2. Cross-cutting concepts: broad organizing ideas such as "energy" which connect topics across different sciences
3. Disciplinary core concepts: big ideas within a scientific area, such as life sciences or earth sciences.

The inherent multidimensionality of these standards, with their emphasis on authentic ways of doing and cross-cutting understanding of core ideas, shows recognition of the importance of a sophisticated epistemology and the complexity of cognition—an influence of LS. The standards also emphasize a clear focus and purpose—an influence of ID, in our view. For example, NGSS documents provide guidance on how to select disciplinary core concepts. Such guidance may be a key to organizing a discipline, may provide a tool for solving complex problems, may relate to the interests and life experiences of students, and may be teachable and learnable over time with increasing depth. The enterprise of implementing new standards like the NGSS also maintains a clear distinction between standards, curriculum, information, instructional materials, and assessment—another ID influence.

Both LS and ID recognize the range of knowledge types within the cognitive domain (Anderson et al., 2001) embedded in each standard, and concur with the principle that different learning experiences (or instructional strategies) are optimum for teaching and learning each of the different knowledge types. Both LS and ID lead us to elaborate these knowledge types and structures as part of early analysis, and then to use this analysis as one input into a design process consistent with a logic model (or theory of action) which also includes specification of the learner profile and role, the teacher's role, the context, and the affordances of the learning environment. Furthermore, both fields would lead us additionally to consider domains of learning beyond the cognitive (including the psychomotor, as well as affective domain constructs such as social and emotional learning, confidence, persistence, extrinsic and intrinsic motivation, and so on).

We propose the diagram below (Figure 5.1) as a common logic model of factors in a complete design of a full learning environment.

Starting from the bottom left, both LS and ID would draw on **Foundations** in psychology, cognitive science, and related disciplines. Foundations include basic scientific findings and theories that would influence the effectiveness of any design. From these foundations, one infers or supports prescriptive principles for design of the learning environment.

Further, both fields create overview documents to guide the design process; here we term these as **Blueprints**. Blueprints often include an analysis of the domain to be learned, which can include documents (like the NGSS) that define learning standards. Blueprints may also include knowledge structures, learning progressions, and assessment frameworks, as well as analysis of learner characteristics (profiles). Taken together, these blueprints clarify and specify the key structural elements of the design.

Based on the foundations and blueprints, either an LS or an ID process designs new **Inputs** to the learning process. These can include new learning materials or resources (i.e., videos, books, podcasts), tools (i.e., simulations, interactive visualizations, data analysis tools, scientific workbenches), workspaces and learning environments, and instructor capabilities (often enhanced through professional development, coaching, and scaffolding for the teachers, coaches, mentors, parents, tutors, or other people who support the learners). Additional classes of inputs are the resources and constraints of the environment within which the learning environment must operate, such as time and place requirements, administrative policy, and organizational requirements. Each input typically has its own design tool and

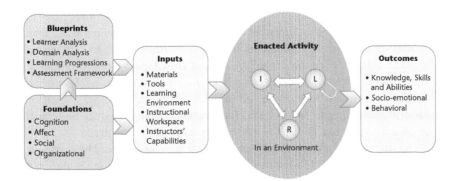

FIGURE 5.1 Proposed consensus logic model for teaching and learning

authoring process: thus, as an example, storyboards and templates define scripts, which are then produced using appropriate authoring tools.

Neither LS nor ID believes that the inputs directly cause learning. Rather, learning happens when learners (and often, instructors) **enact activities** with the inputs. Hence, the quality of enactment (or quality of implementation) can significantly mediate the learning process and outcomes. Further, characteristics of the individuals and the setting may moderate outcomes. In a classic school-based logic model (Cohen et al., 2003), teachers ("I" for instructor in the figure) and students ("L" for learner in the figure) together use resources ("R") in an environment.

Perhaps the arrow from Inputs to the Enacted Activity is an oversimplification: in many important senses, the design of inputs not only references foundations and blueprints but also includes moderating and mediating factors related to enactment. For example, a key class of blueprints models the *learners*: a design needs to anticipate their prior knowledge and skills; goals and interests, frame of reference, affect, attitudes, and beliefs; home environment and socio-economic status; and, of course, their age, gender, culture, language, and other background factors. Furthermore, learners interact not just with an instructor and resources, but with each other (hence, the returning arrow in the figure).

With regard to *instructors* (and other supportive people), a design needs to anticipate and develop, coach, and scaffold their content knowledge, pedagogic knowledge, and technology knowledge. The design may also need to take into account many of the same moderating factors as listed for learners. In collaborative, self-guided, and informal learning environments with no formal instructor role, the design needs to include a means to provide the essential learning environment components that would otherwise be provided by an instructor.

With regard to *resources*, these may be conceptualized in many ways as informational, instructional, communications-oriented, expressive, or creative, or as working tools of the discipline.

Also, the conceptualization of the overall *environment* for learning is important. Is it informal (i.e., primarily oriented to interest or the immediate needs of a work task) or formal (i.e., primarily oriented to specified learning outcomes)? Does it emphasize self-directed or instructor-directed learning? What supports are there for managing instruction (including allocation of time, space, and resources)? What capabilities or features of the physical and virtual space support (or inhibit) interactions and feedback among learners, instructors, and resources? With regard to technology, the environment can often be fruitfully conceptualized as a *platform* that structures the basic opportunities for enacting learning activities. Some such environments automate functions otherwise performed by instructors.

The interactions among these elements are highly important. Do instructors get information from the resources to adapt instruction? How are the resources used in activities to engage students in learning? What is the nature of the discourse among learners and between learners and the instructor?

Finally, the enacted activity leads to *outcomes* that may be some combination of cognitive, socio-emotional, behavioral, or psychomotor, or of a different nature. There may be outcomes for instructors as well as learners. In a well-conceived theory of action, everything that precedes the outcomes is coherent with the intended learning gains. For example, a design which seeks a non-cognitive outcome would likely build on non-cognitive research foundations, address non-cognitive considerations in blueprints, and design inputs which are likely to change learning activities to influence non-cognitive outcomes. Indeed, these are called logic models, because the strength of the logic connecting each element is essential to the quality of the design.

Of course, there may be feedback loops at any level of the figure.

The point of this logic model is that we think both LS and ID would agree on the importance of these components, regardless of the type or intent of learning, the profile of the learner, the platform's technology, and the affordances of the learning environment. Further, the logic model makes the complexity of the design problem clear. Outside the domain of education and training, many design case studies relate to consumer products, and these designs typically must satisfy only the single individual who will use the product. Design cases in education, by way of contrast, typically can succeed only when they lead to extended activities which are enactments by multiple people who vary considerably in their backgrounds and ways of engaging in a learning activity. Because of this complexity, successful designs in education rarely result from a single, unitary thrust, but rather involve *bricolage* of many different elements and approaches which together encourage successful enactment of learning activities.

We can also return to our earlier contrast between the goals of LS and ID by reiterating that a design science research project (whether done by an LS or ID researcher) may choose to ignore some dimensions of this complexity, but development projects meant to scale in the real world cannot. This attention to the entire scope of design complexity required is one of the biggest reasons for the difference in purpose of LS and ID.

We will now turn our attention to three areas of common interest and challenge, which we feel are particularly in need of collaboration of LS and ID, if the state of the art is to advance: learning of domain knowledge, assessment, and scalability. Our intent in this discussion is only to illustrate the kind of collaboration that we think is needed. Many other examples of potential areas of collaboration can be easily identified.

Learning of Domain Knowledge

Societal expectations for learning are advancing rapidly. Over much of the 20th century, advancing expectations were mostly related to "attainment": the expectation that everyone should complete high school came first, followed by the expectation that many would complete college, and then leading to increases in how many people obtained advanced degrees. However, in the 21st century it is unreasonable to add more years of schooling (or more time in training) and yet more learning is needed. This is leading to an *intensification* of expectations for the quality of learning at every level. For example, in mathematics, where the middle school curriculum was once a consolidation and formalization of primary school mathematics, it is now widely expected to propel students into algebraic thinking and disciplinary practices of mathematical argumentation.

The intensification of learning expectations focuses on knowledge, skills, and abilities specific to a domain (or discipline): in English Language Arts, critical analysis is featured; in mathematics, algebraic reasoning has risen to the fore; and in science, developing foundational understandings and using them in inquiry. Similar examples can be found in training domains as well: for example, whereas conventional 20th century training might focus on accurate application of procedures to fix equipment (Mager, 1982), now there would likely be more emphasis on diagnostic reasoning and collaborative problem solving. In this case, shared domain knowledge often includes a structural knowledge of the device (perhaps expressed as a block diagram), principles of why it works as designed, failure modes and their frequencies, diagnostic procedures and their costs and risks, and manipulation of a mental model of the device not only in normal operation, but in abnormal and failure modes (Steinberg & Gitomer, 1992). This intensification is driving instruction beyond the simple cultural patterns of teaching and learning, such as "I do, we do, you do," and requiring more complex instructional designs that aim to develop related dimensions of knowing and doing over time.

Cognitive theory of knowledge has provided a language to describe the dimensions of disciplinary knowledge that are now important. For example, memory theory identified a distinction between declarative knowledge, procedural knowledge, and metacognition (executive function) (Anderson, 2013). Stemming from this work are well-established and efficient instructional strategies for teaching facts, concepts, principles, and well-structured procedures. These strategies have been extended to diagnosis (through error analysis) and correction of misconceptions. Work over the past generation on well- and ill-structured problem solving has established the central importance of domain knowledge, with components of all types of knowledge, organized for the purpose of efficient problem solving in the domain, and shared among participants in a community of practice. This theoretical framework has been applied across a broad range of content areas, such as school mathematics and science, engineering, troubleshooting, combat, medical diagnosis, design, sports, and leadership.

The intensification of learning expectations and diversification of desired gains in knowledge, skills, and abilities is requiring the invention of new ways to engineer complex instructional approaches. This, in turn, leads to important problems of learning theory, analysis, and design that must be addressed to advance the state of the art. For example, we believe there is important work to be done in a number of areas:

Knowledge structures, mental models, and learning trajectories. The central aspects of the complex of learning environments now needed are ways to build more extensive, coherent, interlinked knowledge structures over time. As before, we must help the learner to build a personally useful version of the shared knowledge structure for the domain being studied. However, now the complexity of the target knowledge structure and the amount of time needed to develop them has grown: we may be aiming for a span of learning experiences to develop a cohesive mix of perceptions, principles, approaches, abilities to use tools, modeling practices, and aesthetics of a quality solution. When designing instruction, this knowledge structure drives construction of presentations, examples, activities, investigations, practice and feedback, collaborative teamwork, and assessment. Difficult issues surround how to design a progression of learning experiences, as well as how to plan adaptations to that progression when a student does not progress as expected. Both LS and ID have developed a broad array of analytical techniques, ranging from Gagné's learning hierarchies (Gagné, 1985) to a range of representations used in various assessment systems, expert systems, electronic performance support systems, and intelligent tutors (Heller et al., 2013) as well as curriculum design tools and learning management systems, and to the current efforts at specifying learning trajectories (Clements & Sarama, 2014). However, these analytical techniques have generally proven to be inefficient to use and idiosyncratic in result: no two analysts would produce the same product when using an analysis technique, and attempts to demonstrate empirically that an analysis is valid enough to generalize have often proven difficult. Thus, specification of domain knowledge structures remains more of a craft than a technology. Meeting this challenge clearly requires a multi-field, multidisciplinary effort involving not only LS and ID, but related work in computer science and information science, assessment, and learning psychology (as well as cognitive neuroscience).

Instructional strategies for teaching domain knowledge also need further refinement. We believe most researchers in LS and ID would recognize that full solutions require some mix of direct instruction (e.g., explanation, modeling and practice with feedback) and inductive learning (e.g., through collaborative learning and exploratory strategies). However, despite development of unified models of instructional strategy (e.g., Van Merriënboer et al., 2002; Van Merrienboer & Sweller, 2005), there is little consensus among LS and ID on domain knowledge teaching strategies that are both effective in building domain expertise and efficient in doing so—especially for complex, ill-structured problem solving. We believe this challenge requires collaboration across both fields.

Far transfer. Most educators would agree that their goal is for the learner to use what is learned well beyond the learning environment. Despite this, however, it is still rare in school contexts for assessment of efficacy to extend beyond the initial learning experience—whether done by researchers in LS or ID. In training contexts, particularly those that are planned as part of a Human Performance Improvement (HPI) intervention (Van Tiem et al., 2012), assessment of on-the-job effects of training are somewhat more common. In both education and training, efficacy research suggests that far transfer is quite difficult to attain reliably.

We believe there are two important challenges limiting advancement of the state of the art for far transfer. At the level of underlying learning theory, we don't have a robust causal model of what far transfer is and how it occurs. While work on mechanisms such as analogical reasoning are promising (Vendetti et al., 2015) there is still much to be done to get to a robust model of prescriptive use. Likewise, there is promise in re-conceptualizing transfer in terms of preparation for future learning (e.g., Schwartz & Martin, 2004). This reconceptualization reorients from the older expectation that students would *learn* at time 1 in order to *perform* at time 2, while the more recent expectation of lifelong learning is students learn at time 1 (in a more-supported context) so they can *learn more* at time 2 (in a less-supported context). Consequently the measure of transfer shifts from performing in a new context to how effectively a student can later learn in a new (related) context.

In LS, this could lead to application of principles of cognitive apprenticeship, informal learning, and communities of practice beyond the learning environment. The current work on productive failure (e.g., Kapur, 2008) is also relevant. Meanwhile, ID and HPI have increasingly focused on moving parts of the learning environment into the performance environment, through use of strategies such as electronic performance support systems, just-in-time training (often embedded in the work environment by using mobile devices), structured mentoring, and coaching.

An example of needed collaboration on transfer is in emerging theories to support design of simulation and serious games, to which both LS and ID have contributed. We believe research attention should shift from short-term transfer experiments, to long-term study of development and transfer. We also believe it is time for LS and ID to collaborate on systematic design of complete learning solutions that allow the learner to move seamlessly from learning environments to performance environments and back, thus breaking down the walls between classroom and work, at every level of learning. Our goal should be to get learners at every level up to full expert level performance in real-world environments, whether or not the details of the performance can be specified in advance. And, we need to design solutions that can do so reliably, effectively, with a sound cost-benefit, at scale.

Assessment

There can be little doubt that in education and training, the rhetorical pendulum has swung from summative (assessment of learning) to formative (assessment for learning), and from assessment as a discrete test, to assessment of performance done in real or realistic environments (Gordon, 2013). However, robust prescriptive theory and design principles have yet to catch up to the rhetoric. Since ICT plays an important role in providing improved alternatives to conventional paper tests, LS and ID's experience with technology is particularly relevant here. From a theoretical view, we believe that among the most important challenges both LS and ID face are:

- *Construct validity of performance measures.* Typically performance-based measures depend only on face validity: resemblance to features of the corresponding real-world performance. Longitudinal study may allow validation of the measures against real-world performance, as measured by independent indicators. However, to be fully useful, it is important for performance measures also to be able to make inferences about domain knowledge and far transfer. For this purpose, Mislevy's Evidence-Centered Design (ECD) (Behrens et al., 2013) holds promise. Indeed, the kind of analysis required by ECD methodologies strongly parallels the analyses done within an ID framework using methods such as cognitive task analysis.
- *Inference of knowledge structures.* If the assessment is to be of use in prescribing adaptations of the learning environment to build domain knowledge and correct misconceptions of each learner, then the assessment system must be able to draw inferences about the learner's knowledge structure in its current vs. desired form. This, in turn, requires a robust method of analysis of knowledge structures (see the discussion of domain knowledge analysis, above). This kind of inference has only been attained so far within certain kinds of intelligent tutors (e.g., Ritter et al., 2007). We believe both LS and ID are needed to resolve this challenge, and until it is, use of assessment to guide learning will be limited to particular, non-generalizable projects where the architects substitute their intuition for a set of validated design practices.
- *Reliability of measurement.* Research projects, such as *SimScientist* (Quellmalz et al., 2013) and the work on "stealth assessment" (Shute & Becker, 2010), are demonstrating that it is possible to achieve acceptable levels of measurement reliability using performance measures, at least in simulation and game environments. However, reliability at a level suitable for high-stakes use is still more costly and difficult to attain efficiently than is the case with conventional tests.

Scalability

In developed countries, problems of access to ICT infrastructure are well on their way to being solved in schools, and are by now completely eliminated in the post-secondary and training worlds. The availability of universal, standardized ICT infrastructure creates unprecedented opportunities to scale innovative teaching and learning approaches quickly and widely. However, despite this near-universal access, the typical quality of learning solutions using ICT is far from the state of the art. What has scaled most rapidly and widely (for example, MOOCs which expand conventional university courses) has also yielded unprecedented levels of student attrition due to lack of high quality supports for learning.

Indeed, for 50 years, research on the efficacy of educational uses of technology has yielded a pattern of modest effect sizes on average when compared to "business as usual" classroom teaching (Tamim et al., 2011), with occasional promising strong effects that appear only in unusual circumstances. Further, these effect sizes often diminish or disappear as approaches are further scaled from highly controlled (and better resourced) implementations to everyday, ordinary implementations. Similarly, the long-predicted transformation of the school through use of ICT simply has not occurred. The most common ICT applications in classrooms are merely one-for-one substitutions for existing teaching practices, so the predicted major changes are yet to be seen except in isolated projects run by early adopters (for example, a careful evaluation of the Khan Academy's much talked-about "flipped classroom" approach found strong implementation among a few chosen earlier adopters, but that other implementations were highly variable and looked much more like conventional teaching) (see Murphy et al., 2014). In short, even what we *do* know about designing and delivering high-quality learning environments has not proven to be easily scalable.

We also believe it is a misconception that scaling up small-scale projects is a straightforward matter. Projects at scale differ not only in size, but in quality from smaller research projects. It is simply untrue, in our view, that the means and methods used to build and implement a learning solution for experimental use in a handful of classrooms (often with volunteer teachers who are early adopters), with no more than a few hundred students, can be directly scaled to tens of thousands of classrooms and millions of students. We argued above that designing for scale must take into account the full complexity of the learning environment represented in Figure 5.1. Thus, designing for scale involves solving larger and more complex problems than designing for a few carefully selected and nurtured classrooms or other learning spaces.

Furthermore, the sheer size of a large-scale design project requires different considerations and methods. Since the requirements of large-sized projects are not widely recognized by researchers, we offer this list of size risk issues we have encountered in our work:

- *Robust design methods.* For the typical small research project, design is a one-off task. By contrast, large-scale projects need design methods that are replicable, well-defined, and standardized enough so multiple large multidisciplinary teams can use them to produce solutions that reflect a common product architecture, production values and costs, and stylistic conventions—while still preserving the principles of user-centered design.

- *Cost-efficiency.* Large-scale development ought to achieve economies of scale, but these economies are achievable only if they are carefully planned. For example, careful planning is needed to build a library of common learning objects, production editors, templates and tools, graphics and media libraries, programming object libraries, and quality management standards. Our experience suggests that careful planning of this sort can reduce development cost by a factor of at least 50% over the life of the project.
- *Project management.* One does not manage a multidisciplinary team of hundreds in the same way one can manage a research group of a dozen or fewer. Careful risk management, workflow definition and tracking, definition of roles and responsibilities, and management of time and resources are essential to success with high quality and sound innovation.
- *Quality management.* A successful education or training curriculum product must be instructionally effective, of course. However, when working at scale there is a strong preference for design methods that will minimize risk and rework, maximize efficiency, and ensure as much quality as possible in the first version (this applies even in agile development methods, with their use of rapid prototyping and early learner trials to validate design decisions).
- *Software quality.* When operating at scale, there is a premium on software that is cross-platform, robust in typical "messy" user environments, easily installed and configured, reliable, secure, capable of sustaining tens of thousands of simultaneous users, and easily modified and maintained. User technical support requirements must be as close to zero as possible. Furthermore, the software must support a variety of rights management and licensing scenarios. Large project software development is often done by large teams that must work with the same tools sets and to uniform technical standards. By contrast, software developed for research purposes rarely faces these design requirements. Thus, the discipline for design and development of scalable software is substantially different—and more costly—than that for research purposes. This is an important reason why research software rarely goes to scale successfully, even when there is a commercialization attempt.
- *Professional development/user training, adoption and integration.* At scale, the per-user cost of first-time and recurrent professional development and curriculum integration work is often a major barrier to adoption, especially in education. Consequently, scalable products have a major design objective of minimizing professional development and integration/deployment costs to as close as possible to zero. Furthermore, the typical user is a "middle adopter" who may not have highly developed technological and pedagogical content knowledge (Koehler & Mishra, 2009). By contrast, small-scale research projects often can afford to treat professional development and deployment as a one-time project cost. Curriculum integration may not even be an issue. Thus, for PD and integration/deployment, the cost-benefit tradeoffs for scalable solutions are substantially different from those of small-scale research projects.

We believe that design for scalability is a complex, multidimensional challenge that requires contributions from both LS and ID. For example, we believe both LS and ID need to adopt a true user-centered (participatory) design philosophy; all too often, both researchers and entrepreneurs are seduced by their own visions, and as a result, their work is not designed to meet the needs of large numbers of "middle adopter" users in typical real-world education and training environments. A focus on design-based implementation research (DBIR) has emerged as a correction to this, with the emphasis on implementation signaling greater research and design focus on solving problems of implementation that arise at scale (Fishman et al., 2013). Yet there is still much to be done to develop DBIR from a research emphasis to an engineering approach. By contrast, requirements of design for scalability and size are familiar to ID (e.g., Gibbons, 2013). We believe bringing the lessons from LS to the larger scale, multilayer designs common in ID would benefit the state of the art.

Concluding Remarks

The issues discussed above are admittedly only a few examples chosen from a much larger body of important and complex issues in need of collaborative study from the perspectives of LS and ID. For example, a full discussion of differentiated instruction (including individualization, personalization, adaptive instruction, and formative assessment) would clearly benefit from collaborative work of many fields, but even a superficial discussion of the issues involved would exceed the scope of this chapter.

What do all these issues have in common? They are all important to the progress in research on learning and instruction in order to tackle intensification of learning expectations now occurring in every sector of education and training, with larger implications for technology. Their complexity and depth exceed the theoretical frameworks and tools of inquiry commonly used in either LS or ID. Thus, serious progress on any of these problems will require teamwork that is truly multi-field and interdisciplinary. We applaud the goals of this volume, and we view as an encouraging sign the emergence of interdisciplinary research journals such as *Technology, Instruction, Cognition and Learning* (TICL) and *Computers and Human Behavior* (CHB). We would also like to see the major research journals in LS and ID publish more interdisciplinary articles and special issues on topics such as those we have surveyed here.

We also acknowledge, however, that the differences in culture between the two fields can act as a barrier to collaboration. We might say (somewhat facetiously) that LS risks getting more and more detailed about less and less of the scope of the full instruction challenge as discussed here. ID risks creating a clean, well-lighted book that no one wants to read: ID's favorite city might be Singapore (so perfectly engineered); LS's favorite city might be London (as the infrastructure is a nightmare, but there's a story of historic proportions under every manhole cover).

ID risks treating every project like a rocket launch. LS risks treating every project like a novel. These stereotypes are obviously overstated for effect, but perhaps there is a grain of truth in each.

Perhaps the best posture for LS and ID researchers to engage with each other is to adopt humility in the face of the many complex problems that both fields are trying to solve. When the elephant is as formidable as ours, the blind need all the help they can get.

Acknowledgment

This material is based in part upon work supported by the National Science Foundation under Grant No. IIS-1233722. Any opinions, findings, and conclusions or recommendations expressed in this material are those of the author(s) and do not necessarily reflect the views of the National Science Foundation.

References

Anderson, J. R. (2013). *The architecture of cognition*. New York: Psychology Press.

Anderson, L. W., Krathwohl, D. R., & Bloom, B. S. (2001). *A taxonomy for learning, teaching, and assessing: A revision of Bloom's Taxonomy of educational objectives* (Abridged ed.). New York: Longman.

Behrens, J. T., Mislevy, R. J., DiCerbo, K. E., & Levey, R. (2013). Evidence centered design for learning and assessment in the digital world. In M. Mayrath, J. Clarke-Midura, D. Robinson, & G. Shraw (Eds.), *Technology-based assessments for 21st century skills* (pp. 13–53). Charlotte, NC: Information Age Publishing.

Clements, D. H., & Sarama, J. (2014). *Learning and teaching early math: The learning trajectories approach*. Oxon: Routledge.

Cohen, D. K., Raudenbush, S. W., & Ball, D. L. (2003). Resources, instruction, and research. *Educational evaluation and policy analysis, 25*(2), 119–142.

Donovan, M. S., Bransford, J. D., & Pellegrino, J. W. (1999). *How people learn*. Washington, DC: National Academies Press. Retrieved March 20, 2017 from www.nap.edu/catalog/9853/how-people-learn-brain-mind-experience-and-school-expanded-edition?gclid=Cj0KEQjw2LjGBRDYm9jj5JSxiJcBEiQAwKWAC0kcgWb6ajC2CQweKXkF2CzjagTuFil0En2zmtknWc8aAgtU8P8HAQ

Fishman, B., Penuel, W. R., Allen, A., Cheng, B. H., & Sabelli, N. (2013). Design-based implementation research: An emerging model for transforming the relationship of research and practice. *National Society For The Study Of Education Yearbook, 112*(2), 136–156.

Gagné, R. (1985). *The conditions of learning* (4th ed.). New York: Holt, Rinehard and Winston.

Gibbons, A. S. (2013). *An architectural approach to instructional design*. New York: Taylor & Francis.

Gordon, E. W. (2013). *Gordon Commission Report: Panel discussion*. Paper presented at the American Educational Research Association, San Francisco.

Heller, J., Ünlü, A., & Albert, D. (2013). Skills, competencies and knowledge structures. In J.-C. Falmagne, D. Albert, C. Doble, D. Eppstein, & X. Hu (Eds.), *Knowledge Spaces* (pp. 229–242). Verlag Berlin Heidelberg: Springer

Kapur, M. (2008). Productive failure. *Cognition and Instruction, 26*(3), 379–424.

Koehler, M., & Mishra, P. (2009). What is technological pedagogical content knowledge (TPACK)? *Contemporary Issues in Technology and Teacher Education, 9*(1), 60–70.

Mager, R. (1982). *Troubleshooting the troubleshooting course, or debug d'bugs.* Belmont, CA: Pitman Learning.

Murphy, R., Gallagher, L., Krumm, A. E., Mislevy, J., & Hafter, A. (2014). *Research on the use of Khan Academy in schools. Research brief.* Menlo Park, CA: SRI Education.

National Research Council (2013). *Next generation science standards: For states, by states.* Washington, DC: The National Academies Press. doi:https://doi.org/10.17226/18290.

Quellmalz, E. S., Davenport, J. L., Timms, M. J., DeBoer, G. E., Jordan, K. A., Huang, C.-W., & Buckley, B. C. (2013). Next-generation environments for assessing and promoting complex science learning. *Journal of Educational Psychology, 105*(4), 1100–1114. doi:10.1037/a0032220

Ritter, S., Anderson, J. R., Koedinger, K. R., & Corbett, A. (2007). Cognitive tutor: Applied research in mathematics education. *Psychonomic Bulletin & Review, 14*(2), 249–255.

Schwartz, D. L., & Martin, T. (2004). Inventing to prepare for future learning: The hidden efficiency of encouraging original student production in statistics instruction. *Cognition and Instruction, 22*(2), 129–184.

Shute, V. J., & Becker, B. J. (2010). *Innovative assessment for the 21st century: Supporting educational needs.* New York: Springer.

Steinberg, L. S., & Gitomer, D. H. (1992). *Cognitive task analysis, interface design, and technical troubleshooting.* Research Report RR 92-73. Princeton, NJ: Educational Testing Service.

Stokes, D. E. (1997). *Pasteur's quadrant: Basic science and technological innovation.* Washington, DC: Brookings Institution Press.

Tamim, R. M., Bernard, R. M., Borokhovski, E., Abrami, P. C., & Schmid, R. F. (2011). What forty years of research says about the impact of technology on learning a second-order meta-analysis and validation study. *Review of Educational Research, 81*(1), 4–28.

Van Merrienboer, J. J., & Sweller, J. (2005). Cognitive load theory and complex learning: Recent developments and future directions. *Educational Psychology Review, 17*(2), 147–177.

Van Merriënboer, J. J., Clark, R. E., & De Croock, M. B. (2002). Blueprints for complex learning: The 4C/ID-model. *Educational Technology Research and Development, 50*(2), 39–61.

Van Tiem, D. M., Moseley, J. L., & Dessinger, J. C. (2012). *Fundamentals of performance technology: A guide to improving people process and performance* (3rd ed.). San Francisco: Pfeiffer.

Vendetti, M. S., Matlen, B. J., Richland, L. E., & Bunge, S. A. (2015). Analogical reasoning in the classroom: Insights from cognitive science. *Mind, Brain, and Education, 9*(2), 100–106.

6
IMPLICATIONS
Cherishing the Middle Ground

Jan Elen

Introduction

Addressing implications of a phenomenon requires at least some basic understanding of the phenomenon at hand, in this case the existence of two communities with great interest in learning and in supporting learning. In both communities eminent researchers and professionals reflect about what learning is, what it implies, how it occurs in different contexts, and how to design and implement innovative approaches to support learning often with the help of (new) technologies. This reflection gets inspired by an in-depth understanding of learning processes and the impact of context. While this overall ambition seems to be shared by both communities, a different (not necessarily opposite) underlying logic or ambition seems to drive the two communities (see Figure 6.1). While both communities share a fascination for learning, it is my understanding that members of a (sub)community of the learning sciences are predominantly interested in understanding learning whereas members of a (sub)community of instructional design and technology are rather interested in goal-directed interventions. As a side note it is to be mentioned that individuals can be members of both communities.

The prevailing interest in both communities makes them—despite the common interest in supporting learning—rather different and comes with particular features, characteristics, and even challenges or issues. Without any claim for exhaustiveness, some of these are highlighted in view of detecting implications (see Figure 6.1).

As a whole, the community of the learning sciences seems to be primarily interested in understanding learning. This implies that learning gets observed and inferences are made on the variables and factors that affect that learning. This is a very broad scope (see the impressive *Encyclopedia of the Sciences of Learning*,

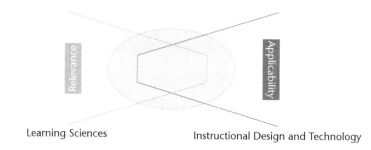

FIGURE 6.1 Two communities interested in learning and supporting learning

edited by Norbert Seel (2012)). Investigations may lead to studies about the psychological and neurological processes at the nano level as well as studies on the role of behavioral, cognitive, and social interaction processes in learning. Given the interest in such processes, this research is characterized by observations in highly controlled (often experimental or quasi-experimental) circumstances. It may also result in studies that focus on the impact on learning of specific changes in the environment (e.g., the work on adjunct aids or on multimedia learning). At the same time, that same interest in understanding learning has also given rise to studies that stress the contextual nature of learning and hence, to studies in which learning is observed in authentic settings. In view of optimally supporting learning in such settings and acknowledging the contextual nature of learning, rich descriptions of learning are an important starting point.

These two approaches to address the ambition to understand learning reveal an underlying issue: the need for relevance both practically and theoretically. From a perspective in which the contextual nature of learning is stressed, studies on detailed cognitive processes might be regarded to be practically irrelevant because they lack ecological validity. While it is fascinating to reveal how in the brain different regions become active when pupils get confronted with specific problems, the immediate implications of such studies for supporting learning in regular settings remain hard to grasp. From a perspective of understanding the underlying cognitive processes, studies that stress the contextual nature might be regarded to be theoretically irrelevant as they—apart from the notion of context-dependency—only seldom offer generalizable abstractions. An important contribution of these studies is the elaboration of a vocabulary to represent the uniqueness of learning in specific contexts.

In view of resolving the tension between theoretical and practical relevance, the growing interest (in both communities) in (different forms of) design-based research is high as it is claimed to offer a way to be at the same time practically and theoretically relevant. While this can be argued to be the case, most who tried to do so have experienced the complexity of the challenge. That should not be surprising given that multiple authors have identified the intrinsic difficulties related to combining theoretical and practical perspectives to relevance (e.g., Phillips & Dolle, 2006).

The community of instructional design and technology seems to be especially interested in supporting goal-directed learning. This implies a relative emphasis on interventions and the effects of these interventions on learning. Within the community of instructional design and technology the interest seems to be mainly directed towards learning that is in line with goals identified prior to the actual learning and not necessarily put forward by the learners themselves. The issue of goals is important not only with respect to the complex issue of selecting important goals for learning, but also with respect to aligning learning goals of learners with instructional goals. Not surprisingly, motivation and how it can be supported is a major issue (e.g. Keller, 2008). Immediately it becomes clear that research on interventions inherently builds on an in-depth understanding of learning (as research on understanding also considers the environment and hence the interventions in which learning occur). In the community of instructional design and technology, interventions are studied, models get elaborated, and the effects of technology use are discussed. As is the case in the community of learning sciences, different positions are taken with respect to a major issue, in this case applicability. On the one hand a multitude of general instructional design models has been elaborated sometimes for specific contexts, but often claiming broad applicability. The broad applicability makes the models "general" and often abstract (e.g., Merrill, 2002). On the other hand, members have tried to highlight the specifics of interventions resulting in detailed, highly complex, and proceduralized recommendations not only about the why and what of interventions but also about the specific requirements for their implementation. An interest in interventions and technology has also brought about a widely criticised focus on technology as such (e.g., Reeves & Reeves, 2015). In numerous studies technology has been focused upon, as if an excellent solution were in search of a decent problem. Applicability can be seen as the major issue in the community of instructional design resulting in broad, general models on the one hand (widely applicable but difficult to implement) and highly specific procedures on the other (directly implementable but only in very specific contexts).

While some issues (relevance, applicability) might be more typical (though not unique) to one of the communities, issues are also clearly shared. Both communities struggle with a problem of terminological confusion and as a consequence with accumulation. Terminological rigor and accumulation may be counterproductive when they narrowly define what might be appropriate research questions and approaches. They may help when they come along with a continuous but explicit and critical discussion of the meaning of terms.

In the following sections an attempt is made to reflect on the implications of the particularities of the two communities. The main question is what it means to build on rich traditions and cherish the middle ground. While distinctions can be made and stressed, it is also clear that neither of the two communities is homogeneous (there are different tendencies and subcommunities in each community). Moreover, while distinctions can be made it is also clear that there is overlap in membership (as there is in research questions and research issues). The reflection in the following sections is made from three perspectives. Each perspective represents a role assumed by the author and each perspective will be discussed from the specific situation of the author. It is assumed that implications are not absolute, but depend on the specific position with respect to the phenomenon one has (at a certain moment). The three roles are teacher of a course on designing learning environments, researcher in the field of instructional design and educational technology, and editor of *Instructional Science, a journal of the Learning Sciences*. We wrap up the chapter by trying to identify some general implications.

Before discussing implications from these three perspectives it is to be acknowledged that in the above a specific interpretation is made of two existing communities. In another interpretation one might refer to the heated debate on the differences between constructivist and objectivist perspectives towards learning and supporting learning. This would imply that learning sciences are more narrowly defined as reflecting a constructivist perspective towards learning and supporting learning. At the same time this would imply that instructional design and technology would necessarily reflect an objectivistic perspective. Although this results in an interesting debate with clear positions (mostly for rhetorical reasons), it also would render the discussion overly simplistic. It would neglect that very different approaches can be taken. This point was nicely illustrated by Cronje (2006) in his argument that constructivism and objectivism could be conceived to be two independent dimensions rather than two extreme positions on one dimension. Furthermore, it would impose a typical American/Anglo-Saxon debate on the international research community. In the remainder we try to cherish the middle ground and highlight the implications for different roles of the existence of multiple communities and perspectives.

Teacher

Confronted with two communities and with the issues of applicability, relevance, and accumulation, one has to wonder how to introduce the field to junior practitioners and scholars in the field. This is especially a challenge in case one aims at fairly representing the communities and highlighting their contributions as well as their specific perspectives and theoretical assumptions. The existence itself of different communities in the field requires that they get adequately represented; at the same time it also implies that a full account of current research in these communities can hardly be given. Ultimately and in order to cherish the middle ground, the implication seems to be that students have to elaborate the skills and perhaps—in Perkins and Ritchhart's (2004) terms—even the disposition to try to integrate insights from both an understanding and an intervention perspective.

In view of boosting that disposition, the following has been attempted for some years now in an actual course on designing learning environments.

patience from all involved. And even when all conditions are met and the research has been carried out rigorously and thoroughly, the result may be disappointing as this type of research enters largely unknown terrain.

Confronted with two communities and cherishing the middle ground seems to be a challenge that induces a lot of humility about what can be accomplished by an individual researcher. Collaboration among researchers from different communities seems more productive than fruitless debates on one's identity.

Editor

Journals are important actors in the academic world. Based on submissions and reviews and on the selection of editors and reviewers, decisions are made on what submissions are regarded to be worthwhile. Decisions are made about what submissions represent research in a field and provide examples of high-quality work. Journals then both reflect and make the field. Confronted with variety in the field, editors cannot but reflect on the implications and make selections. Not surprisingly there is an abundance of journals that reflect the concerns and outcomes from different (sub)communities both in learning sciences and instructional design and technology. The number of journals that cherish the middle ground is limited. One such journal is *Instructional Science*. The name might suggest that the journal stems from the instructional design and technology community. The title and the connotations of the notion "instruction" might even suggest that it holds an objectivistic or teacher-centred perspective. The former editor of the journal (Peter Goodyear) made a tremendous contribution. He added a subtitle to the name of the journal so that it is now known as *Instructional Science, a journal of the Learning Sciences*. The addition can be interpreted in at least two ways. One interpretation might be that the journal covers a broad field and basically encompasses all the research done in both learning sciences (as a broad area) and instructional design and technology (as a broad area). A second interpretation would imply that the journal positions itself in the middle ground. While discussions are still going on, it seems that the second interpretation is most prevalent in the current editorial board. While the scientific relevance and value is acknowledged of research that investigates the impact of specific interventions in controlled environments, provides an account of cases in which learning is supported in innovative ways, reviews the research on specific issues with respect to learning and problem solving, or provides accounts of how instructional design models were elaborated and implemented in specific settings, manuscripts about such research are not very high on the list of wanted manuscripts. However, manuscripts are cherished that embrace the middle ground. Highly preferred articles have high theoretical and practical relevance, and discuss the interplay between alterations in the context (interventions) and learning of either individuals or groups. Preferred articles are characterized by high ecological validity and methodological rigor; they build on and elaborate the existing knowledge base, are very explicit about their research questions, and are methodologically rich. Research results in the preferred articles are both generalizable and immediately applicable in concrete settings. While it might seem that the holy grail of educational research is desired, the "ideal" helps as a leading principle to at least identify what is regarded to be less (or even not) appropriate for the journal. Less appropriate are studies on specific learning processes with no clear relevance for learning in instructional settings (e.g., studies that discuss specific neurological mechanisms as such); descriptions of idiosyncratic reflections; or simplistic studies on learning styles or the direct impact of technology use. Similarly, a discussion of the technological features of a tool with instructional potential or a sociological discussion of agents in instructional contexts is no longer part of the aims and scope. For the rest, assessing and judging whether or not they belong to the field remains a challenge.

The implication of the existence of two communities and of the ambition to be a journal cherishing the middle ground seems to imply that complexity is not avoided but embraced.

Conclusions

Two communities are interested in studying (supporting) learning. Both cover broad areas and share an interest in getting to grips with important issues on learning and supporting learning. While in this contribution an attempt was made to specify the implications of what is common for both communities, the need for a wide variety of studies (as long as they are done well) each providing their own contribution deserves to be recognized. A similar argument was made in 1996 by Gaby Salomon who in his article "Studying the flute and the orchestra" very nicely highlighted the need for research at different levels and the specific issues of research at those different levels.

Cherishing the middle ground has been revealed to be a very challenging endeavor and not only for researchers as such. It is also a fascinating issue for editors of journals and not least, for teachers. Cherishing the middle ground seems to imply the embrace of complexity, not as a burden, but as a constituent. Complexity is not to be avoided, but to be addressed. As Hmelo-Silver et al. (2007) already pointed out, for those in the middle ground the right question is not whether it works, but under what circumstances it works. That sounds like a simple reformulation of the question but it makes a tremendous difference.

Embracing complexity, from my perspective, does not imply that methodological rigor becomes impossible, on the contrary (Elen & Clark, 2006). Complexity should not be an excuse for vagueness. Pointing to the importance of context or to the impact of perceptions cannot be the ultimate purpose of the research. Rather, it is an invitation to specify what aspects of context do matter, what perceptions are indeed relevant and how they work. Embracing complexity implies the need to dig deeper, to look for underlying structures, to reveal the underlying mechanisms. This position calls for even more precision in the formulation of research questions; for even more specific descriptive frameworks (in line with the literature); for the systematic and careful use of the most appropriate research methods; and for consistent reporting in which clear attempts are made to build on, question, and/or strengthen the current knowledge base. It calls for acknowledging the limits of one's own contribution and hence induces the need for collaboration. Embracing complexity reveals the importance of critical thinking and of considering one's epistemological assumptions.

Given the complexity of doing research in the middle ground and given the large number of conditions that have to be fulfilled for doing it right, we might not expect a lot of research to happen there. That is even more reason to cherish those exceptions and look for ways in which groups of researchers can collaborate. Bringing researchers together from different (sub)communities, each with their own insights and perspectives, might be the way to go. To collaborate in full awareness of one's contributions and limitations might be the best way to cherish the middle ground. The presence of different communities enriches the field and only collaboration will foster the field and ensure that our research efforts are not only relevant and applicable, but also meaningful.

References

Cronjé, J. (2006). Paradigms regained: Toward integrating objectivism and constructivism in instructional design and the learning sciences. *Educational Technology Research and Development, 54*, 387–416.

Elen, J., & Clark, R. E. (2006). Setting the scene: Complexity and learning environments. In J. Elen & R. E. Clark (Eds.), *Handling complexity in learning environments* (pp. 1–11). Amsterdam: Elsevier.

Hmelo-Silver, C. E., Duncan, R. G., & Chinn, C. A. (2007). Scaffolding and achievement in problem-based and inquiry learning: A response to Kirschner, Sweller, and Clark (2006). *Educational Psychologist, 42*, 99–107.

Keller, J. M. (2008). An integrative theory of motivation, volition, and performance. *Technology, Instruction, Cognition and Learning, 6*, 79–104.

Merrill, M. D. (2002). First principles of instruction. *Educational Technology Research and Development, 50*, 43–59.

Perkins, D. N., & Ritchhart, R. (2004). When is good thinking? In D. Y. Dai & R. J. Sternberg (Eds.), *Motivation, emotion and cognition: Integrative perspectives on intellectual functioning and development* (pp. 351–384). Mahwah, NJ: Lawrence Erlbaum.

Phillips, D. C., & Dolle, J. R. (2006). From Plato to Brown and beyond: Theory, practice, and the promise of design experiments. In L. Verschaffel, F. Dochy, M. Boekaerts, & S. Vosniadou (Eds.). *Instructional psychology: Past, present and future trends* (pp. 277–292). Amsterdam: Elsevier.

Reeves, T. C., & Reeves, P. M. (2015). Educational technology research in a VUCA world. *Educational Technology, 55*, 26–30.

Salomon, G. (1996). Studying the flute and the orchestra: Controlled vs. classroom research on computers. *International Journal of Educational Research, 14*, 521–531.

Seel, N. (Ed.) (2012). *Encyclopedia of the sciences of learning*. Dordrecht, The Netherlands: Springer.

7
RECONSIDERING DESIGN AND EVALUATION

Andrew S. Gibbons and David D. Williams

> Everything we evaluate is designed. Every evaluation we conduct is designed. Every report, graph, or figure we present is designed. In our profession, design and evaluation are woven together to support the same purpose—making the world a better place.
>
> *President John Gargani*
> *American Evaluation Association*
> *Announcing the Annual Conference theme for 2016*

Design and Evaluation Emerge as Formalisms

Instructional design and educational evaluation have emerged within the last century as formalized systems pertinent to the creation of education and training. The practices of instructional design and educational evaluation should be symbiotically related. But they have become academic silos, which has contributed to a lack of progress of theory and practice in both areas. Design practice is the main loser in this separation of interests. We propose that a more detailed examination reveals the natural value of this relationship, which may lead to advances in our understanding of design. In turn this may lead to advances in the teaching of design and evaluation.

Instructional design as a formal practice began to emerge in the early 1900s. Interest in systematic processes originated in public education (see Gibbons, 2015) and accelerated during both World Wars, joining with psychological, technological, and educational movements that coalesced beginning in the mid-1950s (Finn, 1953; Gibbons, 2014; Saettler, 1968). Following the World War II, new ideas from systems development added new substance and detail to formal instructional design processes (Gagné, 1965), and the field of instructional design began to stabilize as a profession.

In a limited number of introductory sessions instructional design models are presented and their theoretical background is discussed. Next, and assuming they are acquainted with basic insights on learning, students are invited to create an instructional design decision tree. They are asked to specify what advice they would give to practitioners who are about to design a specific learning environment and to reveal the underlying reasoning. Rather than asking the students to design an environment and justify their decisions, they are invited to elaborate a reasoning that can be used to make operational decisions for multiple concrete environments. In view of making the task reasonable some more specific questions and a context are provided. For instance, students are said to be consultants with respect to the design of Massive Open Online Courses (MOOCs) and they have to provide consultancy with respect to a specific question, for example, introducing interaction in MOOCs. Their decision tree has to help them to provide concrete advice on when to provide interaction and of what type. In addition to the design decision tree, students are required to elaborate three argumentation charts. These argumentation charts highlight the reasons why in the decision tree specific decisions are proposed. An argumentation chart is characterized by the inclusion of pro- and contra-arguments that can be theoretical or empirical.

This approach aims at confronting students with the issue of applicability as well as the issue of relevance, giving them an authentic academic task situated in the middle ground. In order to elaborate their design decision tree and argumentation charts, students (in groups) have to consult the (conceptual and empirical) literature. They get to know the heuristic value of instructional design models, the diverse conceptualizations of learning. They are confronted with terminological confusion and idiosyncratic frameworks. They experience that directly relevant research (for their question) can hardly be found and are astonished by the absence of empirical evidence for strong theoretical claims. Otherwise students get confused by the abundance of research on issues of doubtful relevance (from the perspective of their task). Gradually they become aware of the need to take a stance, to think critically, and to elaborate their own reasoning. Confronted with a diversity of perspectives they start to understand the complexity of the issues addressed in the field of learning and supporting learning and come to an awareness that they themselves have to make up their own mind. This implies weighting arguments and hence reflecting on one's own epistemological assumptions.

From a teaching perspective, the existence of multiple communities that address supporting learning and an ambition to cherish the middle ground seem to imply the need for reflection and critical thinking. The existence of multiple communities reveals the need to confront students with different perspectives and the complexity of supporting learning. A task by means of which they are induced to dig into the rich—often conflicting—literature might be a promising starting point.

Researcher

Whereas students might get fascinated by the diversity of the field when they are exploring it, the situation is rather different for anybody who wants to contribute to the development of the field. Any researcher is limited and difficult decisions have to be made with respect to what research to do and how to do it. Whatever decision is made, it is a difficult one. Some people might opt to belong to one specific (sub)community and confront the specific conceptual and methodological issues that are intrinsic to that (sub)community. Setting up a high-quality experimental study is difficult because it implies a thorough understanding of different variables that do play a role and a lot of creativity to specify conditions that differ with respect to one variable only. Just as challenging is designing an ethnographic study as it implies to identify when, where, by whom, and for how long participation is required or desired. One also has to deal with the potentially conflicting roles of participant, observer, and researcher. Research on interventions is at least as difficult. While elaborating an intervention, numerous decisions have to be made, and it is far from easy to specify in detail why specific decisions are made and how these relate to the research question at hand. In research on collaborative learning for instance, one has to decide about the number of students in a group, the use of a script, the distribution of roles and so on. Just as difficult is the challenge of elaborating a model with both theoretical and practical value, while at the same time being applicable. Again, a wide variety of decisions has to be made on the level of granularity of the model, on the theoretical consistency of the different components of the model, on the representation of the model, and on the relationship between the model and its representation. Once a choice is made, consistency seems to be indicated—in full awareness of the relativity of choices made. That relativity does not imply that anything can go. On the contrary, it induces the need for methodological rigor and for forming clear arguments for the methodological approach adopted.

Some researchers cherish the middle ground and aim at doing research at the intersection of different communities. Design-based research has already been mentioned as an interesting approach to combine perspectives and approaches. However, the complexity of design-based research is daunting. It requires unambiguous clarity of concepts, valid and applicable assessment instruments, proper theoretical models to interpret the data, and an in-depth understanding of learning in real settings. Even if design-based research results in theoretically sound and practically relevant solutions, questions about their generalizability and actual effect remain.

While doing research is always both fascinating and challenging, cherishing the middle ground in research is impressively difficult. It is hard to see how it can be done by individuals or even groups in a short period of time with limited funding. Doing this type of research requires acknowledging multiple perspectives and a thorough knowledge of the literature, theoretical complexity, a lot of time, an in-depth understanding of actual practices, methodological sophistication, and

Evaluation as a field of formal study and practice formed and grew much more rapidly, beginning in the mid-1950s. Stimulus for rapid growth came from a new emphasis on accountability occasioned by both a sense of crisis in public education and rapid increases in expenditures on large social programs in the 1960s (McLaughlin & Phillips, 1991; Jardini, 2000).

Evaluation has two embodiments in practice: (a) it is a process of examining the details of a product, process, or phenomenon in order to judge its value, and (b) it is a process carried out during and after instructional design for the purpose of quality control, administration, and product improvement. Evaluation as a design-related practice originated from three different starting points: (a) the introduction of systems design processes developed during the war (Hughes & Hughes, 2000), (b) an empirical approach to the design of programmed instruction that employed a cybernetic build-test-evaluate-revise strategy to improve program effectiveness (Markle, 1969), and (c) educational research into product and program effectiveness (Tyler, 1969; McLaughlin & Phillips, 1991).

The Need for Unifying Theory

Design and evaluation grew up in a climate of expediency, necessity, and intense competition (see, for example, McLaughlin & Phillips, 1991). In both fields the creation of theory trailed practice rather than leading it. In both fields intellectual concepts grew by hypothesizing, rather than by derivation from core principles. Validation of competing approaches, though often recommended in both design and evaluation literatures, was seldom accomplished. Traditional research methods were not suited to the task of verifying technical models for solving highly contextualized and unique problems. Commercial interests of contractors and laboratories often found it more profitable in terms of funding to capitalize on the invention of new terms and approaches than to engage in argumentation from basic principles. Though leading practitioners and theorists in both fields spoke out for empirical verification, change was so rapid that it did not occur.

In this climate of entrepreneurship, and without a firm grounding, terminology in both fields suffered. Concepts in both fields lost precision rather than gaining it, as differences in usage occurred in the literature. Some terms began to refer to different things, and sometimes different terms were used to refer to the same thing.

The Broken Symmetry of Evaluation and Design

Where once in the literature descriptions of design and evaluation referred to each other (Flanagan, 1969; Bloom et al., 1971), the symmetry of the design–evaluation relationship was broken, and opportunities for joint innovation, theory building, and practical user guidance were lost. Today, though instructional designers speak a language of evaluation, it is in relatively shallow and formulaic terms.

Few instructional design graduate programs offer courses dedicated to evaluation design, and formal evaluation literature tends to dismiss interest in evaluation as it is carried out by designers (Scriven, 1991).

Several factors can be identified as contributors to this separation of interests. Among these are (a) a rapid escalation of evaluation economics compared to design in the 1970s, (b) heavier emphasis on theory development and use of theory in the evaluation field, (c) the superficiality of descriptions of evaluation by instructional designers, and (d) a resulting stagnation of the design field's view of evaluation. These and other factors created an imbalance in the mutual contributions these fields should have been making to each other. They also allowed descriptions of both design and evaluation to become increasingly trivialized in the mind of the instructional designer, stultifying further inquiry into the nature of design, and blocking potential insights and contributions from evaluation.

The Rapid Escalation of the Evaluation Economy

The launching of Sputnik in 1957 added impetus to the re-examination of the American educational system. Concern for its status and other social programs reached critical levels in the 1960s (Jardini, 2000). As pressures for reform increased, evaluating the status and impact of programs became a priority, and well-funded evaluation projects were launched. In this period of relative prosperity, evaluation became an industry. Theories of evaluation multiplied as the complexities of carrying out evaluations became more evident. During the same period, though considerable demand for designed curricula also increased, funding tended to go to non-designers and brand-name psychological theorists, and so did not contribute many insights into design practice.

The focus of evaluators during this period was not on the details of product or program design but on the results they produced. There was a distinctly scientific character to the manner in which evaluation studies were carried out. The interest of instructional designers in evaluation stemmed mainly from the need to quality-control products under design, and the value of evaluations performed by designers was either ignored or deprecated by the scientific-minded professional evaluator.

These factors set up a pattern of the isolation of design-related evaluation and its eventual trivialization to being a somewhat adjunctive and optional activity to instructional design. The attention of the evaluation theorist was on diagnosis and causation at much higher levels of concern than the details of product effectiveness. The literature of scientific evaluation slowly became less relevant to the concerns of the designer, so the designer was left to gather out just those concepts relevant to designing, which over time became fewer. Designers began to produce their own practical literature on evaluation and over time became less interested in formal evaluation literature. There was little money available for serious scholarship on evaluation and its deeper relationship to design.

Emphasis on Theory Development in Evaluation

The development of formal evaluation theory expanded, as the complexities associated with evaluations of diverse kinds became apparent. Theory development for large-scale educational assessment increased as well, and so standardized testing also grew into an industry.

A further distraction for evaluators away from design concerns was the migration of evaluation toward social programs for fighting poverty and promoting social change. These competed for evaluation services as well. Increasingly, evaluation became a major professional field, built on competing theories associated with prominent names, perspectives, and philosophies.

Superficiality of Designers' Descriptions of Evaluation

The attention of designers became focused on the development of instructional design models (Andrews & Goodson, 1980; Gustafson, 1981; Gustafson & Branch, 1997, 2002; Gustafson & Powell, 1991). Components of design models became a major competitive issue, and though evaluation was unfailingly included and design models, it was a secondary and less prominent concern. It was not examined as closely as processes for design, development, and media concerns.

Lacking attention from professional evaluators, designers began to create their own literature on evaluation. However, this literature also tended to separate itself from the literature of design and development, so evaluation continued to be considered as a topic held at arm's length from design development. Evaluation books popular with instructional designers, though they have provocative titles, are written to a more general audience and do not examine evaluation in relation to instructional design processes (Worthen & Sanders, 1987; Patton, 2011).

The concerns of designers writing about evaluation were practical rather than theoretical, and pragmatic rather than philosophical. At the same time the trend in design models became less exploratory and more prescriptive. The desire of the military to create large numbers of in-house designers led to the publication of the Interservice Procedures for Instructional Systems Development (Branson et al., 1975), which was intended to simplify and standardize design and development processes to the point where otherwise untrained instructional designers could apply a systematic approach to produce usable instructional material. Design and development procedures had to be simplified in order to address this audience. Evaluation procedures had to be likewise simplified and related directly to development processes for quality control purposes.

From the mid-1950s on, the field of educational technology was responding to a call from Finn for professionalization (Finn, 1953). This led to the publication of a series of attempts to define the professional field (Association for Educational Communications and Technology, 1972, 1977; Ely, 1963, 1973, 1983; Finn, 1953, 1960; Seels & Richie, 1994; see also Januszewski, 2001 for a review of these attempts). These publications laid emphasis on design and development activities and on technology, placing less emphasis on the details of evaluation. Richey, Klein, and Tracey (2011) focus on the instructional design knowledge base but devote attention mainly to the theory of instruction at the expense of evaluation practice or theory. There are some exceptions to the trend of evaluation away from design (Hamilton & Feldman, 2014), but they are just exceptions.

Stagnation of Evaluation in a New Design Literature

In today's instructional design literature evaluation receives little more than cursory attention. Design models themselves are questioned, but no clear new description of design has emerged to take their place. Instead, there is a search for a set of concepts out of which a new description of design can be created. Discussion is beginning to focus on design thinking (Boling & Smith, 2008; Dorst, 2015; Lawson, 1997; Lawson & Dorst, 2009), design imagination (Kelley & Littman, 2001), the social role of the designer (Campbell et al., 2005; Hokanson & Miller, 2009; Kelley & Littman, 2005; Schwier et al., 2004), design as narrative (Parrish, 2006, 2008), and design architecture (Gibbons, 2014). In these discussions evaluation has continued to receive scant attention. One of the purposes of this paper is to renew interest in evaluation and its necessarily close association with the activities of design and development.

Design: Four Definitions and Their Impact

Visualizing the close relationship between evaluation and design depends on how design is described (Gibbons & Rogers, 2009; Gibbons & Yanchar, 2010). We have identified four approaches to describing design that illustrate this:

- Design as a process
- Design as a cybernetic activity
- Design as a logical exercise
- Design beyond logic

Design as a Process

Instructional design is most often described as a process consisting of steps and stages. Some form of process model is employed in virtually every design field, regardless of the content of the field, so instructional design process models are an instance of a larger class of design descriptions. Design process models have many uses: (a) they provide waypoints for marking progress through a design and development project, (b) they provide a general order for design activities, showing which stages must take precedence, (c) they provide security for novice designers who have no other guide, helping them to avoid inadvertently omitting an important step, (d) they facilitate resource and personnel scheduling, and (e) they show convergence points where independent strands of design activity flow together and become integrated.

Design process models are a boon to managers, who must account for schedules, personnel allocation, resource use, and deliverable products. Design process model steps are usually associated imperatives, such as standards for process, quality, and documentation. They also relate to staffing patterns. The downside of process models is that because they are geared to generic standards, they give less guidance for projects that do not fit a standard mold. For this reason, design models are less prone to produce *innovative* design solutions.

Evaluation's role in design process models is to provide quality control at each process step and for each deliverable. Judgments usually comprise product accuracy, effectiveness, acceptance, and accomplishment of initial project goals (budget, time frame, etc.). Sub-assemblies of a product may be subjected to testing by themselves, in intermediate assemblies, and as a whole product. This may occur during design, during rollout, during early implementation, and continuously throughout the lifetime of the product.

This description of the design process and its relationship to evaluation is generic and might as easily be applied to software design, hardware or device design, or the design (and development) of a bridge. The evaluand is the product, its components, and the integrated product's ability to function as planned within its context.

Industrial process models were originally adopted by instructional designers for good reasons. During and after World War II the design of complex engineered systems and the design of training for users, maintainers, and managers had to take place in parallel to ensure that the system and its operator were ready to function together as soon as possible (Gibbons et al., 2014). As instructional designers witnessed the effectiveness and efficiency of process models for engineers, they began to adopt them for their own work. Evidence of this adoption into the instructional design world can be seen in the work of Gagné (1965) and Briggs (1967, 1970) and later in the Interservice Procedures for Instructional Systems Development (Branson et al., 1975). As in the industrial models, the close coupling of evaluation with instructional design models was an unquestioned necessity.

However, this relationship has become somewhat loose. Though design must still be carried out, under the pressures of time and money, evaluation processes for low-stakes projects can, and often are, given lower priority.

Among designers in industry, evaluation is devalued except for high-stakes projects and military and government contracts that specify evaluation standards. Much of evaluation today in commercial and corporate practice is conducted using *smile sheets* that remove the threat of embarrassing failures for corporate project managers and sponsors.

Design as a Cybernetic Activity

Originally, a primary theme of instructional design process models was a cybernetic cycle between design acts and evaluation acts. The most visible application of the cybernetic principle in instructional design emerged in the 1960s, advocated by Markle (1964, 1967) for the proving of programmed instruction products. Each frame of a program under development might become an evaluand, as well as the program as a whole. As instructional programming was adopted by a wider population of designers, time and resource pressures became more confining, and the close cybernetic link between design and evaluation was in most cases lost; designers began to follow formulae rather than conducting product tests. The quality of programs declined, and eventually designers and clients lost interest in a demanding design process that required too many resources.

As design models trended upward and programmed instruction trended downward, interest in the cybernetic principle was strong, and it became one of the selling points for the acceptance of design models. As instructional goals were created, they were subjected to reviews and checks to ensure completeness, accuracy, and proper form. As instruction was created, it was tested and revised until it supported instructional goals. This corrective cybernetic closure was written into most design models, usually for each product element and process stage of the design. As sub-assemblies of the product were completed, they were subjected to testing, followed by whole-product testing. This cybernetic principle that was at one time a major selling point of design models can still be easily detected in some of the earlier instructional design textbooks (Banathy, 1968; Dick & Carey, 1976; Gagné & Briggs, 1979; Romiszowski, 1981; Smith & Ragan, 1999). Over time, as it became apparent that many customers were not prepared to pay for evaluations that could be embarrassing, design theorists soft-pedaled evaluation as a core topic in design, but have done very little new research on the relationship with design.

The cybernetic principle is still used today, but in modified form in design models that include agile design, rapid-cycle design, and prototype-test methods (Kelley & Littman, 2001; Krippendorff, 2007; Schrage, 1999; Scott et al., 2007; Tripp & Bichelmeyer, 1990). In design models of this type, which are popular in the software development field, the design and development processes are cycled rapidly to produce a testable product. After testing a design is modified according to the result; it is then produced in modified form and is tested again. This cycle continues until an acceptable product architecture and featuring emerges. In design systems of this type evaluation is elevated in importance and given the role of informing the design and providing data for its improvement. In this kind of design environment, evaluation cannot be treated as a secondary process because the design cannot move forward without it.

Design Thinking and Design as a Logical Exercise

The design process can be described at multiple levels. Over the past decade there has been heightened interest in describing design as a reasoning process. One approach has been to analyze it at the level of logic and reason. Rittel (1987/1988) addresses design at this level:

> Many forms of mental activity take place in the course of design.... A very significant part of design happens under conscious intellectual control. Since design is intentional, purposive, [and] goal-seeking, it decisively relies on reasoning. (p. 2)

Among instructional design theorists, there is evidence of a change in focus away from high-level process descriptions of design and toward more detailed descriptions of how designs are formed. Rittel proposes that in this perspective, "the designer's reasoning appears as a process of *argumentation*" (p. 3, emphasis in the original). He proposes that "the process appears as one of formation of judgment, alternating with the search for ideas" (p. 5). In this view, evaluative judgment becomes quite frequent and takes place at many levels of design decision-making: at high levels related to gross features, and at the smallest level of detail.

Schön (1987) describes an oscillation that takes place in the reasoning of the designer between ideation and evaluation prior to confirming a design commitment. What is notable is the length of time that a decision can remain tentative, before being made firm. It is also notable that even once a firm decision is reached, it can be undone and re-made later. Schön describes the design thinking of an architectural tutor named Quist during a problem solving session with a student:

> Quist spins out a web of moves, subjecting each cluster of moves to multiple evaluations drawn from his repertoire of design domains. As he does so, he shifts from embracing freedom of choice to accepting implications, from involvement in the local units to a distanced consideration of the resulting whole, and from a stance of tentative exploration to one of commitment. He discovers in the situation's back talk a whole new idea, which generates a system of implications for further moves. (p. 64)

For Schön, "designing takes the form of a reflective conversation with the situation" (p. 56):

> Each move [tentative decision] has consequences described and evaluated in terms drawn from one or more design domains. Each has implications binding on later moves. Each creates new problems to be described and solved. Quist [the designer] designs by spinning out a web of moves, consequences, implications, appreciations, and further moves. (p. 57, emphasis added)

Schön's design "conversation" involves back-and-forth movement between active *decision-making* and *evaluation* of the impact of new decisions on an emergent design that consists of nothing more than prior decisions.

At this detailed level of description of design, the relationship between design and evaluation becomes readily apparent, as in the description by Schön above. What is surprising, however, is the degree to which evaluation becomes prominent. For example, Schön's account makes it clear that before any firm commitment is made, there is considerable back-and-forth movement between hypothesizing a decision and then stepping back from it to reconcile it with other decisions and possible influence on future ones. Even once a decision is made firm, it can be unmade, and the process of designing can proceed forward from there again.

Dorst (2015) gives an even more detailed account of design, which he calls "frame design." It shows clearly the major role of evaluation in decision-making. Although his description is illustrated with applications at a macro level, its parallels with Schön's description at the micro level are informative.

A frame, according to Dorst, is a pattern of relationships between design elements that a designer can select or create (much like Schön's *cluster of moves*) and then use to explore solution options. A frame is an abstraction with parametric positions that can be filled by substitution with different *hows*. The point of Dorst's frame concept, and the origin of the name, is that the process of framing is one step that can lead to workable, practical, and sustainable design decisions. It is significant that the majority of the steps in this framing process are evaluative, rather than committal.

Dorst's process of frame creation includes:

- Archaeology—An in-depth investigation of the apparent problem, as well as previous attempts at solutions
- Paradox—Identification of the "core paradox": the combination of forces that has kept a solution from being found
- Context—Exploration of the practices, and the values, of key stakeholders of a solution
- Field—Definition of the playing field or force field where cultural, economic, social, and symbolic assets are exchanged between players [stakeholders]
- Themes—Identification of the deeper factors that underlie the needs, motivations, and experience of the players: the basis of the assets exchanged
- Frames—Finding the set of themes shared by stakeholders and using them to create frames
- Futures—Reshaping proposed themes and frames through a process of negotiation to fit the requirements of all stakeholders
- Transformation—A critical evaluation of the short-term and long-term prospects of the proposed themes and frames
- Integration—A final negotiation *to produce a decision* acceptable to all interests

At a societal or organizational level these steps are intuitively sound. What is not as apparent is the degree to which they can be applied also to decisions about individual features or clusters of features for a specific design for a specific learning experience. What changes is not the sequence of considerations, but the fact that it can be an individual designer carrying out the evaluation and decision processes, sometimes alone.

The narrative below shows the plausibility of application at the detailed level of individual frame innovation decisions:

- Archaeology—Most instructional designs are created to solve a problem previously unsolved. Previous attempts to solve the problem may have missed the mark, the problem itself may have been misidentified, or the problem may not yet have been identified as a problem. In any case, pausing to search the true nature of the problem has value. Why have previous designs failed, or why can the desired outcome not be achieved? Very minor differences in design impact the effectiveness of designs (McDonald, 2006; McDonald & Gibbons, 2009).
- Paradox—An unsolved problem, whether at the macroscopic or microscopic level, presents an undiscovered and yet discoverable paradox: a positioning of forces that either through tradition or active opposition resists a solution. These forces can be thought of in tectonic terms. At the level of societal problems there are clearly problems locked in by opposing agendas. Is there not an analogous situation within the learner that can be addressed by understanding the forces at work? Can a higher degree of flow be achieved by knowing and avoiding what is opposing it?
- Context—Finding the existence of a paradox, a designer will work to reveal the traditions, habits, and motives that hold the opposing forces in place. The context explicitly addresses the interests of all of the stakeholders of a decision. In a learning design, these interests include not only those of the learner and the designer, but the producer, distributor, and delivery system for produced artifacts. In addition, there are the concerns of those supporting the learner (parents, community), and administrators (parents, school administrators). Each of these is capable of imposing a constraint, as well as being part of a solution for an individual learner.
- Field—The *currencies* exchanged in the learning place are often psychological where the individual learner is concerned. Currencies—perhaps best called *micro-currencies*—that should be given extra consideration by instructional designers are described in detail by Kahneman (2011) and Immordino-Yang (2015).
- Themes—Transactional currencies of instruction lead to themes that provide the basis for building up frames that can lead to solutions. The work of instructional researchers is to seek themes that provide clues to design solutions through traditional and design-based research.

Identifying themes leads a designer to the vast body of research results and instructional theory.
- Frames, Futures—From themes should flow a set of frames that can be reconciled among stakeholders, providing a tool for the negotiation of varied interests. For the individual designer, the identification of frames and the negotiation of futures takes place within the designer's personal reasoning space and represents the personal judgments of the designer. For design teams, the formation of frames and their reconciliation takes place in the group's discussions in a manner described by Bucciarelli (1994).
- Transformation—Finding workable frames and futures is, finally, the beginning of a *commitment* process. Frames and futures represent tentative commitments that can be negotiated in the manner described by Schön earlier. Transformation represents a further step toward the commitment in which final "sanity checks" can be performed in the terms used by all of the stakeholders.
- Integration—Final adjustments lead to firm commitments: decisions made.

Two things are striking about Dorst's description of the framing process: (a) that it describes a process that is a plausible description of design decision-making at different levels of scale, and (b) that it is made up mainly of *evaluative* acts rather than *committal* ones. This speaks directly to the main theme of this chapter, which now becomes clearly discernible at this level of design description: that design and evaluation are symbiotically, inextricably related and that evaluation decisions are equally if not more crucial to design success than final decisions about features and properties. At this level of detail the term evaluation achieves a deeper meaning for the designer. Seeing evaluation from this perspective should perhaps result in a tectonic shift in the amount of attention a designer should pay to each decision.

Design beyond Logic

The importance of acknowledging the key role of evaluation during design does not end with recognition of its *logical* implications: there is an *illogical* or *emotional* aspect as well. Design is often described in terms that go beyond rational, intellectual, and objective (Boling et al., 2015; Kim & Ryu, 2014; Norman, 2005).

Miller, Galanter, and Pribram (1960, hereafter MGP), propose that decision-making is an agentive process and that the influences brought to bear on a decision can be rational, but that they may also include emotional and tacit, or unconscious, influences. In their book, *Plans and the Structure of Behavior*, MGP argue in favor of a basic unit of human behavior capable of subsuming the reflex arc described in the literature of behaviorism. They maintain that this basic unit must feature an expression of will, or choice, and that human behavior is not merely a reflexive response to the environment. Therefore, as MGP make their argument, they revive the concept of agency: "something to bridge the gap from knowledge to action" (p. 11). They propose as the basic unit of human performance a new unit called the TOTE (test-operate-test-exit). The TOTE for them represents a basic unit of human action. The TOTE unit has to be scalable. That is, it has to be a self-similar structure at all levels:

> A proper description of behavior must be made on all levels simultaneously. That is to say, we are trying to describe a process that is organized on several different levels, and the pattern of units at one level can be indicated only by giving the units at the next higher, or more molar, level of description. (p. 13)

The TOTE is a cybernetic element consisting of *test-operate-test-exit*. According the MGP, "the problem is to describe how actions are controlled by an organism's internal representation of the universe" (p. 12). The TOTE portrayal indicates an ongoing test of *congruity* (in the internal or the external environment) that draws attention when an expected state is detected (*incongruity*). An incongruity leads to the selection and execution of a known operation. This is followed by a subsequent test to determine the success of the operation. Though the test and the operation are depicted as separate functions, it is clear that they must proceed in parallel in very close alternation. This brings evaluation and decision-making, alternating with action, into consideration at a most basic level of performance.

MGP speculate on what is represented by the arrows in their diagram. They consider the answer at three levels of abstraction: energy, information, or control. Certainly the brain employs electrical energy in its operations. But at a level of higher abstraction, pulses of energy represent information. At the next level of abstraction, these pulses can be interpreted as control pulses that invoke or neutralize the execution of operations.

> Here we are not concerned with a flow of energy or transmission of information from one [memory] page number to the next but merely with the order in which the "instructions" are executed. At this abstract level of description we are no longer required to think of the test as a simple [reflex arc] threshold that some stimulus energy must exceed. The test phase can be regarded as any process for determining that the operational phase is appropriate. (p. 29)

In order to account for all human behavior, the test element of the TOTE unit must involve both deliberate, rational, intellectual judgments (tests) and action choices (operations), and those below the level of conscious and deliberate control. This can mean that choices made by a designer can involve hunches or unexplainable biases in the designer's thinking. This gives validation to the idea that even though a designer cannot verbalize a rationale for a design decision, it may still have a reasonable basis based on the designer's previous experience.

> In its weakest form, the TOTE asserts simply that the operations [including decisions] an organism performs are constantly guided by the outcomes of various tests. ... When the TOTE has been executed—the operations performed, the test satisfied, and the exit made—the creature may indeed appear to have attained a more desirable state. (p. 29–30)

The concepts of agency and intentionality are a critical part of the MGP argument. MGP deconstruct the concept of motivation, describing it in terms of value and intention:

> The present authors take the position that a motive is comprised of two independent parts: value and intention. A value represents or refers to an Image [of the world held in the individual's mind, capitalization in the original], whereas an intention refers to a Plan [capital in the original]. Presumably, a normal adult human being has constant access to a tremendous variety of plans that he might execute if he chose to do so. ... As long as he is not using them, these various available plans form no part of his intentions. But as soon as the order to execute a particular plan is given, he begins to speak of its incomplete parts ... as things he intends to do. (p. 31)

The value of the TOTE to the present argument is that it opens for discussion a vision of human choice-making and design intimately associated through evaluation with all of the factors that influence human choices, including those that are emotional, unconscious, or tacit. Figure 7.1 illustrates a sampling of the factors that are brought to bear on judging (testing) and choosing operations (operating).

At this level of the design and evaluation relationship, it becomes impossible to see how one of them can be considered in the absence of the other. Eisner's (1976) artistic appreciative approach to evaluation, dismissed by many designers as irrelevant, becomes more of a usable tool. At this level, evaluation may take as its evaluand not just one, but a succession of emotional states as well as the usual succession of intellectual states.

The view of the design–evaluation relationship at this level makes it hard to understand how design can adequately be taught without parallel instruction in evaluation and its close relation to decision-making. This becomes more important in light of the emerging recognition of the impact of emotions on learning (Immordino-Yang, 2015).

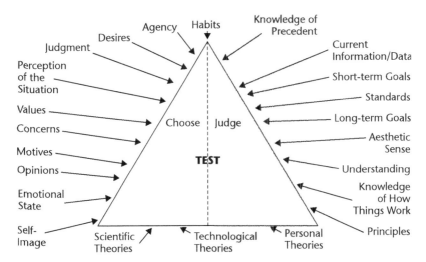

FIGURE 7.1 A sampling of factors, deliberate and tacit, that influence judging (testing) and choosing

Conclusion

In this chapter we have put design and evaluation, as it were, under a microscope with multiple lenses. We are not trying to explain design authoritatively, but rather to use four different snapshots of design, each at a different level of resolution, to reveal new perspectives on the design–evaluation relationship. We have observed that evaluative activity emerges larger and larger in the designer's field of view with each new level of detail. The process we usually perceive as *design* appears to be a fusion of *design and evaluation* processes. The more detailed the level of inspection, the more prominent, judgmental, and evaluative aspects appear to be.

This runs counter to our observation at the outset of this chapter, that at present the worlds of design and evaluation seem to be drifting apart rather than converging, which has led to the formation of separate specialties that show only passing interest in each other's main concerns. It is true that designers have become mainly interested in practical decision-making, followed by fitness checking, while evaluators have become interested in large-scale projects and principled positions on conducting different kinds of evaluations.

Training for new instructional designers tends to emphasize decision-making aspects of design, describing evaluation as a follow-up activity, *after* decisions are made, rather than a process of applying judgment *before* deciding. This finding, should it be confirmed through further research and analysis, should lead to curricula for new designers that give greater weight to the judgmental aspects of design—design thinking, design logic, and most importantly, design judgment. This will require not only creating more detailed descriptions of design activity, but in the process, it will require teasing out the role of value-seeking and value-assigning that they imply. By introducing this change, we will be teaching design thinking and design judgment rather than design process.

Relating Educational Technology and the Learning Sciences through Design and Evaluation

This may point to a path to *rapprochement* between disciplinary areas like the learning sciences and educational technology that now consider themselves only in isolation—areas that have been addressing questions of learning and designing, beginning with different assumptions about the nature of what they are studying and how it can be studied.

Edelson (2002) describes an alternative view of research where:

> Design researchers proceed through iterative cycles of design and implementation using each implementation as an opportunity to collect data to inform subsequent design. Through a parallel and retrospective process of reflection upon the design and its outcomes the design researchers elaborate upon their initial hypotheses and principles, refining, adding, and discarding—gradually knitting together a coherent theory that reflects their understanding of the design experience. (p. 106)

This approach, which is widely recognized as design research, or design-based research, studies the processes of learning and designing simultaneously: teaching the researcher at the same time about designing, the elements of designs, and the elements of learning experiences. Edelson notes that: "an important characteristic of design research is that it eliminates the boundary between design and research" (p. 107).

It may be that "the boundary between design and research" in people's minds has been a major factor separating the interests and communities of the learning sciences and educational technology. The learning sciences, by adopting the term "science" in their identity, subscribe to the metaphors of science and all of the assumptions and associations they imply. Educational technologists carry in their minds the assumptions and associations of the term "technology." However, we submit that in practice neither the learning science researchers nor the educational technology practitioners subscribe solely and exclusively to their nominal metaphors.

One way of understanding the divide that, unfortunately, many accept between the interests of these two communities is to appeal to a more disinterested definition of the common reasoning processes these seemingly disparate schools of thought rely on.

George Klir (1969), a general systems theorist, describes an underlying continuity between scientific and design reasoning that may be a key not only to the design–evaluation relationship but to the learning sciences–educational technology relationship as well. Klir proposes that the common goal of scientists and designers is the study of the properties of systems: "in our experimental [scientific] investigation of objects," says Klir, "we concentrate on ... the search for a simple expression of the time-invariant relation[ships] between ... quantities." He continues:

> In the engineering [design] branches, the system [being studied] has the same traits as in the experimental sciences. As a rule, however, the problems involved are different. The relations between its quantities are usually prescribed [or constrained in some way], and we are to find a suitable manner for implementing them ... or, conversely, a distinct realization [outcome] is given and we are to find the relations between certain quantities [to achieve it]. (pp. 39–40)

For Klir, the systems being studied by scientists and engineers are exactly the same, but scientists and engineers (designers) are solving different problems with respect to them. In general, scientists hold certain system quantities fixed while allowing others to vary so that unknown relationships within the system can be studied. Independent variables are controlled to determine their relationships to dependent variables. In design, what would be to the scientist the dependent variables—the outcomes—become fixed, and the designer's job is to determine what relationships among the scientist's "independent" variables can achieve it.

Given this description by Klir, the examples in the previous section of the reasoning behavior of Quist the designer and Einstein the scientist seem very similar. Both involve making a tentative decision regarding the resolution of forces represented by variables. This is followed by evaluation of the fitness of the decision within its context. The scientist's decision is about what variables to control using designed experimental materials and an experimental design; the engineer's decision is about what variables to involve and how to balance their influence. It is interesting to note that in order to conduct an experiment, the scientist must prepare (design) the experimental materials, the tools of observation, and the measures of outcomes. It is likewise interesting that the designer has no information about the utility of a design without subjecting it to a quasi-experimental trial.

The statement in the inscription by John Gargani, President of the American Evaluation Association, is a realization of the close design–evaluation connection. We wonder whether there might be a similar statement possible relating the learning sciences with educational technology. Making decisions based on judgment, followed by the evaluation of the decisions by trial, lies at the heart of both processes. This not only unifies our concepts of science and engineering, but it also shows the closeness of the design–evaluation relationship, even down to the minutest level of detail, as we have tried to show.

Edelson concludes:

> Taken together, these three arguments present a view of educational research as an applied science that differs from the view of research that is held by the broad community of educational researchers and has been taught in graduate schools of education in the past. Changing that view may be the key to enabling educational research to play a larger role in educational reform in the future. (p. 119)

We believe that the disparate views of designers and evaluators can be resolved by resorting to the middle ground described by Klir. We believe also that the disparate views of educational technologists and learning scientists can be similarly resolved by appealing to the similar principle of Edelson.

References

Andrews, D. H., & Goodson, L. A. (1980). A comparative analysis of models of instructional design. *Journal of Instructional Development, 3*(4), 2–16.

Association for Educational Communications and Technology (1972). The field of educational technology: A statement of definition. *Audiovisual Instruction, 17*(8), 36–43.

Association for Educational Communications and Technology (1977). *The definition of educational technology*. Washington, DC: Association for Educational Communications and Technology.

Banathy, B. H. (1968). *Instructional systems*. Belmont, CA: Fearon.

Bloom, B. S., Hastings, J. T., & Madaus, G. F. (Eds.) (1971). *Handbook on formative and summative evaluation of student learning*. New York: McGraw-Hill Book Company.

Boling, E., & Smith, K. M. (2008). Artifacts as tools in the design process. In J. M. Spector, M. D. Merrill, J. Elen, and M. J. Bishop (Eds.), *Handbook of research on educational communications and technology* (pp. 685–690). New York: Springer.

Boling, E., Gray, C., Dagli, C., Demiral-Uzan, M., Ergulec, F., Tan, V., Altuwaijri, A., Gyabak, K., Hilligoss, M., Kizilboga, R., & Tomita, K. (2015) Judgment and instructional design: How ID practitioners work in practice. *Performance Improvement Quarterly, 28*(3), 25–49.

Branson, R. K., Rayner, G. T., Cox, J. L., Furman, J. P., King, F. J., & Hannum, W. J. (1975). *Interservice procedures for instructional systems development (5 vols.)* (TRADOC Pamphlet 350-30). Ft. Monroe, VA: U. S. Army Training and Doctrine Command, August, 1975. (NTIS Nos. AD-A019 4860-AD-A019 490).

Briggs, L. J. (1967). *Instructional media: A procedure for the design of multi-media instruction, a critical review of research, and suggestions for future research*. Washington, DC: American Institutes for Research.

Briggs, L. J. (1970). *Handbook of procedures for the design of instruction*. Washington, DC: American Institutes for Research.

Bucciarelli, L. L. (1994). *Designing engineers*. Cambridge, MA: The MIT Press.

Campbell, K. Schwier, R. A., & Kenny, R. F. (2005). Agency of the instructional designer: Moral coherence and transformative social practice. *Australasian Journal of Educational Technology, 20*(1), 69–100.

Dick, W. & Carey, L. M. (1976). *The systematic design of instruction (1st ed.)*. Instructional Design and Development Department, College of Education, Florida State University, Tallahassee, FL.

Dorst, K. (2015). *Frame innovation: Create new thinking by design*. Cambridge, MA: The MIT Press.

Edelson, D. C. (200). Design research: What we learn when we engage in design. *Journal of the Learning Sciences, 11*(1), 105–121.

Eisner, E. W. (1976). Educational connoisseurship and educational criticism: Their form and functions in educational evaluation. *The Journal of Aesthetic Education, 10*, 135–150.

Ely, D. P. (1963). The changing role of the audiovisual process: A definition and glossary of related terms. TCP monograph no. 1, *Audiovisual Communication Review*, 11(1), supplement no. 6.

Ely, D. P. (1973). Defining the field of educational technology. *Audiovisual Instruction, 8*(3), 52–53.

Ely, D. P. (1983). The definition of educational technology: An emerging stability. *Educational Considerations, 10*(2), 2–4.

Finn, J. D. (1953). Professionalizing the audio-visual field. *Audio-Visual Communication Review, 1*(1), 6–17.

Finn, J. D. (1960). A new theory for instructional technology. *Audiovisual Communication Review, 8*(1), 84–94.

Flanagan, J. C. (1969). The uses of educational evaluation in the development of programs, courses, instructional materials and equipment, instructional and learning procedures, and administrative arrangements. In R. W. Tyler (Ed.) (1969). *Educational evaluation: New roles, new methods: Sixty-eighth yearbook of the National Society for the Study of Education, Part II* (pp. 221–241). Chicago, IL: University of Chicago Press.

Gagné, R. M. (Ed.) (1965). *Psychological principles in system development*. New York: Holt Rinehart & Winston.

Gagné, R. M., & Briggs, L. J. (1979). *Principles of instructional design* (2nd ed.). New York: Holt, Rinehart and Winston.

Gibbons, A. S. (2014). *An architectural approach to instructional design*. New York: Routledge.

Gibbons, A. S. (2015). Instructional design models. In J. M. Spector (Ed.), *The SAGE encyclopedia of educational technology* (pp. 386–389). Thousand Oaks, CA: Sage Publications.

Gibbons, A. S. & Rogers, P. C. (2009). Coming at design from a different angle: Functional design. In L. Moller et al. (eds.), *Learning and instructional technologies for the 21st century*, New York: Springer Science Business Media.

Gibbons, A. S. & Yanchar, S. C. (2010). An alternative view of the instructional design process: A response to Smith and Boling. *Educational Technology, 50*(4), 16–26.

Gibbons, A. S., Boling, E., Smith, K. M. (2014). Instructional design models. *Handbook of Research On Educational Communications Technology* (4th ed.). New York: Springer.

Gustafson, K. L. (1981). *Survey of instructional development models*. Syracuse, NY: ERIC Clearinghouse on Information & Technology.

Gustafson, K. L., & Branch, R. M. (1997). *Survey of instructional development models* (3rd ed.). Syracuse, NY: ERIC Clearinghouse on Information & Technology.

Gustafson, K. L., & Branch, R. M. (2002). *Survey of instructional development models* (4th ed.). Syracuse, NY: ERIC Clearinghouse on Information & Technology.

Gustafson, K. L., & Powell, G. C. (1991). *Survey of instructional development models with an annotated ERIC bibliography* (2nd ed.). Syracuse, NY: ERIC Clearinghouse on Information & Technology.

Hamilton, J., & Feldman, J. (2014). Planning a program evaluation: Matching methodology to program status. In *Handbook of research on educational communications and technology* (pp. 249–256). New York: Springer.

Hokanson, B., & Miller, C. (2009). Role-based design: A contemporary framework for innovation and creativity in instructional design. *Educational Technology, 49*(2), 21–28.

Hughes, A. C., & Hughes, T. P. (2000). *Systems, experts, and computers: The systems approach in management and engineering, World War II and after.* Cambridge, MA: The MIT Press.

Immordino-Yang, M. H. (2015). *Emotions, learning, and the brain.* New York: Norton.

Januszewski, (2001). *Educational technology: The development of a concept.* Englewood, CO: Libraries Unlimited.

Jardini, D. (2000). Out of the blue yonder: The transfer of systems thinking from the Pentagon to the Great Society, 1961–1965. In A. Hughes and T. Hughes (Eds.), *Systems, experts, and computers: The systems approach in management and engineering, World War II and after.* Cambridge, MA: The MIT Press.

Kahneman, D. (2011). *Thinking, fast and slow.* New York: Farrar, Straus and Giroux.

Kelley, T., & Littman, J. (2001). *The art of innovation.* New York: Crown Business.

Kelley, T., & Littman, J. (2005). *The ten faces of innovation.* New York: Currency Doubleday.

Kim, J. & Ryu, H. (2014). A design thinking rationality framework: Framing and solving design problems in early concept generation. *Human–Computer Interaction, 29*(5-6), 516–553. doi: 10.1080/07370024.2014.896706.

Klir, G. J. (1969). *An approach to general systems theory.* New York: Van Nostrand Reinhold.

Krippendorff, K. (2007). Cybernetics of design and the design of cybernetics. *Kybernetes, 36*(9/10), 1362–1380.

Lawson, B. (1997). *How designers think: The design process demystified* (3rd ed.). Oxford, UK: Architectural Press.

Lawson, B., & Dorst, K. (2009). *Design expertise.* Oxford, UK: Elsevier.

Markle, S. M. M. (1964). Teaching machines and programmed instruction: The Harvard teaching machine project: The first hundred days. *Audiovisual Communication Review, 12*(3), 344–351.

Markle, S. M. M. (1967). Empirical testing of programs. In P. C. Lange (Ed.), *Programmed instruction: Sixty–sixth yearbook of the National Society for the Study of Education: Part II* (pp. 104–138). Chicago: University of Chicago Press.

Markle, S. M. M. (1969). *Good frames and bad: A grammar of frame writing* (2nd ed.). New York: John Wiley & Sons.

McDonald, J. K. (2006). Technology I, II, and III: Criteria for understanding and improving the practice of instructional technology. Unpublished Thesis (Ph.D.), Brigham Young University, Department of Instructional Psychology and Technology.

McDonald, J., & Gibbons, A. (2009). Technology I, II, and III: Criteria for understanding and improving the practice of instructional technology. *Educational Technology Research and Development, 57,* 377–392.

McLaughlin, M. W., & Phillips, D. C. (Eds.) (1991). *Evaluation and education: At quarter century: Ninetieth yearbook of the National Society for the Study of Education, Part II.* Chicago, IL: University of Chicago Press.

Miller, G., Galanter, E., & Pribram, K. (1960). *Plans and the structure of behavior.* New York: Henry Holt & Company.

Norman, D. (2005). *Emotional design: Why we love (or hate) everyday things.* New York: Basic Books.

Parrish, P. (2006). Design as storytelling. *TechTrends, 50*(4), 72–82.

Parrish, P. (2008). Plotting a learning experience. In L. Botturi and T. Stubbs (Eds.), *Handbook of visual languages in instructional design* (pp. 91–111). Hershey, PA: IDEA Group.
Patton M. Q. (2011). *Developmental evaluation: Applying complexity concepts to enhance innovation and use*. New York: Guilford Press.
Richey, R. C., Klein, J. D., & Tracey, M. W. (2011). *The instructional design knowledge base: Theory, research and practice*. New York, NY: Routledge
Rittel, H. W. J. (1987/1988). The reasoning of designers. Paper presented at the Congress on Planning and Design Theory, Boston, August, 1987, and at the *Schrieftenreihe des Instuts fuer Grundlagen der Planung, Universitaet Stuttgart*, 1988.
Romiszowski, A. J. (1981). *Designing instructional systems: Decision making in course planning and curriculum design*. New York: Kogan Page/Nichols Publishing.
Saettler, P. (1968). *A history of instructional technology*. New York: McGraw-Hill.
Schrage, M. (1999). *Serious games: How the best companies simulate to innovate*. Cambridge, MA: Harvard Business School Press.
Schön, D. A. (1987). *Educating the reflective practitioner*. San Francisco, CA: Jossey-Bass Publishers.
Schwier, R., & Dykes, M. (2004). The Struggle for Community and Content in Virtual Learning Communities. *Proceedings of Ed-Media 2004* (pp. 2976–2982), Lugano, Switzerland.
Scott, B., Shurville, S., Maclean, P. & Cong, C. (2007). Cybernetic principles for learning design. *Kybernetes, 36*(9/10), 1497–1514.
Scriven, M. (1991). Beyond formative and summative evaluation. In M.W. McLaughlin and D. C. Phillips (Eds.), *Evaluation and education: At quarter century: Ninetieth yearbook of the National Society for the Study of Education, Part II*. Chicago, IL: University of Chicago Press.
Seels, B. B., & Richey, R. C. (1994). *Instructional technology: The definition and domains of the field*. Bloomington, IN: Association for Educational Communications and Technology.
Smith, P. L., & Ragan, T. J. (1999). *Instructional design* (2nd ed.). Upper Saddle River, NJ: Merrill.
Tripp, S., & Bichelmeyer, B. (1990). Rapid prototyping: An alternative instructional design strategy. *Educational Technology Research and Development, 38*(1), 31–44.
Tyler, R. W. (1969). *Educational evaluation: New roles, new methods: Sixty-eighth yearbook of the National Society for the Study of Education, Part II*. Chicago, IL: University of Chicago Press.
Worthen, B. B., & Sanders, J. R. (1987). *Educational evaluation: Alternative approaches and practical guidelines*. White Plains, NY: Longman.

8

LEARNING SCIENCE APPLICATIONS FOR RESEARCH IN MEDICINE

Susanne P. Lajoie

Delineating What Is Meant by a Learning Sciences Approach

The area of learning sciences is broad in terms of the research questions and constructs studied as well as the methodologies selected to answer questions about learning. Due to the diversity in theories and methodologies for teaching and learning, interdisciplinary approaches can be advantageous. Individuals from psychology (educational, cognitive, neuro, social, motivational, emotion, perception, etc.), computer science (computational linguists, software engineers), and anthropology (ethnographers) and subject matter experts from the teaching and learning domain in question may work together in different configurations to design effective and engaging learning environments. Some of these learning environments are technology rich and some are not. In this chapter the author describes how learning science approaches can be used to foster teaching and learning in the medical domain.

In the section below, descriptions of the learning science constructs that our team has been exploring in medical education are presented along with a reference to the theories that guide our research in this area. We further discuss the type of knowledge that learners are required to learn and how to foster and assess such learning.

Types of Knowledge

Early cognitive science research illustrated that we process different types of knowledge differently and consequently when we plan instruction we need to consider the types of knowledge we want students to acquire in a particular context. In the latest handbook on learning sciences Sawyer (2014) reiterates the importance of defining the type of knowledge that learners are to acquire. In this regard, Bloom's revised learning taxonomies are still relevant today in that they define knowledge types that have specific cognitive processes involved in learning (see Anderson et al., 2001). This taxonomy describes the knowledge dimension consisting of four types of knowledge: declarative, procedural, conceptual, and metacognitive. Declarative knowledge refers to knowledge "of" some thing, i.e., factual knowledge pertinent to a discipline. Procedural knowledge generally refers to "how" to do something, i.e. skills related to performing a specific procedure, in this example. Conceptual knowledge refers to "why" something is important and describes a deeper or more systematic understanding of the interrelationships among concepts rather than knowledge of such concepts in isolation. Metacognitive knowledge refers to awareness and understanding of "what" one knows or does not know about a specific topic.

When learning medical constructs the same types of knowledge apply. Declarative knowledge may be learning definitions, for example, what bilirubin is. A simple fact would be that bilirubin is a brownish substance found in bile (see www.webmd.com/digestive-disorders/bilirubin-15434 for full definitions). Procedural knowledge for this topic would include how to identify if bilirubin is normal, high, or low, the answer being that a blood test is required. Conceptual knowledge would expand on why bilirubin is important. The answer is that a bilirubin test will provide information about liver function and can determine if there is some form of liver disease. Metacognitive knowledge may refer to how a learner searches their sources to see if they understand the totality of what bilirubin can mean in a specific context, for instance, how an abnormal bilirubin level results in jaundice, and if one sees a jaundiced patient, what steps they should take next in determining a diagnosis. When designing specific learning environments we need to consider the manner in which we can scaffold these specific types of knowledge in a particular learning context.

Learning Sciences and Pedagogy: What Are the Mechanisms for Promoting Learning?

All four types of knowledge are important, however, we need to help learners go beyond familiarity with a large database of facts and help them integrate their knowledge in ways that result in deeper conceptual knowledge. In a report for the National Research Council Pellegrino, Chudowsky, and Glaser (2001) recommended that educators focus on learners' prior knowledge as a starting point toward developing deeper conceptual knowledge. Prior knowledge may be partially correct or it may consist of misconceptions that need to be corrected. In both situations instructors need to pay attention to what the learner knows or does not know in the effort to foster a deeper understanding of the topic at hand.

Research on expertise has helped identify what learners need to know in specific areas of study. Specifying what learners need to know provides a starting place for teachers and tutors to assist their students along a learning trajectory towards competence (Lajoie, 2003). Although expertise is domain specific, experts, regardless of their area of expertise, share some things in common: their performance is consistently superior; they are fast and accurate; they are able to identify meaningful patterns and ignore irrelevant information; they have superior memories specific to their field (not in general); and they have better self-regulatory skills where they observe and evaluate their own performance to make improvements (see Chi et al., 1988; Ericsson et al., 2006). The pedagogical question is: how do we help the less proficient acquire these competencies? Additionally, 21st century competencies call for teamwork, collaboration, adaptability, and creativity. Innovative forms of instruction are needed to help foster the development of these competencies. The cognitive apprenticeship framework provides a model for considering the learner and methods of instruction that can facilitate deep conceptual learning in meaningful contexts that represent authentic practices.

Cognitive Apprenticeship

A great deal of learning occurs in the real world outside of formal classroom instruction. We learn from our families or from members of our communities that have skills different from our own. Learning in these informal settings, be it learning how to change the oil in your car or how to cook a family recipe, is often done at the side of a more skilled individual who demonstrates and assists in completing the tasks at hand. These situations are informal apprenticeships, and we see traditional apprenticeships in the workplace where novices are often tutored by team leaders and other team members. Collins & Kapur (2014) discuss why apprenticeships are good learning settings and describe how learning content knowledge can be improved by examining some of the strengths of this model. Having said this, there is a careful delineation between traditional and cognitive apprenticeships that need to be considered (see Brown et al., 1989; Collins et al., 1989 for a full description of the framework). Most importantly, cognitive apprenticeships require the externalization of cognitive domain knowledge and the strategies that can serve as models for novice learners to acquire new knowledge. In traditional apprenticeships, learners can observe others doing a task and then practice those skills while their mentor or group members provide guidance. However, cognitive apprenticeships are more complex since mental activity is difficult to observe unless experts are able to successfully articulate their knowledge or if helpful visualizations are created to represent these cognitive processes.

The cognitive apprenticeship framework provides guidelines for designing learning environments that assist learners in acquiring expertise in a particular area of study. Content, method, and sequencing instructions are described, as is the sociology of learning. Theories of expertise guide the content of instruction since the domain knowledge needs to be specified along with the expert learning strategies that are useful for solving problems or acquiring new facts in that domain. The teaching methods support the assumption that there is a zone of proximal development (Vygotsky, 1978) for every learner, the zone being the area between actual and potential performance. This zone is measured by the difference between what a learner can do without help versus with help. A variety of teaching methods are needed to help learners achieve their potential.

These teaching methods include modeling the processes needed to solve problems so that learners can observe and incorporate these strategies into their own performance. Teachers coach students and provide support when they reach an impasse. Teachers gradually fade assistance as learners demonstrate they can do the task. Students demonstrate their learning by verbalizing their knowledge and teachers can help scaffold learners' concepts in this context. Teachers encourage students to reflect on their learning by helping them compare their performance with others. Finally, teachers include exploration of student-centered learning to encourage independence. Sequencing instruction is important so that appropriate levels of challenge are provided to learners, where difficulty level increases gradually. Diversity is also important so that learners see the multiple contexts in which they can apply what they have learned. Learners have an easier time generalizing their learning if they learn to apply their knowledge in more than one context. This approach allows students to engage in higher order reasoning about the "big picture" and local skills are supported to allow students to think about why the knowledge is important. Lastly, cognitive apprenticeships situate the learning experience in the context of meaningful, realistic tasks where students can experience a situation that might mimic a community of practice where learners work together to accomplish a task. The social aspect of learning in this context help learners share multiple perspectives and build their argumentation skills, helping them to critically evaluate solutions and evaluate their own understanding and process of learning.

Designing a Learning Environment for Clinical Reasoning Using the Cognitive Apprenticeship Model

As discussed earlier, there are different types of knowledge but deep understanding occurs when students are learning in a context that is realistic or has concrete applications to the real world. There is a large repository of declarative knowledge to be acquired in medical education; however, such knowledge is more meaningful when there is a context in which to apply the new knowledge, i.e., a patient case. Using knowledge in a specific context will result in better long-term recall (Whitehead, 1929). A great deal of informal learning in medicine occurs in the hospital where students learn in an apprenticeship-like setting from physicians and more skilled peers who guide them in their decision-making. However, traditional apprenticeships are outcome driven, in the case of medicine, as saving or attending to a patient takes priority over instructing the learner. A cognitive apprenticeship mimics a traditional apprenticeship but has the added value of creating an optimal learning environment where students can practice their skills deliberately with feedback from experts to assist in achieving proficiency (Ericsson et al., 1993).

BioWorld is a technology-rich learning environment (TRE) designed to assist medical students as they learn clinical reasoning skills in the context of diagnosing virtual patient cases (Lajoie, 2009). A cognitive apprenticeship framework guided the design of this TRE where learning is situated in a virtual-hospital setting where students see a patient, make observations, order diagnostic tests, and make diagnoses. A short description of the domain content, teaching method, sequencing of instruction, and social characteristics that are supported in this system is presented.

Defining the Content

Specific domain knowledge is pertinent to the patient cases in question. Consequently, the TRE was created to support the acquisition of knowledge pertaining to specific diseases, be it hepatitis, diabetes, etc. In this regard, the TRE was created so that learners could acquire an understanding of many diseases. The learning was situated around the patient case, where learners could collect information about the patients' symptoms, habits, and case history. These isolated concepts can be interpreted in the context of making a diagnosis, helping learners situate their thinking about the case. An online library was available for students to acquire new knowledge by looking up words they did not understand or by reading about specific diseases to discover the specific concepts, facts, procedures, and specific diagnostic tests that could be ordered to confirm a diagnosis. By studying expert physicians we determined the types of knowledge required to solve a case and then we designed the cognitive tools to support learners in BioWorld as they try to solve virtual cases. Patient cases were created and verbal protocols were collected from physicians and analyzed to determine the types of problem-solving processes involved in reaching a diagnosis. We used these expert paths and activities in our assessments of students to see where they might need help in the context of solving cases.

Methods of Instruction

Once expert performance models are identified for each case we can then show learners different ways of going about diagnosing the patient. We use these models as benchmarks of performance where teaching points can occur when we coach and scaffold concepts for learners in the context of the processes they use to solve a problem. For example, students may conduct diagnostic tests to confirm a diagnosis. In the case of suspected diabetes type I, learners would expect elevated blood glucose test results. If, however, the test result indicated normal glucose levels, the students might need assistance at this point in time in the form of scaffolding. The scaffolding may take the student back to the patient's symptoms to review the case or point them to the library to different types of tests. Students are asked to articulate what evidence was most important for solving the case and then reflect on this evidence in comparison to an expert solution and case summary. The expert feedback provided by the computer tutor serves in the place of a human tutor or partner who provides guidance toward solutions. External models of expertise help scaffold the learner by helping learners reflect on their own actions in comparison to more skilled individuals.

Types of Methodologies Used to Provide Evidence of Learning

Learning science methodologies provide a variety of approaches that help illustrate the cognitive, behavioral, and emotional processes that occur in the context of learning, resulting in different types of evidence as to when and perhaps why learning occurs or does not occur. Both instructors and researchers make decisions regarding the type of data they see as best forms of evidence based on either their instructional or research goals. Using a combination of methodologies i.e., self-report, log files, think-aloud protocols, electro-dermal activation, automated facial expression coding, and video-screen capture measures can provide a more nuanced assessment of the learner that reveal the underpinnings of student reasoning. Using these different data channels has allowed us to examine learning from a variety of angles and draw different insights.

As an example, I present the methods used to examine learning outcomes as well as the learning processes students take to reach a diagnosis using BioWorld. Diagnostic accuracy in solving patient cases is an obvious learning outcome and increasing diagnostic accuracy is a goal of instruction. Students enter their differential hypotheses in BioWorld and a final diagnosis when they complete the case. These diagnoses are logged and recorded as accurate or inaccurate. However, one may obtain an accurate diagnosis (learning outcome) without having a deeper understanding of the case. For instance, students may guess the right diagnosis or take random solution paths that do not reveal meaningful learning.

For this reason, we must study the process of learning not just the outcomes. The cognitive and metacognitive processes taken to reach a successful outcome reveal different types of evidence of learning. We study the learning paths and processes individuals take in the context of solving patient cases and compare their processes with that of experts. Some of our research is conducted using think-alouds with physicians who are considered experts and medical students who are still novices in their field of study. Participants are asked to think out loud as they are solving the virtual patient cases. In other words they are asked to verbalize whatever spontaneously comes into their attention without trying to explain or interpret their thoughts. These think-alouds are then analyzed to determine the types of goals and strategies used to solve patient cases. In particular, we looked for patterns among experts and how they differed from novices so that we could contrast and compare learner differences (Gauthier & Lajoie, 2014). The think-alouds help us determine why certain actions were taken. For instance, as students solve a case in BioWorld, we ask several questions. Are they regulating their behavior? Do they spend time orienting themselves to understand the case history prior to planning and action? When they execute an action, do they monitor the results of their actions and evaluate whether that was the correct move or not? We code the protocols for evidence of this metacognitive activity and then examine whether more proficient learners are higher in self-regulated learning than less proficient learners and found that those rated high in self-regulated learning outperformed the lower performers (Lajoie et al., 2013).

Another method of examining learner differences is to analyze log files. BioWorld logs each action a learner takes and compares their actions with expert trace files. These comparisons provide measures of efficient problem solving and help document changes in the strength of their solution paths. In other words, do students make the most relevant patient observations, notice the correct patient symptoms and history, and order the right tests? BioWorld records such actions and assesses learners while they are solving a case. We found that students spend more than twice as much time monitoring their learning behavior before asking for help (consult) (Lajoie et al., 2013). Moreover, consults are most often requested after conducting a lab test that does not return the expected result and when diagnosing rare diseases. Proficient learners requested consults to gain advice on how to rule out alternative diagnoses, whereas the less proficient asked for help when an impasse occurred (Jarrell et al. 2015). Patterns of library searches reveal that searching for related materials on a specific disease can lead to accurate diagnoses (Poitras et al., 2014a). Overall, BioWorld has a positive effect on enhancing the reasoning processes of students based on the number of cases they solve using it. With practice, students become more expert-like in the steps they take to solve a problem.

Medical students and physicians are required to write patient case reports that are used by the next physician who sees the patient. Students using BioWorld write case summaries as well and we compare these written documents with expert reports as a method of comparing learner performance. Recently we generated a predictive model that was able to accurately classify the correctness of case summaries and the underlying disease identified by the learner at a recognition rate of 92% and 98%, respectively (Poitras et al., 2014b). This classification model is a first step towards developing automated assessments of case summaries written in BioWorld.

Other questions may pertain to the level of student engagement, motivation, or positive affect experienced while learning. Learning scientists are interested in engaging and sustaining learning so it makes sense to understand if positive emotions are related to better performance or learning. For instance, do students experience positive emotions while learning with BioWorld? Do those students who experience higher positive emotions perform better in Bioworld? Do students with different achievement goals, such as mastery or performance goal orientations, have different emotions when they receive feedback in BioWorld? We have combined different methodologies to examine the relationship between affect and learning in BioWorld. Using FaceReader 6.0 (by Noldus, 2014) we have been able to identify the basic emotions (anger, disgust, sadness, scared, surprise, happy, neutral) that individuals experience while learning. Using a BioPack electrodermal activation bracelet we record skin conductance responses that provide useful data regarding the level of emotional arousal during learning. These behavioral and physiological measures are used in concert with self-report measures of student achievement emotions and confidence levels. Together these measures tell a more realistic story of what is occurring while learning.

Multiple methods were used to determine the types of emotions learners experienced using BioWorld. In general, students report high levels of curiosity and a predominance of positive emotions (Jarrell, 2015; Naismith, 2013) using BioWorld. However, emotions varied based on performance and feedback. Achievement emotions have been closely linked to performance outcomes (Pekrun, 2006) and we were interested if this were true in the case of BioWorld. Using an adapted version of the achievement emotions questionnaire (AEQ) (see Pekrun et al., 2011 for description of the AEQ) we found that emotions varied according to the accuracy and efficiency with which the cases were solved (Naismith, 2013; Jarrell et al., 2015), supporting other research that demonstrated positive emotions follow feedback about success, while negative emotions follow feedback about failure (Pekrun, 2006; Pekrun et al., 2007). In fact, medical students who were classified as performance oriented (as opposed to mastery oriented) experienced more anger when they received feedback that their performance did not match an expert solution (Naismith, 2013). In addition to self-report data we examined student arousal or stress level by measuring electrodermal activation during their learning experience with BioWorld. Using this method along with FaceReader analyses we were able to determine if arousal, self-reported emotions, and facial expressions of basic emotions (Ekman, 1972) converged. Using these combined methods, Jarrell (2015) found convergence across these multi-componential measures of emotions in BioWorld. Specifically, emotions experienced and expressed varied depending on when student's hypotheses and actions were confirmed as accurate or inaccurate. For example, when students ordered diagnostic tests and the results of those tests were not what they expected, they experienced higher levels of arousal. When the test results were anticipated there was less arousal and more expressions of neutral as indicated by FaceReader analyses, and more positive emotions as reported in a retrospective interview (Jarrell, 2015).

Concluding Remarks

By definition, the field of learning sciences encompasses many disciplines and consequently embraces many theories and methodologies. However, the overall goal of learning science is to improve learning. This chapter illustrates how some of the theories and methodologies can be used to support learning in medical education. A case is made that educators and researchers alike must first decide what type of knowledge they are trying to impart or study respectively. Once that decision is made instructors or designers must consider the best pedagogical methods for promoting learning along with innovative assessments that provide evidence of such learning.

First, decisions are made as to what to teach in terms of domain content, but just as importantly we need a model of best performance or competence on such content in order to model expertise and make assessment criteria more transparent so that learners can become more aware of what needs to be accomplished. For this reason, expertise research has been helpful in identifying the types of domain knowledge and strategies, be they learning or control strategies, that help learners effectively regulate their learning.

The cognitive apprenticeship model was discussed as a framework for situating learning in meaningful contexts along with strong methodologies for fostering learning by modeling, coaching scaffolding, and fading assistance once learners articulate their understanding in a meaningful manner. As an example, BioWorld was described in terms of how a technology-rich learning environment was created to support the clinical reasoning of medical students about virtual patient cases.

A description was provided of how theories pertaining to learning led the design of BioWorld. An account is provided of how diverse learning science methodologies are used to document what learning occurs, how and when it occurs, along with the co-occurrence of learning and affect in this situation. In particular, these methods were used to describe how learning outcomes along with cognitive, metacognitive, and emotional processes could be examined using different time scales and learning events that occur using a technology-rich environment.

There are enormous possibilities for using learning science approaches to improve learning and assessment in medical education. This chapter merely touches the tip of the iceberg of medical possibilities. Technological innovations in medical education are also burgeoning, ranging from mobile apps, serious games, intelligent tutoring systems, and virtual reality environments to both high- and low-fidelity simulations. Interdisciplinary approaches to the improvement of teaching and learning will continue to carve out new territory for the betterment of nuanced assessment of learning.

Acknowledgments

The research reported in this chapter was made possible by continued support from the Social Sciences and Humanities Research Council of Canada. The author acknowledges the support of members of her Advanced Technologies for Authentic Learning Laboratory, past and present.

References

Anderson, L. W., Krathwohl, D. R., Airasian, P. W., Cruikshank, K. A., Mayer, R. E., Pintrich, P. R., Raths, J., & Wittrock, M. C. (2001). *A taxonomy for learning, teaching, and assessing: A revision of Bloom's taxonomy of educational objectives (Complete edition)*. New York: Longman.

Brown, J. S., Collins, A., & Duguid, P. (1989). Situated cognition and the culture of learning. *Educational Researcher, 18*(1), 32–42. doi:10.3102/0013189x018001032

Chi, M. T. H., Glaser, R., & Farr, M. (1988). *The nature of expertise*. Hillsdale, NJ: Erlbaum.

Collins, A., & Kapur, M. (2014). Cognitive apprenticeship. In R. K. Sawyer (Ed.), *The Cambridge handbook of the learning sciences* (pp. 109–127). New York: Cambridge University Press.

Collins, A., Brown, J. S., & Newman, S. E. (1989). Cognitive apprenticeship: Teaching the craft of reading, writing, and mathematics. In L. B. Resnick (Ed.), *Knowing, learning, and instruction: Essays in honour of Robert Glaser* (pp. 453–494). Hillsdale, NJ: Erlbaum.

Ekman, P. (1972). Universals and cultural differences in facial expressions of emotions. In J. K. Cole (Ed.), *Nebraska symposium on motivation* (pp. 207–283). Lincoln, NE: University of Nebraska Press.

Ericsson, K. A., Charness, N., Feltovich, P., & Hoffman, R. R. (2006). *Cambridge handbook of expertise and expert performance*. Cambridge, UK: Cambridge University Press.

Ericsson, K. A., Krampe, R. T., & Tesch-Römer, C. (1993). The role of deliberate practice in the acquisition of expert performance. *Psychological Review, 100*(3), 363–406. doi: 10.1037/0033-295x.100.3.363

Gauthier, G., & Lajoie, S. P. (2014). Do expert clinical teachers have a shared understanding of what constitutes a competent reasoning performance in case-based teaching? *Instructional Science, 42*(4), 579–594. doi:10.1007/s11251-013-9290-5

Jarrell, A. (2015). *The emotional twists and turns of problem solving: An examination of learners' behavioural, physiological and experiential emotion responses to unexpected events during problem solving* (Unpublished Master's Thesis). McGill University, Canada.

Jarrell. A., Doleck, T., Tressel, T., Poitras, E., & Lajoie, S. (2015, August). *Towards adaptive help-seeking: Asking for help while problem solving in a computer based learning environment*. Paper presented at the Junior Researchers Pre-conference of the European Association for Research in Learning and Instruction, Limassol, Cyprus.

Jarrell, A., Harley, J. M., Lajoie, S. P., & Naismith, L. (2015). Examining the relationship between performance feedback and emotions in diagnostic reasoning: Toward a predictive framework for emotional support. In C. Conati & N. Heffernan (Eds.), *Lecture notes in artificial intelligence: Vol. 9112. Artificial intelligence in education* (pp. 657–660). Switzerland: Springer.

Lajoie, S. P. (2003). Transitions and trajectories for studies of expertise. *Educational Researcher, 32*(8), 21–25. doi: 10.3102/0013189x032008021

Lajoie, S. P. (2009). Developing professional expertise with a cognitive apprenticeship model: Examples from avionics and medicine. In K. A. Ericsson (Ed.), *Development of professional expertise: Toward measurement of expert performance and design of optimal learning environments* (pp. 61–83). Cambridge, UK: Cambridge University Press.

Lajoie, S. P., Poitras, E., Naismith, L., Gauthier, G., Summerside, C., Kazemitabar, M., Tressel, T., Lee, L., & Wiseman, J. (2013). Modelling domain-specific self-regulatory activities in clinical reasoning. In C. H. Lane, K. Yacef, J. Mostow, & P. Pavik (Eds.), *International artificial intelligence and education proceedings* (pp. 632–635). Berlin, Heidelberg: Springer-Verlag.

Naismith, L. (2013). *Examining motivational and emotional influences on medical students' attention to feedback in a technology-rich environment for learning clinical reasoning* (Unpublished Doctoral Dissertation). McGill University, Canada.

Pekrun, R. (2006). The control-value theory of achievement emotions: Assumptions, corollaries, and implications for educational research and practice. *Educational Psychology Review*, *18*(4), 315–341. doi: 10.1007/s10648-006-9029-9

Pekrun, R., Frenzel, A. C., Goetz, T., & Perry, R. P. (2007). The control-value theory of achievement emotions: An integrative approach to emotions in education. In P. A. Schutz, & R. Pekrun (Eds.), *Emotion in education* (pp. 13–36). Massachusetts: Academic Press.

Pekrun, R., Goetz, T., Frenzel, A. C., Barchfeld, P., & Perry, R. P. (2011). Measuring emotions in students' learning and performance: The Achievement Emotions Questionnaire (AEQ). *Contemporary Educational Psychology*, *36*(1), 36–48. doi:10.1016/j.cedpsych.2010.10.002

Pellegrino, J., Chudowsky, N., & Glaser, R. (2001). *Knowing what students know: The science and design of educational assessment*. Washington, DC: National Academy Press.

Poitras, E., Jarrell, A., Doleck, T., & Lajoie, S. (2014a). Supporting diagnostic reasoning by modeling help-seeking. In *Proceedings of 9th International Conference on Computer Science & Education (ICCSE)* (pp. 10–14), Vancouver, BC, Canada. doi:10.1109/iccse.2014.6926422

Poitras, E., Naismith, L., & Lajoie, S. P. (2014b, April). Automated assessment of writing proficiency: Can text mining of argumentative texts lead to more nuanced assessments? Paper presented at the Innovative Practices for Assessment in Computer-Based Learning Environments Symposium at the *Annual Meeting of the American Educational Research Association Conference*, Philadelphia, PA, USA.

Sawyer, K. (2014). The new science of learning. In R. K. Sawyer (Ed.), *The Cambridge handbook of the learning sciences* (pp. 1–18). NY: Cambridge University Press.

Vygotsky, L. S. (1978). *Mind in society: The development of higher mental processes*. Cambridge, MA: Harvard University Press.

Whitehead, A. N. (1929). *The aims of education*. New York: The Free Press.

9
AN ASIAN PERSPECTIVE ON THE DIVIDE

Allan H. K. Yuen

Introduction

Instructional design and technology (IDT) has been developed and practiced in the context of the education and business sector. The field of IDT encompasses the analysis of learning and performance problems, and the design, development, implementation, evaluation, and management of instructional and non-instructional processes and resources intended to improve learning and performance in a variety of settings, particularly educational institutions and the workplace (Reiser, 2012). Over the years, a generic description of the design process called ADDIE (analysis, design, development, implementation, evaluation) has evolved (Spector et al., 2014a). Moreover, the research in learning sciences (LS) aims to understand the nature of learning at all levels of scientific inquiry, focusing on how learning varies as a function of learner characteristics as well as how learner characteristics interact with different environments to produce variation in learning outcomes (Bransford et al., 2000; Hoadley & Van Haneghan, 2012; Sawyer, 2006).

During the past two decades, there has been an exponential growth in the use of information and communication technology (ICT) in all aspects of everyday life. It is undeniable that ICT is changing how we live, how students learn, and how teachers teach. In addition to the growth of ICT use, the emergence of the knowledge and skills students need in the twenty-first century has brought about a greater emphasis on education (Resta, 2002). In response to these challenges, policies on education reform and ICT in education have been established around the globe since the mid-1990s (Anderson & Plomp, 2008; Pelgrum & Anderson, 1999). In many Asian countries/regions such as Japan, South Korea, Singapore, Taiwan, China, and Hong Kong, governmental initiatives to support and facilitate the adoption of ICT use in schools have been launched

(Plomp et al., 2009). More importantly, there are many different stakeholders involved with the development and implementation of ICT in education, including policy-makers, government officials, academics, administrators, teachers, students, parents, and educational practitioners. Thus, a review of the development and implementation of ICT in education provides a lens to understand the beliefs and experiences of stakeholders.

This chapter aims to explore an Asian perspective on the divide between the communities of IDT and LS. A divide is a difference or separation between two things. The central goal of this chapter is to identify specific areas in the development and implementation of ICT in education in an Asian context that characterize the differences in the orientation, thinking, and approach between the fields of IDT and LS. The exploration focuses on a study of two Asian countries/regions, Singapore and Hong Kong. They share similar developmental stages since the launch of their first ICT masterplan for education and ICT in education strategy in 1997 and 1998 respectively. The development of ICT in education policies in Singapore and Hong Kong is summarised in Table 9.1.

A perspective refers to a way of thinking about something or regarding situations. The following review focuses on four aspects: policy-driven development,

TABLE 9.1 ICT in education policies in Singapore and Hong Kong

Singapore	Hong Kong
1997–2002: First ICT Masterplan for Education (MP-1) aims to provide a blueprint for the use of ICT in schools and access to an ICT-enriched school environment for every child	1998–2003: Information technology for learning in a New Era: five-year strategy (ITE1) aims to promote a paradigm shift in school education
2003–2008: Second ICT Masterplan for Education (MP-2) focuses on the pervasive and effective integration of ICT into the curriculum for engaged learning	2004–2007: Empowering learning and teaching with information technology (ITE2) aims to encourage students, teachers, schools, and other stakeholders to use ICT effectively as a tool for enhancing learning and teaching
2009–2014: Third ICT Masterplan for Education (MP-3) focuses on both students and teachers as learners	2008–2013: Right technology at the right time for the right task (ITE3) aims to enable teachers to use the right technology at the right time for the right task
From 2015: Fourth ICT Masterplan for Education (MP-4) aims to put quality learning in the hands of every learner empowered with technology	From 2014: Realising IT Potential, Unleashing Learning Power (ITE4) aims to unleash the learning power of all our students to learn how to learn and to excel through realizing the potential of ICT

the focus of learning, understanding ICT in education, and research and practice. The questions to be asked here are: What are the beliefs or experiences reflected in the development and implementation? Is there a different way of thinking about the fields of IDT and LS in research and practice?

Policy-Driven Development

The first systemic introduction of ICT into education took the shape of the first ICT Masterplan for Education in 1997, and it was part of an ongoing national effort to use ICT for day-to-day activities in Singapore (MoE, 1997). The education landscape in Singapore had already reached a good level of ICT maturity and was ready for the widespread injection of ICT into education (Kong et al., 2014). The MP-1 laid a strong foundation for schools to harness ICT, particularly in the provision of basic ICT infrastructure and in equipping teachers with a basic level of ICT integration competency, which achieved a widespread acceptance for its use in education. The implementation of MP-1 attempted to bring about a pervasive and systematic use of ICT for interactions in teaching and learning, in order to level the entire system up to a point where the use of ICT was effective and pervasive (Kong et al., 2014). It has done well in promoting and facilitating the integration of ICT in schools (Lim, 2007). By the end of MP-1, Singapore had succeeded in laying a firm foundation that enabled all its schools to integrate ICT into their curriculum. Students who were surveyed indicated that they had the necessary skills to complete ICT-based projects/assignments. All schools were provided with the necessary physical and ICT infrastructure for ICT-based teaching and learning. Teachers acquired basic competencies in integrating ICT into the curriculum. Most importantly, teachers accepted ICT as a pedagogical tool in the classroom.

The Hong Kong Government announced its first ICT in education policy statement in 1998 (EMB, 1998). It can be seen as one step in realizing the Government's commitment for Hong Kong to become "a leader, not a follower, in the information world of tomorrow," as declared in the Chief Executive's Inaugural Policy Address in 1997 (EMB, 1998, p. i). Four missions were laid down: to provide sufficient ICT facilities for students and teachers so that they could access information from the Internet; to encourage teachers to undertake the challenges of their respective new roles; to meaningfully integrate ICT into school education through the necessary curriculum and resource support; and to foster the emergence of a community-wide environment conducive to cultural change. These missions indicated the policy makers' determination to integrate ICT in education.

This policy could build up and strengthen Hong Kong's competitive edge by empowering its citizenry with the know-how to use ICT, when some other economies had already introduced plans to promote ICT in education. Another consideration driving this policy was the realization that the exponential growth in the use of ICT in the past decade had made a tremendous impact on the society at large, both in the workplace and in our daily lives, while comparatively little change had taken place in teaching and learning practices in schools. It was felt that ICT would have great potential in transforming the way education is delivered in schools (Pelgrum & Anderson, 1999). Also, two research studies (Law et al., 2001; Kwan et al., 2005) were commissioned by the Education Bureau to review and evaluate the progress and achievements made under ITE1. These studies identified areas requiring attention in the implementation of ICT in education, which informed the policy makers in their formulation of the next strategy.

The emergence of ICT has always been an opportunity for the IDT field to guide its introduction in a school context (Suzuki & Jung, 2012). Like most Asian countries/regions, Singapore and Hong Kong have channelled substantial resources into the development of ICT in education to empower their citizenry with competitiveness. In ITE1 and MP-1, the emphasis on the development of infrastructure and curriculum resources, teacher training, and use of ICT in the classroom encouraged the application of IDT concepts and techniques, such as the systems approach and ADDIE process. The development and implementation of ITE1 and MP-1 took an IDT orientation to improve students' learning and performance. However, it seems the notion of LS was overlooked in the initial stage of development.

The Focus of Learning

The four pillars of learning, learning to know, learning to do, learning to live together, and learning to be, proposed in the UNESCO report entitled *Learning: The Treasure Within* (Delors et al., 1996) has stimulated a lot of discussion and put learning at the forefront of education. It is worth noting that this report is a milestone for the Hong Kong education reform launched in 2000. The aims of education advocated in the reform document entitled *Learning for Life, Learning through Life* (EC, 2000) is to prepare the younger generation for life in the twenty-first century:

> To enable every person to attain all-round development in the domains of ethics, intellect, physique, social skills and aesthetics according to his/her own attributes so that he/she is capable of life-long learning, critical and exploratory thinking, innovating and adapting to change; filled with self-confidence and a team spirit; willing to put forward continuing effort for the prosperity, progress, freedom and democracy of their society, and contribute to the future well-being of the nation and the world at large. (EC, 2000, p. 4)

While global influences were one of the contributing factors, the education reform was the contextual factor having the most critical impact on the development of ICT in education policies in Hong Kong. Educational practices using ICT have been increasingly embedded within a broader framework of the reform that aimed to develop students' capacities for self-learning, problem-solving, information seeking and analysis, and critical thinking, as well as the ability to communicate, collaborate, and learn, abilities that figured much less importantly in previous Hong Kong school curricula (EDB, 2008; EMB, 2004).

The vision of ITE1 was to promote a "paradigm shift" in school education from a traditional textbook-based teacher-centered approach to a more interactive and student-centred approach. However, there appeared to be very little evidence to indicate a paradigm shift occurring from preliminary evaluations (Law et al., 2001; Yuen et al., 2010). Alongside the advocacy of the education reform (EC, 2000), ITE2 put forth a comprehensive plan to further promote the use of ICT in teaching and learning with a clear educational vision. The strategic focus was on the further integration of ICT into the teaching and learning process to facilitate student-centered learning and pedagogical innovations. Later, the goal of ITE3 was to maximize the potential of ICT as one of many mediators of learning and teaching, achieved through a balance between ICT-enabled learning activities and systematic guidance by teacher and parents (Yuen et al., 2010). Recently, student learning is central to ITE4. As an ongoing initiative, the goal of ITE4 is to unleash the learning power of all our students to learn how to learn and to excel through realizing the potential of ICT in enhancing interactive learning and teaching experiences.

In Singapore, the development of lifelong learning culture is already taking shape since the launch of the national vision of *Thinking Schools, Learning Nation* in 1997. Under this vision, the Ministry of Education has shifted away from an efficiency-driven education towards an ability-driven one that aims to develop and harness the abilities and potential of students. An ability-driven education approach requires a responsive education structure, the creation of a student-centred learning environment, the inculcation of values, and the nurturing of thinking skills and creativity through formal and informal curricula. Teaching and assessment methods have been reviewed and modified to nurture thinking skills and creativity, and to encourage knowledge generation and application (Lim, 2007). Additionally, the vision of MP-3 focuses on both students and teachers as learners. It captures the primary affordance of ICT in enabling them to shape their personal learning experience, both as individuals and in collaboration with others. It envisages that through the use of ICT, learning will not just take place in the classroom, but wherever and whenever the learner chooses. The outcome goal focuses on self-directed and collaborative learning, which requires learners to exercise a good range of twenty-first century skills and dispositions that will lead to the desired outcomes of education (MoE, 2008). The goal of the recent MP-4 is to put quality learning in the hands of every learner empowered with ICT.

The focus of learning is clearly demonstrated in ICT in education polices in Singapore and Hong Kong. The concepts and application of LS and IDT were found in implementation and practice, whereas the difference between the communities of IDT and LS was not obvious.

Understanding ICT in Education

It is apparent that there are different interpretations of ICT in education and how ICT improves learning performance. ITE1 identifies the need for changes to the mind-set and culture among teachers, parents, and students that were essential for affecting the aforementioned paradigm shift. Examples of ICT use are provided in ITE1 to illustrate the implications of ICT for classroom teaching, teachers, and students (EMB, 1998). However, these examples are presented in a fairly implicit manner, without elaborating on the practical steps to connect to the meaning of ICT in education. In ITE2, the meaning and scope of ICT in education was again not explicitly defined. However, there was a clear emphasis on pedagogy and the goals of the education reform as drivers for ICT in education.

The meaning of ICT in education differs from context to context (EDB, 2008). Following on the first two strategic plans, ITE3 aimed to consolidate and extend the changing learning environment to offer greater flexibility and interactivity to students. It provided an explicit statement about the meaning of ICT in education that included the use of ICT for increasing the efficiency and effectiveness of school administration, the enhancement of students' information literacy, and the improvement of students' learning outcomes across the curriculum. It further pointed out that the focus for ITE3 was on the effective integration of ICT into learning and teaching, which had the potential to create the greatest positive impact on student's learning outcomes (EDB, 2008). The document further noted that the strategic focus for ITE3 was the human factor in creating and implementing more interactive, student-directed learning environments, though the need to provide extra resources and increasing flexibility in the use of existing operational grants are also acknowledged. It highlighted the need to take account of the influencing factors at different levels and their interactions in a holistic manner:

> There are push factors encouraging teachers to use IT to perform their tasks and pull factors discouraging them from doing so. If the push factors are overwhelmingly offset by the pull factors, it is unlikely that a teacher will use IT even though he/she recognizes that IT is the most effective mediator. Our strategy is to strengthen the push factors while reducing the pull factors. (EDB, 2008, p. 17)

In Singapore, MP-2 built on the foundation of MP-1 to strive for an effective and pervasive use of ICT in education by, for example, strengthening the integration of ICT into the curriculum, establishing baseline ICT standards for students, and seeding innovative use of ICT among schools. The vision of MP-2 is that ICT will be pervasively and effectively used to enhance educational processes and structures. By leveraging on ICT as a tool to customize education to meet the needs and abilities of our pupils, we will be able to support and develop lifelong learners as we work towards the overall vision of *Thinking Schools, Learning Nation* (MoE, 2003). MP-2 encouraged schools to *"seed"* innovations that built on the foundation established in MP-1. These schools also received additional funding to carry out ICT in education experimentation primarily for selected classes across education levels or for classes within the same education level. While these experimentations tended to be of smaller scale compared to those schools for the Future Schools at Singapore (FS@SG) program launched in 2007, there were few restrictions on the experimentation boundary as long as they stayed within the school curriculum and the teaching and learning context (Kong et al., 2014). The vision of MP-3 focuses on both students and teachers as learners. It captures the primary affordance of ICT in enabling them to shape their personal learning experience, both as individuals and in collaboration with others. It continues to focus on innovative teaching and learning practices through bringing the practices established, such as from the FS@SG program, into the system (Chen & Looi, 2011).

From the above review, the strategies reflected different understandings of the meanings of ICT in education. The complexities involved in realizing the educational potential of ICT, the strategic importance of human factors and experimentations in ICT implementation, and the need for effective change strategies are recognized and discussed in each policy. The application of IDT and LS concepts in the implementation was vague and general. It is noted that a divergence of views on IDT and LS fields was not evident.

Research and Practice

In Singapore, MP-1 has established a university-level institute to spearhead the national research and development of pedagogical aspects in e-Learning and worked with other agencies and industrial partners to explore technological innovations for e-Learning (Kong et al., 2014). The realization based on the implementation of MP-1 and MP-2 is that for effective transformation of learning to take place enabled by ICT, educators need to go back to the basics of understanding learning from scientific and inter-disciplinary perspectives (Looi et al., 2004). At the National Institute of Education (NIE), the Learning Sciences Lab (LSL) was set up to transform ICT-enabled pedagogy in schools. Through a continuous spiral process of experimentation to workable ideas and developed prototypes, the LSL thus:

> Disrupts traditional pedagogical mind-sets and spurs individuals to innovative thinking and life-long learning. Fosters experimentation with emerging technologies to transform learning and pedagogy in the future. Engages in

> transformative capacity building and empowerment while translating experimentation to curriculum redesign and education at the NIE and in schools. (Looi et al., 2004, p. 92)

The LSL is the first center for LS in the Asia-Pacific region. There are unique dimensions of ICT adoption and cultural underpinnings in this part of the world. First of all, Looi and his colleagues (2004) recognized the unique learning epistemologies held by Asian cultures, which are oriented toward family and social values and traditions. Compared with Western traditions, there are strong impartation-of-knowledge assumptions within the Asian culture and context. A similar point is made by Zhang (2007) that the Eastern cultural tradition, together with other social factors, has shaped a group-based, teacher-dominated, and centrally organized pedagogical culture.

The LSL is designed to tackle issues of the ICT mind-set that are rooted in the Asian culture and context, and to collaborate with the emerging centers for the science of learning set up in the United States and other parts of the world. In the LSL's view, the two communities, learning science and instructional systems, are convergent especially for the researchers from both communities who have kept themselves up-to-date in the fields. Drawing too many distinctions between the two fields or communities may be unnecessary (Looi et al., 2004). Thus, it is LSL's hope to balance the perspectives of learning sciences and instructional systems.

> Learning sciences are concerned with issues of context, cognition, design, theory, and methodology. Learning sciences cultivate a disposition for expansive thinking about learning, whereas instructional systems provide the methodologies, tools, and strategies for affecting actual teaching and learning. The learning sciences field can benefit from the how-to of instructional systems, which includes evolving strategies and pedagogies applied to learning contexts. The challenge is to bring theories of situated cognition to the level of practitioners and teachers without reducing situated cognition to a procedure-rule level. Unless we at LSL can achieve such an end, we may remain only academics in the ivory tower. (Looi et al., 2004, p. 98)

In Hong Kong, the Centre for Information Technology in Education (CITE) was established in 1998 at the University of Hong Kong (HKU) to provide intellectual leadership and support to promote the use of ICT for quality education. CITE continues to be a center of excellence and serves as a focal point for collaboration and innovation, providing a platform for individuals and institutions, dreamers and experts, to come together and build new knowledge about learning and the transformative uses of technology, to contribute to the improvement of educational practices, and to excel in research and knowledge exchange (www.cite.hku.hk).

CITE has conducted numerous local as well as international research and development projects. Areas of focus include (1) designing, implementing, and evaluating learning technologies that support inquiry, social networking, collaboration, and knowledge building; (2) research on establishing and scaling up knowledge-building teacher communities for sustained curriculum innovation; (3) investigating the implementation and good practices of ICT use in schools and tertiary institutions, and building models and theories of technology-supported pedagogical innovation and educational change; and (4) investigating the social, cultural, and contextual aspects of students' experiences with ICT and new media.

In addition, the HKU Sciences of Learning Strategic Research Theme (SoL-SRT), hosted by the Faculty of Education, is designed as a platform to foster interdisciplinary research and to advance the field of LS by constructing multilevel models or theories of learning that build on an understanding of and methodologies used for diverse aspects of learning (such as neural physiological, functional, cognitive, and socio-affective aspects of learning). It is expected that the scope and impact of learning technologies research will be greatly enhanced if accomplished through collaboration with researchers in allied disciplines (Spector et al., 2014b).

Singapore and Hong Kong showcase how Asian cultures and values were transformed by colonization and modernization. Due in part to this history and background, collaboration, cultural diversity, and a commitment to making effective use of ICT and learning theories are the hallmarks of ICT in education development in Hong Kong and Singapore. In addition to focusing on interdisciplinary approaches, research at NIE and HKU more generally has embraced cultural differences and different research communities such as IDT and LS. Spector and colleagues made a remark about the research at HKU: "... there are not strong distinctions between instructional systems, learning sciences, and performance technologies that one often finds at American universities ..." (Spector et al., 2014b, p. 40). No doubt the same is also true for NIE.

Towards a Dialectical Perspective

In the review of the development and implementation of ICT in education in Singapore and Hong Kong, we summarize our observations as follows. First, there is an encouraging trend of an IDT approach, i.e., using systematic instructional design procedures and employing a variety of instructional media to improve students' learning performance. Similar IDT implementation trends were also observed in Japan and Korea (Suzuki & Jung, 2012). Second, the implementation also stressed the importance of learning as well as teaching processes, providing opportunities for learners to engage in reflection, and designing environments that are student-centered. Third, LS research was considered in the pedagogical design throughout the implementation. The practices of IDT and LS worked together for their mutual benefit.

This chapter explored an Asian perspective on the divide between the communities of IDT and LS. A review of two Asian countries/regions showed that the concepts and practices of IDT and LS co-exist. It seems stakeholders including researchers have embraced and balanced the fields of IDT and LS in the development and implementation of ICT in education. We characterize this as a "dialectical" perspective on the divide.

Nisbett (2015) argues that all cultures in East Asia have roots in the Confucian tradition. He also notes that the system of thought that Chinese developed has been called "dialectical reasoning" (p. 224), which is characterized by three intimately linked principles:

> Principle of change – reality is a process of change; what is currently true will shortly be false. Principle of contradiction – contradiction is the dynamic underlying change; because change is constant, contradiction is constant. Principle of relationships – the whole is more than the sum of its parts; parts are meaningful only in relation to the whole. (p. 225)

The dialectical tradition would produce different reactions to deal with conflicting views and changes. To illustrate: if things are constantly changing, one better pay attention to the circumstances surrounding a given event. This explains in part why East Asians are more attentive to context.

The influence of Confucian tradition and values is evident in Asian societies with different political structures, such as mainland China, Hong Kong, Taiwan, and Singapore (Rao & Chan, 2009). Singapore and Hong Kong are definitely showcases of Confucian heritage in Asian countries/regions. The dialectical tradition is evident in the review of their development and implementation of ICT in education.

What is an Asian perspective on the divide? In conclusion, a dialectical perspective on the divide between the communities of IDT and LS is proposed, which emphasizes a pragmatic and holistic orientation, recognition of change, acceptance of differences, attentiveness to contextual aspects, and striving for harmony (Nisbett, 2015). A dialectical perspective may help synthesize conflicting views and deal with changes. We also suggest that the dialectical perspective deserves further exploration to unpack the complex synergy between the fields or communities of IDT and LS.

References

Anderson, R. E., & Plomp, T. (2008). National contexts. In N. Law, W. J. Pelgrum & T. Plomp (Eds.), *Pedagogy and ICT use in schools around the world: Findings from the IEA SITES 2006 study* (pp. 37–66). Hong Kong: Springer and CERC.

Bransford, J. D., Brown, A. L. & Cocking, R. R. (Eds.). (2000). *How people learn: Brain, mind, experience, and school* (expanded ed.). Washington, D.C.: National Academy Press.

Chen, W., & Looi, C.-K. (2011). Active classroom participation in a Group Scribbles primary science classroom. *British Journal of Educational Technology, 42*(2), 676–686.

Delors, J., et al. (1996). *Learning: The treasure within*. Paris: UNESCO.

Education and Manpower Bureau (EMB). (1998). *Information technology for learning in a new era: five-year strategy 1998/99 to 2002/03.* Education and Manpower Bureau, Hong Kong SAR Government.

Education and Manpower Bureau (EMB). (2004). *The second strategy on IT in education: empowering learning and teaching with information technology.* Education and Manpower Bureau, Hong Kong SAR Government.

Education Bureau (EDB). (2008). *The third strategy on IT in education: Right technology at the right time for the right task.* Education Bureau, Hong Kong SAR Government.

Education Commission (EC). (2000). *Learning for life, learning through life: Reform proposal for the education system in Hong Kong.* Education Commission, Hong Kong SAR Government.

Hoadley, C. & Van Haneghan, J. P. (2012). The learning sciences: Where they came from and what it means for instructional designers. In R. A. Reiser & J. V. Dempsey (Eds.), *Trends and issues in instructional design and technology* (3rd ed.) (pp. 53–63). Boston, MA: Pearson.

Kong, S. C., Chan, T. W., Huang, R. & Cheah, H. M. (2014). A review of e-Learning policy in school education in Singapore, Hong Kong, Taiwan, and Beijing: Implications to future policy planning. *Journal of Computer Education,* 1(2–3), 187–212.

Kwan, K. P., Leung, C. K., Ng, T. Y., Tam, S. F., Chan, C. F., Chiu, C. S., et al. (2005). *Overall study on reviewing the progress and evaluating the Information Technology in Education (ITEd) projects 1998/2003.* Hong Kong: The Hong Kong Polytechnic University Project Team.

Law, N., Yuen, H. K., Wong, K. C., Li, S. C., & Lee, Y. (2001). *Preliminary study on reviewing the progress and evaluating the Information Technology in Education (ITEd) Projects.* Hong Kong: The Centre for Information Technology in School and Teacher Education (CITE), Faculty of Education, The University of Hong Kong.

Lim, C. P. (2007). Effective integration of ICT in Singapore schools: Pedagogical and policy implications, *Educational Technology, Research and Development,* 55(1), 83–116.

Looi, C. -K., Hung, D., Bopry, J. & Koh, T. -S. (2004). Singapore's Learning Sciences Lab: Seeking transformations in ICT-enabled pedagogy. *Educational Technology, Research and Development,* 52(4), 91–99.

Ministry of Education (MoE) (1997). *1st ICT Masterplan for Education.* Singapore: Ministry of Education.

Ministry of Education (MoE) (2003). *2nd ICT Masterplan for Education.* Singapore: Ministry of Education.

Ministry of Education (MoE) (2008). *3rd ICT Masterplan for Education.* Singapore: Ministry of Education.

Nisbett, R. E. (2015). *Mindware: Tools for smart thinking.* New York: Farrar, Straus and Giroux.

Pelgrum, W. J., & Anderson, R. E. (Eds.). (1999). *ICT and the emerging paradigm for lifelong learning: A worldwide educational assessment of infrastructure, goals and practices.* Amsterdam: International Association for the Evaluation of Educational Achievement & the University of Twente.

Plomp, T., Anderson, R. E., Law, N. & Quale, A. (Eds.). (2009). *Cross-national information and communication technology: Policies and practices in education* (revised 2nd ed.). Charlotte, NC: Information Age Publishing, Inc.

Rao, N. & Chan, C. K. K. (2009). Moving beyond paradoxes: Understanding Chinese learners and their teachers. In C. Chan & N. Rao (Eds.), *Revisiting the Chinese learner: Psychological and pedagogical perspectives* (pp. 3–34). Hong Kong: Comparative Education Research Centre, The University of Hong Kong, Springer.

Reiser, R. A. (2012). What field did you say you were in? Defining and naming our field. In R. A. Reiser & J. V. Dempsey (Eds.). *Trends and issues in instructional design and technology* (3rd ed.) (pp. 1–7). Boston, MA: Pearson.

Resta, P. (2002). *Information and communication technologies in teacher education: A planning guide*. Paris: UNESCO: Division of Higher Education.

Sawyer, R. K. (2006). *The Cambridge handbook of the learning sciences*. Cambridge: Cambridge University Press.

Spector, J. M., Johnson, T. E. & Young, P. A. (2014a). An editorial on research and development in and with educational technology. *Educational Technology, Research and Development, 62*(1), 1–12.

Spector, J. M., Yuen, A. H. K., Wang, M., Churchill D., & Law, N. (2014b). Hong Kong perspectives on educational technology research and practice. *Educational Technology*, September-October, 35–41.

Suzuki, K., & Jung, I. (2012). Instructional design and technology in an Asian context: Focusing on Japan and Korea. In R. A. Reiser & J. V. Dempsey (Eds.), *Trends and issues in instructional design and technology* (3rd ed.) (pp. 239–247). Boston, MA: Pearson.

Yuen, A. H. K., Law, N, Lee, M. W., & Lee, Y. (2010). *The changing face of education in Hong Kong: Transition into the 21st century*. Hong Kong: Centre for Information Technology in Education, The University of Hong Kong.

Zhang, J. (2007). A cultural look at information and communication technologies in Eastern education. *Educational Technology, Research and Development, 55*(3), 301–314.

10
THE COLLABORATION IMPERATIVE
Ellen B. Meier

Introduction

Research has played a vital role in the development of modern society. Advances in science, medicine, technology, and many other fields have been driven by research investments and discoveries. Educational research, however, has been supported unevenly according to the National Research Council (2002). The Council notes that several issues have influenced both funding and progress for researchers in the educational field including the value-laden nature of education, the struggle over the meaning of "scientific evidence," the fragmented nature of various fields within education, the simplistic expectations for research-based reform, and the segregation of educational research and practice (p. 14).

Paradoxically, the conditions for promoting educational research have never been better. Advances in the sophistication of brain imaging, coupled with breakthroughs in neuropsychology and cognitive neuroscience have deepened our understanding of brain function in ways that have direct relevance for learning (Zimmer, 2016). Educational policy-makers increasingly emphasize the importance of research in improving educational practice (Coburn & Penuel, 2016) and research-based concepts are *de rigueur* in school reform proposals. Despite the obvious need to build the research base however, educators continue to maintain research silos and perpetuate lateral barriers, even in closely related fields such as the learning sciences and educational technology.

These two discrete domains, the learning sciences and educational technology, hold particular importance for educators today because of our growing understanding of the process of learning and the rapid development of digital tools. The field of learning sciences, which studies learning environments and the basic science of learning, formally emerged in the early 1990s (Nathan & Sawyer, 2014; Sawyer, 2014b). Educational technology, dating from the 1930s, has historically been focused on educational tools and their relevance to learning (Reeves & Oh, 2016).

Today the lines between the two fields are blurring, and they can no longer be described in such discrete terms. There is overlap, as the learning science scholars frequently include technology as a part of their studies and educational technologists increasingly include learning science approaches in their discussion of digital tools (Dede, 2008; Lowyck, 2014; Meier, 2015). Traditionally, the learning science field has been considered more theoretical, educational technology more applied (Reeves & Oh, 2016). Recently however, learning science scholars claim that their field is more "use inspired" than basic sciences such as cognitive psychology (Nathan & Sawyer, 2014, p. 21). At the same time, educational technology is increasingly focused on learning theories to guide the development and use of technology (Lowyck, 2014).

At a time when the two fields already overlap in such significant ways, and when the needs of education are so great, close cooperation between researchers is essential. Scholars from these two fields—both committed to the study of emerging learning approaches and tools for improving learning—need to work together to create more effective, equitable learning environments for twenty-first century students. Such collaboration is not just a good idea; it is an imperative for educational advancement.

This chapter describes key concepts that might shape such collaboration and explains an approach taken by a research and development center that intentionally incorporates perspectives from both fields. This approach demonstrates the effectiveness of applying theoretical understandings to develop learning environments supported by current technology.

Definitions and Implications

The definitions of learning sciences and education technology are changing as these fields continue to evolve. Researchers are developing their understandings of the learning process even as new technology tools are developed. A short synopsis of each field provides a cursory overview of the learning science and education technology fields and how they are changing.

Educational Technology

According to the Association of Computing and the Association for Educational Communications and Technology (AECT), educational technology is focused on the study of learning through the use of technology and its related educational theories (2004). The roots of this field go back nearly a century (Reeves & Oh, 2016). Originally, the research in educational technology was focused on proving the effectiveness of media and technology as teaching tools. More recently, education technology is defined as "the study and ethical practice of facilitating learning and improving performance by creating, using, and managing appropriate technological processes and resources" (Januszewski & Molenda, 2008, p. 1).

Early on, educational technology research was focused on the affordances and the possibilities of tools for learning. Behavioralism shaped the learning stance of the early educational technologists, who thought that "knowledge and skill are transferred as learned behaviors" (Dede, 2008, p. 46). Many educators still believe that behavioralism shapes technology use. This perception has been cited as a limitation for the field, resulting from society's expectations that technology can solve learning problems with a machine (Lowyck, 2014). The proliferation of Computer Assisted Instructional (CAI) programs, for instance, reflects this behavioralist approach (Cuban, 1986, 2001; Dede, 2008; Lowyck, 2014). Going further, Lowyck claims that, "The interplay between behaviorist learning theory and technology ultimately resulted in inflexible and didactic instruction" (Lowyck, 2014, p. 5). Since then, theorists have introduced cognitivist, constructivist, and socio-constructivist perspectives, and subsequently, technology educators have been turning their attention to using technology as tools for these new learning approaches.

AECT (2004) noted that:

> [I]nquiry programs in educational technology have been influenced by growth and change in major theoretical positions in learning.... For example, the theoretical lenses of cognitive and constructivist theories have changed the emphasis in the field from teaching to learning. (p. 2)

In this shift from teaching to learning, educational technologists have increasingly emphasized the use of technology tools for inquiry and problem solving, concepts that the learning science field has helped to introduce (see Bransford et al., 2000).

The Learning Sciences

The roots of the "science of learning" can be traced to the end of the nineteenth century, when "systematic attempts were made to study the human mind through scientific methods" (Bransford et al., 2000, p. 6). Officially, the field of learning sciences was established in 1991, with the first international conference and the initial publication of the *Journal of the Learning Sciences* (Sawyer, 2014b)

The Cambridge Handbook of the Learning Sciences defines the field as follows:

> The Learning Sciences is an interdisciplinary field that emerged from a historical intersection of multiple disciples focused on learning and learning environment design. Consequently, learning sciences blends research and practice – and views the two approaches as synergistic. (Nathan & Sawyer, 2014, p. 38)

Learning sciences researchers design new learning approaches to serve as a basis for larger theories about how children learn (Penuel & Spillane, 2014). Their overall goal is to understand the processes, both cognitive and social, that lead to more effective learning and to use this information to inform the broader design of better learning environments (Sawyer, 2014b, p. 1).

Today technology is a core element of the conversation in the learning sciences: it is seen as a critical learning tool. "If we are to succeed in creating the schools of the future, educational innovation and technology must be grounded in the learning sciences" (Sawyer, 2014a, p. 729). And yet, while schools proudly trumpet their use of technology as a sign of their modernity, they are often using this technology simply to support very traditional teaching practices, practices which often reflect the belief that knowledge can simply be transmitted didactically (Meier, 2011, 2015). Two Canadian scholars who base their work on learning science principles, Marlene Scardamalia and Carl Bereiter (2014), position students as "knowledge builders"—individuals who are actively engaged in building their understandings through collaborative inquiry-based learning. They also embrace the broader notion of digital tools as "thinking tools" for finding information and solving problems. From this perspective, technology should be used in ways that support emerging learning opportunities for students.

Implications for Collaboration

While at this time there may be broad acceptance for the idea that both educational technology *and* learning sciences perspectives are essential for educational researchers in these fields, there is precious little evidence of collaboration to date. In a well-known study, Nolen (2009) analyzed four years of educational psychology journals (2003–2007) and found that only a small percentage of the articles actually linked learning theory and technology. Concrete initiatives are needed, supported with policy encouragement and funding. A rationale for such collaborations can be found in a widely recognized framework, Pasteur's Quadrant.

Pasteur's Quadrant and Its Relevance for Collaboration

Earlier in this volume, Reeves and Oh note that educational technology generally takes a more applied research stance, while the learning sciences emphasize more basic science. Many researchers share this perception. Lowyck (2014) notes that "the nature of learning sciences and instructional technology reflects two separate endeavors with different conceptual frameworks, methods and goals often labeled as fundamental versus applied" (p. 12). Although the fields have distinctly different roots and research traditions, increasing the flow of knowledge between the two fields requires educational technologists to be knowledgeable about emerging findings in the learning sciences. At the same time learning sciences researchers need to be aware of emerging discoveries and ongoing research in the educational technology field.

Stokes (1997) discussed the importance of transforming the scientific paradigm from a dichotomy between basic and applied research to one in which both *use* and *fundamental understandings* are considered in the scope of work. Figure 10.1

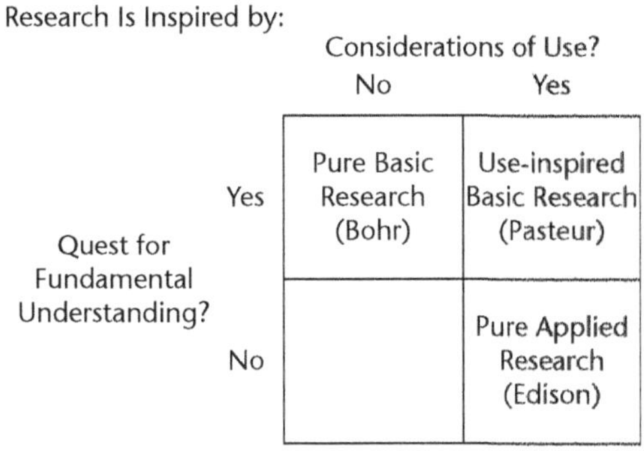

Research Is Inspired by:

	Considerations of Use?	
	No	Yes
Quest for Fundamental Understanding? Yes	Pure Basic Research (Bohr)	Use-inspired Basic Research (Pasteur)
No		Pure Applied Research (Edison)

FIGURE 10.1 Pasteur's quadrant
Source: Pasteur's Quadrant (Stokes, 1997, p. 73).

illustrates Stokes' vision. The upper right-hand cell includes basic research that seeks to extend the frontiers of understanding but is also inspired by considerations of use. It is known as Pasteur's Quadrant in view of Pasteur's clear drive toward both understanding and use: Pasteur's work illustrates the combination of both basic and applied goals (Stokes, 1997).

Figure 10.1 depicts a way of categorizing research approaches and inspires a different way of thinking about both basic and applied research by showing the relevance of each approach to the other. Pasteur's Quadrant reveals the potential for synergy between the two approaches and as such, reflects the importance of each perspective and the need for each field to engage with the goals and objectives of the other.

If, as the definitions above state, learning science researchers "blend research and practice" (Nathan & Sawyer, 2014, p. 38) and educational technologists promote appropriate uses of technology that incorporate more recent learning theories, then both should be inclined to embrace what Stokes would describe as "use-inspired basic research," or Pasteur's Quadrant. These two different aspects of learning—thinking processes and tools for thinking—are naturally allied and have great collaborative potential.

Improving Education during Unsettled Times

From the perspective Pasteur's Quadrant then, the overriding goal is the development of new theoretical knowledge about learning and technology and the eventual adoption of research findings to improve schools throughout the United States and perhaps beyond. Therefore, it is important to ask how the research agendas address the needs of teachers, administrators, and students. The relevance of the research and the research findings themselves depend on school circumstances. Effective research involving technology and the learning sciences requires a deep understanding of the lives of those in the classroom.

Since the 1980s, the schools have been on the front lines of dramatic changes, with at least three major waves of innovation impacting schools across the states. First, in the 80s and 90s, schools began a broad investment in technology with the assumption that teachers could easily incorporate these digital tools in their teaching. Second, individual state standards were introduced in the late 1980s and 90s and the Common Core State Standards (CCSS) were introduced in 2010. The CCSS established a common set of standards that most states voted to adopt in order to establish similar, and therefore more equitable, learning opportunities across states for all students. Third, the No Child Left Behind Act of 2001 introduced annual testing for all students in grades 3–8. States were charged with making adequate progress each year toward statewide proficiency goals (U.S. Department of Education, 2004).

Teachers and administrators experienced the introduction of all three innovations in waves over the last two decades. Each innovation demanded new understandings, new approaches in the classroom, even new beliefs about teaching, and the use of new materials—technological or otherwise (Fullan, 2007).

Digital Tools

Technology was first introduced into schools in 1970s, but equipment began to proliferate throughout the late 80s, 90s, and early 2000s, greatly increasing the amount of technology available in the schools. The expectations were high: it was thought that digital tools would "revolutionize" teaching and learning, primarily because there was "faith in electronic pedagogy" (Tyack & Cuban, 1995, p. 111). Many inside and outside education were hoping—and many still do hope—that the machines themselves would bring about increased engagement and greater learning achievement. There were "high hopes riding on an assumed causal relationship between installing computers … in classrooms and improved student learning outcomes and standardized test scores" (Knobel & Kalman, 2016, p. 7). The actual results have fallen far short of these expectations (Cuban, 2013).

Teachers have faced a number of barriers in *implementing* technology. Typical professional development programs introduce teachers to the technology itself, but do not explain how to *teach* with the tools (Bostock et al., 2016; Hew & Brush, 2007; Lawless & Pellegrino, 2007; Penuel et al., 2007). Teachers are rarely given professional development that links technology to new approaches for teaching or even specific teaching techniques. They are very rarely given the *ongoing* support needed to integrate technology with new ideas about teaching and learning. This type of support, however, is where the greatest potential for substantive classroom change exists (Lowyck, 2014).

In addition, findings from the learning science field are rarely a part of technology professional development. Collaborative learning is an example of a learning activity supported by learning sciences findings that lends itself to the use of technology (Bransford et al., 2000; Stahl et al., 2014). Introducing the technology that might facilitate collaborative learning is not enough to help teachers implement effective collaborative learning. Teachers need to know how to use the software to scaffold thoughtful, intellectual collaboration (Kuhn, 2015; Nussbaum et al., 2009; Zurita & Nussbaum, 2004). If teachers do not learn how to restructure "classroom as usual" practices, or how to take advantage of learning science discoveries more generally, digital tools often simply "digitize the status quo" (Meier, 2015, p. 5).

Perhaps the most serious issue in the area of technology is that of equity. High-need urban and rural schools typically receive far less support than wealthier schools (Blanchard et al., 2016; Warschauer & Matuchniak, 2010).Serious equity problems continue to be reflected in the lack of access to working technology; the lack of access to high-speed Internet connections; the limited types of software purchased for the schools; and the limited number of teachers prepared to *use* the technology effectively (Anderson, 2009; Blanchard et al., 2016; Margolis, 2008; Warschauer & Matuchniak, 2010).

In summary, the first wave of innovation involved the introduction of digital tools but there have been several challenges for educators: first, the technology has not been supported with effective professional development for teachers and administrators; second, technology has been implemented *without* an explicit link to the learning sciences; and most importantly, it has not been adopted or implemented equitably. Digital tools have been introduced *as the innovation* rather than as a powerful resource for supporting the true innovation: the creation of authentic inquiry-driven learning environments.

Common Core State Standards

The second innovation wave came in 2009 with the development of the Common Core State Standards (CCSS) (Common Core State Standards Initiative, 2011). During the 1990s individual states began developing their own standards with the passage of the Elementary and Secondary Education Act of 1994. Soon, all the states except Iowa had developed their own set (Wenglinsky, 2005, p. 18). The expectations for students were quite uneven across the states, however, and policy-makers were concerned that the U.S. needed a more coherent set of standards.

The Common Core State Standards (developed by a core group of educational experts and teachers and supported by the National Governors Association and the Chief State School Officers) were intended to be a set of standards which each state would vote on to adopt. To date, 42 states have adopted the Common Core State Standards (www.corestandards.org/).

To encourage adoption of these "Common Core" standards, federal budget support for the states was partially tied to their adoption of the standards. Through the *Race to the Top* legislation, the federal government awarded funding to states that made a commitment to, among other things, "developing and implementing common, high-quality standards" (U.S. Department of Education, 2009, p. 3).

While the CCSS standards themselves were clear, teachers needed help in learning how to implement them in their classrooms (Meier & Sánchez, 2013). Few states provided substantive, ongoing technical assistance to support their Common Core implementation plan: "…[S]tates were struggling to provide CCSS training of sufficient quality and quantity, with less than a majority of teachers in adopter states having participated in such professional development" (Cristol & Ramsey, 2014, p. 1).

The promise of CCSS was the shared set of expectations and learning goals across states: many other countries enjoy the benefits of a common set of standards. CCSS presented a coherent body of content standards and yet processes for implementing the standards were not defined and varied widely from state to state and district to district (Cristol & Ramsey, 2014). Teachers were challenged with both learning the standards and thinking about best practices for their implementation. To "incentivize" the teachers, many states and districts implemented formulas for evaluating teachers based in part on their students' test scores (Porter, 2015).

High-Stakes Testing

The high-stakes testing introduced during the early 2000s represents the third innovation wave. Traditionally, test scores had been used to provide parents and educators with helpful information, but there was a shift to use test scores for accountability purposes starting during the 1970s with minimum competency testing (Koretz, 2008). The No Child Left Behind (NCLB) (No Child Left Behind Act, 2002) legislation doubled down on this shift by defining test results as a way to evaluate school systems and hold teachers accountable. "It is hard to overstate the impact NCLB has had on elementary and secondary education" (Koretz, 2008, p. 23).

Although test results have always been a concern for teachers, students, and administrators, the high-stakes pressure that came with the annual NCLB testing requirements was unprecedented, according to many educators (Cristol & Ramsey, 2014, p. 1). Teachers and administrators were now accountable for "annual yearly improvement" of test scores for grades 3–8; they could face serious consequences for low scores, consequences that became more severe each year (Kirp, 2015). Teachers could be let go, principals reassigned, and whole schools closed as a result of poor test scores (Koretz, 2008). By 2010, some states used student test performance for 50% of the assessment of teacher effectiveness (Baker et al., 2010), and by the 2016–17 school year, all but six states were expected to use tests to assess teachers (Porter, 2015). Predictably, teachers and administrators have made test preparation a priority in a growing number of schools.

A Perfect Storm of Interventions

In the context of this combination of external interventions, one could argue that teachers and administrators need the help of the entire educational community— especially educational researchers—to help make sense of these demands and determine how best to implement changes in the classroom (Cristol & Ramsey, 2014). Both learning scientists and educational technology researchers have important insights for school personnel regarding the use of technology, the implementation of the common core standards, and appropriate use of assessment.

Beyond the world of the school, technology advances continue. However, the exponential growth of hardware and software does not necessarily result in exponential growth in student learning. In an article summarizing emerging educational technologies, Spector (2013) notes: "It is clear that powerful educational technologies exist and will continue to emerge. What is not clear is how well we will be able to make effective use of those technologies" (p. 27).

Effective use of digital tools will depend on educators' ability to situate technology's use in research-based learning approaches, with a clear understanding and appreciation for the context of real schools and ongoing policy initiatives. To accomplish this ambitious goal, partnerships between learning scientists and educational technology researchers are needed.

The next section describes the opportunity that design-based research (DBR) presents for bringing together researchers from learning sciences and educational technology in partnerships with schools. The rationale for using DBR is presented as a preface to describing a concrete example of a research organization that attempts to address the partnership challenge.

Design-based Research: A Structural Opportunity for Collaboration

Opportunities are needed to blend the theoretical and applied worlds of both the learning sciences and educational technology fields. Opportunities are also needed to develop partnerships with schools. Design-based research (DBR) provides a pathway for researchers and school personnel to collect and study data together and to use the data to continue to improve the quality of learning. Design-based research typically uses both quantitative and qualitative methodologies to explore educational contexts in ways that maximize the "translation of educational research into improved practice" while emphasizing the development of educational theory (Anderson & Shattuck, 2012, p. 16).

Design-based research is an approach for collecting data and studying interventions in collaboration with local school agencies. It is an effective tool for building rapport between researchers and school-based educators (Gutierrez & Penuel, 2014; Penuel et al., 2011). DBR also provides a means of studying emerging innovations and improving the interventions through iterative cycles of research and implementation. Learning science researchers and educational technologists can address real problems and explore potential solutions in school settings with research providing ongoing feedback about the innovation.

> Design-based research strives to generate and advance a particular set of theoretical constructs that transcends the environmental particulars of the contexts in which they were generated, selected, or refined. This focus on advancing theory grounded in naturalistic context sets design-based research apart from laboratory experiments or evaluation research. (Barab & Squire, 2004, p. 5)

Professional development (PD) is often an implicit feature of design-based research as researchers prepare teachers and administrators for an innovation or new approach to teaching. Many educators have written about the importance of well-designed professional development (Borko, 2004; Darling-Hammond, 1998; Desimone, 2009; Loucks-Horsley et al., 1998; Penuel et al., 2007). Professional development represents a structured opportunity for researchers to create a dialogue with the field and share emerging research findings. At the same time, these sessions help teachers keep up with changes in the field or learn to make relevant changes in their classroom (Guskey, 2000). Professional development is key to teacher learning (Blanchard et al., 2016; Desimone, 2009) and yet lamentably, it often falls short of what is needed to prepare teachers. Thoughtful, well-designed, professional development is needed to support teachers and administrators in making the transitions that are required to address successive waves of change such as those described above.

At the same time, researchers gain from this opportunity by creating a channel of communication with the field that also helps the researchers better understand the context of the classroom teacher and school administrator. This can, in turn, help ground research efforts in reality-based perceptions of the problems facing schools today and inform researchers' study designs and dissemination plans.

Design-based research, particularly design-based research that features high-quality professional development, provides learning scientists and educational technology researchers with rich partnership opportunities. The challenge is to find ways to collaborate as technologies continue to emerge and as researchers learn more about learning in order to craft the most effective pedagogies for today's students. A concrete example of a research organization entity that attempts to address this challenge is described below.

An Opportunity for Collaboration: The Center for Technology and School Change

The Center for Technology and School Change (CTSC), at Teachers College, Columbia University, is engaged in research, evaluation, and professional development. The Center is committed to the creation of innovative learning environments for all students. Recognizing the potential of technology as a catalyst for transforming instruction, the Center engages in research and practice to reimagine approaches to equitable education (http://ctsc.tc.columbia.edu).

The Center was founded in 1996 with the goal of introducing technology to schools in ways that harmonized with the learning approaches reflected in what researchers were learning about learning.

The promise of technology was that it would be a catalyst to improve teaching and learning. However, exactly *how* that could—or should—happen has largely remained a black box (Cuban, 2013). CTSC researches key issues around positioning teachers as designers of their classroom learning environments, approaches focused on creating student understandings, and introducing digital tools as thinking tools for project-based work. Related research questions reside in both the learning sciences and educational technology worlds.

Over the last fifteen years, the Center has embarked on a series of design-based research cycles to investigate questions related to helping teachers use technology effectively. One overriding finding that has emerged from the Center's work with schools: teachers need a design process to help them use the technology in ways that introduce authentic, inquiry-driven learning environments.

A teacher's interest in learning the technology can serve as the motivator, but Center research shows that teachers need help in learning how to *use* the technology. They need *a process* for integrating the technology—a design process that shifts the pedagogical focus from "covering" material to creating interactive learning environments for students. Without design help, educators often simply add a technology activity to their existing routines (Meier, 2011, 2015), falling far short of the catalytic potential that technology promises (Cuban, 2001, 2013). If technology is to be a transformative tool for pedagogy and for classroom learning more generally, then teachers need help in learning to *design* new ways of working in their classroom with the technology.

The work of Marlene Scardamalia and Carl Bereiter has provided a conceptual foundation for CTSC's work. Their theoretical approach positions students as "knowledge-builders" (Scardamalia & Bereiter, 1994, 1999, 2006, 2014). This knowledge-building concept emerged from the learning sciences and envisions knowledge as "… created, rather than, as older epistemologies viewed it, discovered" (Scardamalia & Bereiter, 2014, p. 397).

Project-based learning (PBL) provides a practical, purposeful approach to helping teachers think differently about their classroom activities. It positions teachers as *designers* (Wiggins & McTighe, 2005) and provides a structure that supports the development of engaging learning opportunities and opportunities to integrate technology meaningfully (Meier, 2011). Others have written about the strong connections between PBL and the learning sciences (Darling-Hammond, 2010; Lowyck, 2014; Penuel & Gallagher, 2009). Project-based learning presents teachers with opportunities, for example, to explore student preconceptions or misconceptions and to provide students with opportunities to reflect on their learning goals and progress. These are both activities supported in learning science principles (Bransford et al., 2000, pp. 14–18). PBL focuses on big understandings and uses authentic problems to frame the work. Teachers can help students scaffold their learning and assess that learning in new and creative ways (Wiggins & McTighe, 2005).

Professional Development Design

Over a period of fifteen years, using design-based research, the Center has refined a professional development model that reflects learning sciences and educational technology findings, as well as research-based findings about professional development. Concepts such as situating the learning, creating "authentic" projects to engage teachers and model interactive, knowledge-building processes, and creating opportunities for reflection and meta-cognition are all found in the learning science and professional development literature (Borko, 2004; Desimone, 2009; Fishman et al., 2003; Garet et al., 2001; Lawless & Pellegrino, 2007). Moreover, research shows that the active construction of meaningful tasks, using social interaction and cognitive tools, such as those often found in technology, all lead to more meaningful learning and deeper understanding of subject matter (Krajcik & Shin, 2014).

What has been relatively unexamined is the link between the use of design practices and the introduction of technology within a learning science framework. To understand this link, it has been important to learn how to reach teachers effectively. "[R]esearchers are increasingly concerned with describing the linkage between the design and conduct of professional development and subsequent improvements to both teacher practice and student learning outcomes" (Penuel et al., 2007, pp. 920–921).

The Center explores the connections between teacher design practices, technology use, professional development, and school improvement. Findings include the understanding that learning sciences principles are necessary for introducing technology to ensure that teachers are using these powerful tools in ways that support how children learn best.

Through design-based research, conducted over time with many dozens of schools, administrators, and hundreds of teachers, the Center identified key elements for a new model. The CTSC model for *Innovating Instruction* (see Table 10.1) guides the work at the Center and provides a basis for new theoretical understandings of change.

The *Innovating Instruction* model was designed to provide a means of contextualizing change by first identifying key factors known in the literature regarding effective learning, effective technology use, and effective organizational change. Design-based research then helped refine and evolve the CTSC approach for helping teachers make important shifts in their classroom, with the support of administrators at the school and district levels. New practices, particularly practices involving the use of technology, and particularly new practices in urban schools, require a good "fit" between the idea, the culture of the school, and

TABLE 10.1 The CTSC model: Innovating Instruction ©

	*DESIGN – Engage teachers as designers of student-centered, authentic learning experiences*
1. Embrace a Design Approach	Model and support a backwards design approach to project planning that creates meaningful learning experiences for students.
2. Enrich Content Knowledge	Provide opportunities for deepening teachers' understanding of content, including cross-curricular connections, learning standards, and student misconceptions.
3. Integrate Assessment Practices	Facilitate the design of authentic assessment and data use to identify and respond to student needs.
4. Leverage Digital Tools	Teach the integration of digital tools as part of the design process to facilitate interactive student learning and to enrich content.
	*SITUATE – Create learning experiences for teachers that foster professional respect while adapting the learning for their particular school and situation*
1. Contextualize Teacher Learning	Situate the design work in the professional lives of teachers in order to connect deeply to the realities of teachers' classrooms and their students.
2. Model Effective Practice	Provide interactive, hands-on professional development that engages teachers and models project-based learning with available tools and resources.
3. Individualize Support	Co-construct project plans based on particular student and curricular needs, provide ongoing support for classroom implementation, and facilitate reflection on teaching and learning.
	*LEAD – Support leaders in guiding and sustaining change initiatives, while positioning teachers as agents of change*
1. Envision Change	Prioritize instructional leadership and develop actionable goals to promote change in self-identified areas of need.
2. Empower Leadership at All Levels	Provide a forum for identifying leaders—administrators, teachers, and community members—who can spearhead efforts that contribute to the common vision.
3. Sustain a Culture For Innovation	Scaffold educators' efforts toward instructional innovation to realize goals beyond the immediate scope of the professional development.
4. Research	Lead research that informs the transformative use of technology in existing and emerging practices in schools, while contributing to evolving scholarship on innovations for teaching and learning

technical capacities (Penuel et al., 2011, p. 333). Design-based research was particularly helpful in refining this aspect of the model.

Key change issues that are part of the model such as giving teachers agency as designers, situating the professional development by adapting the work to the needs of each school, and developing leadership to support an ongoing learning community are all essential aspects of the organizational change literature (Fullan, 2007; Leithwood et al., 2006; Leithwood et al., 2004; Senge, 2006; Sergiovanni, 2000). These concepts were built into the CTSC model and refined in various design-based research iterations in dozens of schools.

The *Innovating Instruction* model consists of three phases: Design, Situate, and Lead. Each phase plays an essential role in helping to structure and ground the approach taken in the schools. The implementation of the model is crafted and designed for each professional development encounter by a professional team at the Center to situate the work for that particular audience. The CTSC professional development facilitators consists of graduate students, or students who have already graduated with master's or doctoral degrees, who are all formerly teachers or administrators. The Center sits in the Mathematics, Science, and Technology Department, and typically collaborates within the department and with other Teachers College or Columbia University departments as particular types of expertise, such as engineering, are needed.

The *Design* phase consists of four key elements: teaching teachers the design process, developing teachers' content knowledge, introducing new perspectives in assessment with an emphasis on formative assessment, and learning about the appropriate use of technology. These four components are central to the development of teacher-designed projects. Project-based learning typically positions teachers to guide student learning through the exploration of content-rich authentic problems, grounded with an essential question. This often takes teachers out of their content comfort zone by going beyond "covering" a particular content. To help with this shift, the inquiry process must be modeled for teachers, as the professional developers facilitate the process of learning for the teachers. Thus, the CTSC facilitators work with teachers through the implementation of a model project and then, after reflection and further training, help teachers learn to design and implement their own project. Small group collaboration, formative assessment strategies, and appropriate use of technology are all modeled for the teachers by the professional development facilitators during the professional development sessions.

The *Situate* phase contextualizes the professional learning in the lives of the specific group of teachers via workshops, school planning sessions, and formal and informal meetings. Facilitators model the use of technology-infused, project-based learning, and later, provide individualized classroom support for teachers. This customized aspect of the professional development underscores the importance of each teacher, school, student body, and administrator. "Successful scaling, most policy researchers agree, depends on local actors—especially district administrators, school leaders and teachers—who need to make continual coherent adjustments to programs as they work their way through educational systems (Penuel et al., 2011, p. 331; Weinbaum & Supovitz, 2010). By adapting the professional development and building the projects around the needs and interests of individual schools, administrators, teachers, and students, CTSC facilitators provide teachers with the knowledge and skills to pursue the design of authentic, CCSS-aligned, technology-enhanced projects.

The *Lead* component emphasizes the importance of institutionalizing change. It underscores the need to envision change, especially as it relates to how leaders understand instructional leadership. Historically, unrealistic demands have been put on building leaders to become instructional leaders. Bryk (2015) describes a common plight: "Principals [are] urged to become instructional leaders even though demands on their time [are] already excessive and few or no modifications [are] offered to relieve those demands" (p. 468). Building leaders are invited to attend all professional development sessions to learn more about changing instructional practices, and regular meetings to update administrators are a routine part of the work of the facilitators. Facilitators encourage building leaders to support teachers involved in the efforts so that the ideas can move beyond the professional development sessions to become a part of the school culture. Facilitators frequently encourage ongoing research at the building level, so that schools are able to study and continue to learn from their improvement efforts. CTSC's work has resulted in institutional changes such as the reorganization of schedules to provide more time for technology-infused project work, and the reorganization of teacher teams to provide more school coherence for a project-based approach to learning. Below, a specific example of a professional development effort with an urban school district helps show the CTSC process in action.

Innovating Instruction in the Field

CTSC facilitators have worked each summer for the past four years with a high need urban district. In a summer school setting, envisioned as a "Learning Lab," facilitators work alongside teachers for four hours per day, over a four-week period. The goal is two-fold: to provide a summer opportunity for students and to provide teachers with an in-depth professional development opportunity to design an authentic project using technology as a powerful learning tool for students.

During the last weeks of school, orientation sessions for teachers are conducted at the end of the school year with afterschool workshops, followed by three pre-program professional development days just before the start of summer school. When the summer sessions begin, the learning is sustained through teacher meetings during the day, in-class mentoring while the teachers are teaching, and after-school teacher workshops for a total of 60 hours of professional development.

During the professional development sessions, the teachers implement a model project designed by the CTSC facilitators. After reflecting on the experience, they learn to design their own projects. These workshops are hands-on, interactive, engaging sessions, focused on the particular Common Core State Standards important to the district, based on test scores and other feedback from the past school year.

Before summer school begins, facilitators scaffold the development of new projects with the teachers, supporting them as they begin designing their own projects. These projects are then implemented in their classrooms during the summer session with students. The CTSC facilitators follow the teachers into the summer school classrooms, working alongside them in the classroom during the school day, helping them to carry out the projects and modeling the management of project-based learning elements, such as the appropriate use of technology. After class in the afternoon, the facilitators lead workshops for the teachers to focus on particular aspects of the design process or technology, such as the use of technology for formative assessment. The building administrators are encouraged to attend workshops and visit the classrooms frequently. At the end of the summer sessions, an open house is held for parents and district administrators to see the students' work and celebrate the projects.

Preliminary findings from the design-based research indicate that the professional development provided teachers with the support they felt they needed to make changes in areas significant to both researchers and the district. The work was designed around the needs and interests of the school district and individual teachers, situated in the schools, and supported with ongoing discussions with building administrators to discuss how teachers would take the work forward in their classrooms and home buildings. Importantly, equity discussions were an explicit aspect of the work, as facilitators worked with teachers to get technology into the hands of the urban students, students who sometimes do not have direct access to the technology tools. Facilitators helped teachers manage the use of the technology and showed teachers how to use digital tools with students in the design and implementation of the projects.

The overall goals for the work at the Center are aligned with learning sciences lessons regarding the need for engaging students in meaningful, authentic learning opportunities. In CTSC's approach, technology is used to support and deepen these opportunities, and teachers are given the tools to become designers of learning environments. The *Innovating Instruction* model, situated in the needs of particular districts and classrooms, holds promise for reaching and empowering teachers and students. The Center continues its design-based research, and the model continues to evolve, supported by National Science Foundation funding and other federal, state, and local district funds.

The Way Forward

In the harried world of real schools, teachers and administrators are eager to find effective ways to reach students. Everyone wants to be more successful as a teacher or an instructional leader. At the same time, researchers in the learning sciences and educational technology fields are eager to develop theories and test them in real school "learning laboratories."

This chapter has outlined the need for more collaboration between the two closely related fields of educational technology and the learning sciences to advance the school reform agenda and promote greater equity by providing students with the tools for knowledge-building and engaged learning. "Pasteur's Quadrant" highlights the potential for "use-inspired basic research," and provides a possible solution to the traditional "either-or" dilemma of basic or applied research. Understanding the real-world context for the research is important, however, and researchers must appreciate the recent real-world innovation waves that have shaped the stress-filled agenda for schools throughout the United States.

Meaningful partnerships between researchers and practitioners are enhanced through design-based research. The work of the Center for Technology and School Change demonstrates the potential for using principles from the learning sciences to inform the use of technology, as well as the possibility of collaborating with schools through professional development, using design-based research.

The chapter began with a discussion of the vital role that research plays in our modern society. Nowhere is research needed more than in the field of education. Coburn and Penuel (2016) note that there is currently "more talk than ever" about the importance of research in the improvement of educational practice (p. 48). Nolen (2009) noted that:

> For educational technology research to help solve real-world educational problems, we advocate that studies increasingly reflect two qualities. One is to achieve balance between rigor (internal validity) and relevance (external validity). The second is to focus on meaningful application topics that deal directly with teaching and learning challenges and practices in today's classrooms. (p. 24)

One issue that can unite researchers, school personnel, technology advocates, and those interested in the learning sciences is the issue of equity. The overarching rationale for the work of educators is to bring more equitable learning opportunities to our students. If the educational community can commit to creating learning environments to support the learning needs of *all* students, then there is motivation to collaborate around the use of technology to support new approaches to learning and the design of new dynamic learning environments.

Going forward, it will be important to design policy that "targets persistent problems of practice and employs participatory approaches to design and research" (Coburn & Penuel, 2016, p. 661). Educational technology and learning science researchers need to be partners in such efforts: a discriminating sense for the appropriate use of technology tools is of paramount importance in a time of rapidly expanding technology resources. A partnership between the learning sciences and educational technology researchers is needed to capitalize on technology's creative power as a catalyst to support the creation of authentic, engaging, robust learning environments. Collaboration is imperative in an era filled with change.

The author would like to gratefully acknowledge Caron Mineo, Dawn Horton, Rita Sanchez, Sharmin Hakim, Jessica Yusaitis-Pike, Kenny Graves, and others at the Center for Technology and School Change who have been extensively involved in the development and implementation of this work at the Center.

References

Anderson, N. (2009). *Equity and information communication technology (ICT) in education*. New York: Peter Lang.

Anderson, T., & Shattuck, J. (2012). Design-based research: A decade of progress in education research? *Educational Researcher, 41*(1), 16–25. doi:10.3102/0013189X11428813

Association for Educational Communications and Technology. (2004). *The definition of educational technology*. Association for Educational Communications and Technology. Unpublished draft for a book chapter.

Baker, E., Barton, P., Darling-Hammond, L., Haertel, E., Ladd, H., Linn, R. . . . Shephard, L. (2010). Problems with the use of student test scores to evaluate teachers, *EPI Briefing Paper #270*. Washington D.C.: Economic Policy Institute.

Barab, S., & Squire, K. (2004). Design-based research: Putting a stake in the ground. *The Journal of the Learning Sciences, 13*(1), 1–14.

Blanchard, M., LePrevost, C., Tollin, A. D., & Gutierrez, K. S. (2016). Investigating technology-enhanced teacher professional development in rural, high poverty middle schools. *Educational Researcher, 45*(3), 207–220.

Borko, H. (2004). Professional development and teacher learning: Mapping the terrain. *Educational Researcher, 33*(3), 3–15.

Bostock, S., Lisi-Neumann, K., & Collucci, M. (2016). Doing-it-ourselves development: (Re)defining, (re)designing and (re)valuing the role of teaching, learning, and literacies. In M. Knobel & J. Kalman (Eds.), *New literacies and teacher learning* (pp. 43–64). New York: Peter Lang Publishing.

Bransford, J., Brown, A., & Cocking, R. (Eds.). (2000). *How people learn: Brain, mind, experience, and school, expanded edition*. Washington, DC: National Academy Press.

Bryk, A. (2015). Accelerating how we learn to improve. *Educational Researcher, 44*(9), 467–477.

Coburn, C., & Penuel, W. (2016). Research-practice partnerships in education: Outcomes, dynamics, and open questions. *American Educatational Research Jounal, 45*(1), 48–54. doi:10.3102/0013189X16631750

Common Core State Standards Initiative. (2011). *Common Core State Standards*. Retrieved from www.corestandards.org/

Cristol, K., & Ramsey, B. (2014). *Common Core in the districts*. Washington, D.C: The Thomas B. Fordham Institute.

Cuban, L. (1986). *Teachers and machines: The classroom use of technology since 1920*. New York: Teachers College Press.

Cuban, L. (2001). *Oversold and underused: Computers in the classroom*. Cambridge, MA: Harvard University Press.

Cuban, L. (2013). *Inside the black box of classroom practice: Change without reform in American education*. Cambridge, MA: Harvard Education Publishing Group.

Darling-Hammond, L. (1998). Teacher learning that supports student learning. *Educational Leadership, 55*, 6–11.

Darling-Hammond, L. (2010). *The flat world and education: How America's commitment to equity will determine our future*. New York: Teachers College Press.

Dede, C. (2008). Theoretical perspectives influencing the use of information technology in teaching and learning. In J. Voogt & G. Knezek (Eds.), *International handbook of information technology in primary and secondary education* (pp. 43–62). New York: Springer Science+Business Media LLC.

Desimone, L. (2009). Improving impact studies of teachers' professional development: Toward better conceptualizations and measures. *Educational Researcher, 38*(3), 181–199.

Fishman, B., Marx, R., Best, S., & Tal, R. (2003). Linking teacher and student learning to improve professional development in systemic reform. *Teaching and Teacher Education, 19*(6), 643–658.

Fullan, M. (2007). *The new meaning of educational change* (4th ed.). New York: Teachers College Press.

Garet, M., Porter, A., Desimone, L., Birman, B., & Yoon, K. (2001). What makes professional development effecftive? Results from a national sample of teachers. *American Educational Research Journal, 38*(4), 915–945.

Guskey, T. (2000). *Evaluating professional development*. Thousand Oaks, CA: Corwin Press.

Gutierrez, K., & Penuel, W. (2014). Relvance to practice as a criterion for rigor. *Educational Researcher, 43*(19), 19–23.

Hew, K. F., & Brush, T. (2007). Integrating technology into K-12 teaching and learning: Current knowledge gaps and recommendations for future research. *Educational Technology Research and Development, 55*, 223–252.

Januszewski, A., & Molenda, M. (2008). *Educational technology: A definition with commentary*. New York: Routledge.

Kirp, D. (2015, December 10). Why the new education law is good for children left behind. *New York Times*. Retrieved from www.nytimes.com/2015/12/10/opinion/why-the-new-education-law-is-good-for-children-left-behind.html

Knobel, M., & Kalman, J. (2016). Teacher learning, digial technologies and new literacies. In M. Knobel & J. Kalman (Eds.), *New liteacies and teacher learning* (pp. 1–20). New York: Peter Lang Publishing.

Koretz, D. (2008). *Measuring up: What educational testing really tells us*. Cambridge, MA: Harvard University Press.

Krajcik, J., & Shin, N. (2014). Project-based learning. In R. K. Sawyer (Ed.), *The Cambridge handbook of the learning sciences* (pp. 317–334). New York: Cambridge University Press.

Kuhn, D. (2015). Thinking together and alone. *American Educatational Research Jounal, 44*(1), 46–53.

Lawless, K., & Pellegrino, J. (2007). Professional development in integrating technology into teaching and learning: Knowns, unknowns, and ways to pursue better questions and answers. *Review of Educational Research, 77*(4), 575–614.

Leithwood, K., McAdie, P., Bascia, N., & Rodrique, A. (2006). *Teaching for deep understanding: What every educator should know*. Thousand Oaks, CA: Corwin Press.

Leithwood, K., Seashore-Louis, K., Anderson, S., & Wahlstrom, K. (2004). *How leadership influences student learning*. Minneapolis, MN: Center for Applied Research and Educational Improvement.

Loucks-Horsley, S., Hewson, P., Love, N., & Stiles, K. (1998). *Designing professional development for teachers of science and mathematics.* Thousand Oaks, CA: Sage.

Lowyck, J. (2014). Bridging learning theories and technology-enhanced environments: A critical appraisal of its history. In J. M. Spector, M. D. Merrill, J. Elen, & M. J. Bishop (Eds.), *Handbook of research on communications and educaitonal technology* (pp. 3–20). New York: Springer.

Margolis, J. (2008). *Stuck in the shallow end: Education, race and computing.* Cambridge, MA: The MIT Press.

Meier, E. (2011). New millennium leadership for 21st century learning environments. *IMPACT on Instructional Improvement, 36*(1), 37–42.

Meier, E. (2015). Beyond a digital status quo: Reconceptualizing online learning opportunities. *Bank Street Occasional Papers, 34.* Retrieved from www.bankstreet.edu/occasional-paper-series/

Meier, E., & Sánchez, R. (2013). *Data-driven instruction: What can assessment data offer urban educators?* Paper presented at the National Council of Teachers of Mathematics, Denver, CO.

Nathan, M., & Sawyer, R. K. (2014). Foundations of the learning sciences. In R. K. Sawyer (Ed.), *The Cambridge handbook on the learning sciences* (2nd ed., pp. 21–43). New York: Cambridge University Press.

National Research Council (Ed.) (2002). *Scientific Research in Education.* Washingon, D.C.: National Academy Press.

No Child Left Behind Act, 20 USC 6311(b)(3)(C) C.F.R. (2002).

Nolen, A. L. (2009). The content of educational psychology: An analysis of top-ranked journals from 2003–2007. *Educational Psychology Review, 21*(3), 279–289.

Nussbaum, M., Alvarez, C., McFarlane, A., Gomez, F., & Claro, S. (2009). Technology as small group face-to-face collaborative scaffolding. *Computers & Education, 52,* 147–153.

Penuel, W., & Gallagher, L. (2009). Preparing teachers to design instruction for deep understanding in middle school earth science. *Journal of the Learning Sciences, 18*(4), 461–508.

Penuel, W., & Spillane, J. (2014). Learning sciences and policy design and implementation: Key concepts and tools for collaborative engagement. In R. K. Sawyer (Ed.), *The Cambridge handbook of the learning sciences* (pp. 649–667). New York: Cambridge University Press.

Penuel, W., Fishman, B., Cheng, B., & Sabelli, N. (2011). Organizing research and development at the intersection of learning, implementation, and design. *Educational Researcher, 40*(7), 331–337.

Penuel, W., Fishman, B., Yamaguchi, R., & Gallagher, L. (2007). What makes professional development effective? Strategies that foster curriculum implementation. *American Educational Research Journal, 44*(4), 921–958.

Porter, E. (2015, March 25). Grading teachers by the test. *The New York Times.* Retrieved from http://nyti.ms/1BhHQtJ

Reeves, T., & Oh, E. G. (2016). Comparing the goals and methodologies of learning scientists and educational technology researchers. In L. Lin & J. M. Spector (Eds.), *The sciences of learning and instructional design: Constructive articulation between communities* pp. 52–64. New York: Taylor-Francis/Routledge.

Sawyer, R. K. (2014a). The future of learning: Grounding educational innovation in the learning sciences. In R. K. Sawyer (Ed.), *The Cambridge handbook of the learning sciences* (2nd ed., pp. 726–746). New York: Cambridge University Press.

Sawyer, R. K. (2014b). Introduction: The new science of leanring. In R. K. Sawyer (Ed.), *The Cambridge handbook of the learning sciences* (pp. 1–20). New York: Cambridge University Press.

Scardamalia, M., & Bereiter, C. (1994). Computer support for knowledge-building communities. *The Journal of the Learning Sciences, 3*(3), 265–283.

Scardamalia, M., & Bereiter, C. (1999). Schools as knowledge-building organizations. In D. Keating & C. Hertzman (Eds.), *Today's children, tomorrow's society: The developmental health and wealth of nations* (pp. 274–289). New York: Guildford.

Scardamalia, M., & Bereiter, C. (2006). Knowledge building: Theory, pedagogy, and technology. In R. K. Sawyer (Ed.), *Cambridge handbook of the learning sciences* (pp. 97–118). New York: Cambridge University Press.

Scardamalia, M., & Bereiter, C. (2014). Knowledge building and knowledge creation. In R. K. Sawyer (Ed.), *The Cambridge handbook of the learning sciences* (2nd ed., pp. 397–417). Cambridge, UK: Cambridge University Press.

Senge, P. (2006). *The fifth discipline.* New York: Currency Doubleday.

Sergiovanni, T. (2000). *The lifeworld of leadership.* San Francisco: Jossey-Bass.

Spector, J. M. (2013). Emerging educatonal technologies and research directions. *Educational Technology & Society, 16*(2), 21–30.

Stahl, G., Koschmann, T., & Suthers, D. (2014). Computer-supported collaborative learning. In R. K. Sawyer (Ed.), *The Cambridge handbook of the learning sciences* (pp. 479–500). New York: Cambridge University Press.

Stokes, D. (1997). *Pasteur's quadrant.* Washington, D.C.: Brookings Institution Press.

Tyack, D., & Cuban, L. (1995). *Tinkering toward utopia.* Cambridge, MA: Harvard University Press.

U.S. Department of Education. (2004). Executive summary of the No Child Left Behind Act. Retrieved from www2.ed.gov/nclb/overview/intro/execsumm.html

U.S. Department of Education. (2009). Race to The Top: Executive summary. Retrieved on April 2, 2017 at www2.ed.gov/programs/racetothetop/executive-summary.pdf.

Warschauer, M., & Matuchniak, T. (2010). New technology and digital worlds: Analyzing evidence of euqity in access, use, and outcomes. In N. Pinkard & V. Gadsden (Eds.), *Review of research in education: What counts as eidence in educational settings? Rethinking equity, diversity, and reform in the 21st century* (Vol. 34, pp. 179–225). Thousand Oaks, CA: Sage.

Weinbaum, E., & Supovitz, J. (2010, April). Planning ahead: Making program implementation more predictable. *Phi Delta Kappan, 91*(7), 68–71.

Wenglinsky, H. (2005). *Using technology wisely: The keys to success in schools.* New York: Teachers College Press.

Wiggins, G., & McTighe, J. (2005). *Understanding by design* (2nd ed.). Alexandria, VA: Association for Supervision and Curriculum Development.

Zimmer, C. (2016, July 21). Updated brain map identifies nearly 100 new regions. *The New York Times.* Retrieved from www.nytimes.com/2016/07/21/science/human-connectome-brain-map.html?_r=0

Zurita, G., & Nussbaum, M. (2004). Computer supported collaborative learning using wirelessly ineronnected handheld computeres. *Computers & Education, 42,* 289–314.

11
SYNTHETIC ENVIRONMENTS FOR SKILLS TRAINING AND PRACTICE

Robert Hubal and Thomas Parsons

Overview

Today's technologies—from Web 3.0 and beyond to mobile devices to game engines to immersive and augmented virtual systems—offer great potential for students to train and practice the physical and cognitive components of hands-on social interaction skills in safe, diverse, and controllable contexts. Systematic training and practice opportunities in the real world are, at best, difficult to set up in typically resourced educational settings, but for many skills it is critical to validate students before they experience uncontrolled and unseen situations. Synthetic environments (SEs), the term used in this chapter, involve a human–computer interface that facilitates the student interaction with and engagement in computer-generated activities and resources, whatever the platform. SEs offer the potential to deliver systematic learning opportunities with (virtual) objects and people in precisely controlled, dynamic situations. SE paradigms allow for the sophisticated, objective, real-time measurement of students' behaviors and training outcomes, such as changes in performance or focus of attention (Parsons, 2015a). Continual cost reductions in, and improved capabilities of, SE technologies promise the advancement of more accessible, usable, and relevant SE applications to address an increasingly wider range of physical and cognitive training and practice conditions (Parsons, 2016; Parsons & Phillips, 2016; Bohil et al., 2011).

This chapter discusses the development, presentation, and measurement of SEs for training and assessment. We have been involved with the design, implementation, study, and application of many SEs, and, as a result of our experience, we have come to view SEs as supporting a cycle that relates motivation and retention to performance as portrayed in Figure 11.1. The engaging nature of well-designed SEs encourages students to explore the environment and demonstrate behaviors

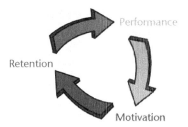

FIGURE 11.1 Benefits of engaged learning

as they would or should in a real situation. This performance leads to retention of content, but also motivation to continue learning that extends the cycle. One of the theoretical bases for use of SEs in training and assessment is the constructivist approach advocated by Mayer (2009) and others. We view learning as an active role taken on by students, in environments that emphasize realistic tasks and dynamic feedback and guidance. Further the cognitive components of gaining knowledge and behavioral aspects associated with learning a skill suggest that the careful design of SEs is critical to creating a platform for successful learning.

SEs have traditionally been used for training of hands-on skills. Early systems focused on the physical elements of these skills, using costly setups that were nevertheless necessary to train on skills that were logistically complex or outright dangerous (Stone, 2001). Some subsequent SEs have continued this trend, particularly in surgical simulation (McElhinney et al., 2012). Others have focused more on strategies and procedures, using representative if not fully realistic physical manipulation, but using the rapidly advancing technology intelligently and applying it across a huge range of domains (Hale & Stanney, 2015).

In contrast, our more recent work reflects a growing trend in SEs in their use of intelligent virtual human (VH) agents for social and interaction skills training. These systems consist of artificially intelligent characters that have realistic appearances, can reason and behave much like people in similar situations, and can express themselves both verbally and non-verbally (Hubal, 2008a; Hubal & Frank, 2001; Hubal et al., 2007; Kenny & Parsons, 2011; Parsons, 2011b).

No matter the domain, SEs afford desired training features such as standardization, potential cost reduction, dynamic tailoring to the individual student, readily adapted content, and faithful administration of assessments. The remainder of this chapter discusses these and other features of SEs as they apply to skills training and assessment.

Development

A key component to training and assessment through SEs is development of educational materials, including resources and activities. Material development is by now quite well understood. The use of computer-based instruction for strict drill and practice and straight conversion of print-based materials to electronic form is, thankfully, past; materials designers now understand how to employ advanced technology in their applications. Here we offer insight gleaned from past experience designing and evaluating SE-based skills training applications.

Learning Objectives

As students interact in the virtual situations that are portrayed by the SE the effects and consequences of their actions (positive or negative) can be carefully assessed. The realism of interactions can be varied and the SE can control the pace and complexity of exposure to learning contexts. This allows for a degree of individualized design with regard to the SE-based practice of skills.

It is critical the materials designer first understand what is to be learned. Commonly, these goals are called learning objectives (LOs). LOs should be definable and measurable. Because they can be defined and measured, they can be labeled, saved, and reused. The need is for the designer to develop materials that help the student meet LOs. The designer should carefully weigh alternative approaches that meet the requirements. For instance, objectives that are well-defined, structured, and well-understood, such as gaining skills at troubleshooting machines (Hubal, 2005), can be met using structured, ordered materials with content-relevant help. In contrast, objectives that are ill-defined, unstructured, or poorly understood, such as gaining interaction skills (Hubal & Frank, 2001; Hubal, 2008a), can better be met using more free-form instructional materials with context-sensitive help.

Further, there should be a train-up of skills, increasing the ambiguity, complexity, uncertainty, and/or volatility of what is meant to be learned (e.g., the "task classes" of van Merriënboer et al., 2002). Ideally, an intelligent tutoring system would control this scaffolding (Jackson et al., 1998; Lane & Johnson, 2008), providing decreased assistance as the difficulty—and student competency—increases. Put another way, the SE should support students as they move from orientation, in which relatively simple problems are presented, to inquiry that encourages exploration and understanding of the complexity of the content, to policy formulation that demands that students develop rules and heuristics to perform successfully on a given problem and generalize to new ones (Milrad et al., 2003). As will be expanded further below, types of assistance that systems can provide to support students in achieving LOs include direct, extrinsic support (tutoring, highlighting, help functions), encouragement to reflect on learning that often leads to deeper understanding as well as realization of gaps in knowledge, and internal or intrinsic support (such as reducing task complexity or providing hints within the flow of the simulation) (Wray & Woods, 2013).

Tie to Strategic Needs

Effective learning needs to be tied to the needs of the students. Though this statement appears straightforward, it underlies an important ingredient to training success: students will be motivated to learn if they are able to immediately envision ready application of the knowledge and skills gained (Garris et al., 2002). The needs of students almost always extend beyond basic skills. As the basic skills are acquired, the SE must adapt, such as increasing the difficulty (to address more advanced LOs). Features such as materials reuse, modular design, and adaptive presentation can ensure that new and evolving knowledge and skills can be acquired just-in-time. Ease of distribution is also important; convenient access to learning content not just in the classroom but also across the Internet and via mobile devices, with encouragement provided through social media, implies a greater ability to access new knowledge and to practice skills flexibly, just-in-place.

Gain-Practice-Demonstrate

A staged model for providing learning opportunities uses a gain-practice-demonstrate framework (adapted from Frank et al., 2000 and Hubal & Pina, 2012). The concept holds that students first gain whatever knowledge is specific to the topic, then they acquire basic skills and iteratively practice them, ultimately demonstrating competence or mastery on performance measures during assessments. Figure 11.2 shows this approach schematically.

Becoming knowledgeable in to-be-learned material implies acquiring declarative information about concepts, capabilities, and characteristics relevant to what is being studied. Declarative knowledge is factual, overt, well-understood, basic information about skills and contexts. This part of the process is relatively passive; knowledge can be gained, for instance, by absorbing a presentation or through reading. But it forms the basis for skills acquisition. Acquiring a skill is learning techniques and procedures, at first a relatively passive endeavor but becoming active as students perform the skills. Later stages of acquisition can be achieved in an SE, as can the practice (often called proceduralization) through which the student internalizes techniques and procedures. Procedural abilities are thus gained during acquisition, and they are automated during practice. For instance, driving a vehicle first requires knowledge of clutches, exhaust systems, road signs, rights

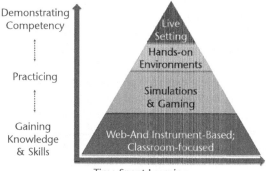

FIGURE 11.2 Gain-practice-demonstrate approach

of way, etc. With practice, this knowledge becomes routine, a skill (often, as in this case, largely a motor skill) that demands decreasing exertion to accomplish. Some demonstration of competency can be done in an SE, or one augmented by a physical device as described next, but typically students are assessed and their skills validated in a live environment, when available. The more realistic the setting in which skills are demonstrated, the more confidence both instructor and student will have in their successful application.

Part-Task Trainers

The gain-practice-demonstrate framework applies to training of social interaction skills—the bulk of our current work—but also to hands-on skills, particularly when SEs are augmented by physical training devices such as part-task trainers (PTTs). PTTs can be integral components of learning environments and useful adjuncts to SEs. It is easy to see how efficient and effective SEs can be for acquiring and practicing physical, even spatial, elements of a skill when PTTs are added. Though obviously applicable to the learning of physical and motor skills, PTTs can also be used for cognitive and strategic skills.

PTTs are usually limited-functionality, high-fidelity mockups of part or all of a live environment. For PTTs to be used effectively, it has long been established that training guidelines should map task action verbs to knowledge and skills being trained (Gagné, 1962). But it is reasonable to conceive of these devices not only as training environments in their own right but also as components within an SE, in which case they are more like appended devices. For instance, having a joystick or game controller integrated into an SE helps the student learn when such movement is necessary (Hubal, 2005) and helps to capture observations and reactions in a convenient manner (Hourani et al., 2011). Similarly, interacting with a life-sized VH projected into the room offers a level of immersion that makes rapid decision-making vital (Schaffer et al., 2013), in line with the tension felt by medical students engaging with standardized patients (Parsons et al., 2008; Parsons, 2011a; Pataki et al., 2012).

It is this latter example that hints at how PTTs can support learning of cognitive and strategic skills. Practice requires repeated performance in an environment that alters to reflect performance outcomes. In understanding when and how to apply knowledge, and in realizing gaps in knowledge that need to be filled for particular tasks, a student demonstrates strategic knowledge. In performing the skills under realistic conditions, a student experiences the breadth of content associated with the skill. For instance, deciding which of multiple paths to take to reach point B from point A requires application of a strategy. This observation is as true of a motor skill like driving (e.g., in a military vehicle, accounting for terrain, fortifications, and support systems) as it is for engaging in dialog with another individual (e.g., during the conversation, accounting for topics covered, topics to be avoided, and dyadic norms; Hubal et al., 2015b). That is, one strategically applies declarative or procedural knowledge (or both) and experiences consequences. The ability to demonstrate skills is enhanced in ever more realistic contexts such as those provided by PTTs.

Augmented and Mixed Systems

To this point we have purposefully avoided rigorously defining the "synthetic" in SE, because there are different means to present the environment, and we feel our ideas apply across them. Indeed, we have shown that, for many applications, relatively simple desktop simulation systems are satisfactory (Hubal, 2005, 2009). To be complete, though, here we outline some common intensive, more complex approaches for SEs.

In traditional virtual reality (VR), the individual is engaged in a fully immersive experience designed to instill a sense of presence. As an example, the VR environment may involve a head-mounted display (HMD) and data gloves that together present the full experience to the wearer. The HMD may have such features as a highly resolved camera, a depth sensor, tracking sensors via a 9-axis inertial measurement unit (IMU), and 3D audio. The depth sensor would be important for recognizing and segmenting body parts, particularly hands, during manipulations while the student demonstrates virtual hands-on skills. A good camera is important (in concert with the IMU) to accomplish closed-loop tracking of the student and environment. It may present the student with a 6-degree of freedom (DOF) view, "inside looking out" around a scene, or, depending on the task, an "outside looking in" configuration that represents 5-DOF.

Not all VR experiences, though, require these gadgets. For instance, several researchers have developed systems in which the student stands in front of a projected display and engages with objects and elements of the presented environment, with environmental trackers monitoring motion and interaction (e.g., Bowyer et al., 2008; Hays et al., 2012; Shapiro et al., 2015). Meanwhile, in augmented reality (AR) (Caudell & Mizell, 1992), the system overlays information onto the physical environment, perhaps, for example, via a pass-through camera, but does not otherwise interact with the physical environment. AR is based on geospatial locaters and other sensor data that act as fiducial markers for body positioning and visual overlays. A kind of combination of VR and AR is sometimes called mixed reality. In this environment, the system registers the real world digitally then overlays virtual content, and uses motion trackers and scanners for objects and boundaries to the current physical environment. This is technology with which one can bounce a virtual ball on a real table. Instead of fiduciary markers, mixed reality usually is focused on video, infrared signals, and depth capture of the scene. As such, it currently tends to track better on static objects.

The tools and techniques involved in VR, AR, and mixed reality—as well as other platforms for SEs such as the Web and even game consoles and smartphones—are advancing rapidly, blurring the lines of what is immersive and what is desktop. What required a large processor and bulky HMD some years ago that still resulted in jittery, time-delayed images now involves small, lightweight, fast mechanisms that yield ever-more-real depictions. While technological advancement enhances the effectiveness and versatility of mediated environments, researchers are also investigating how endogenous characteristics (personality traits, immersive tendencies, openness to experience) of individuals relate to the ways in which mediated environments are experienced (Parsons et al., 2015a). We do not know exactly where the technology will lead, but because they all are focused on increasing engagement of a user in a realistic experience, we are confident that the concepts associated with the SEs we have used will apply to future environments as well.

Student Control and Tutoring

Tutorial Roles

Good instructional technology that leads to experiential learning has the ability to support instructors and even replace some of their tutorial responsibilities. For an SE, as with any educational setting, it is important to address the amount of control given to the student, the scaffolding alluded to above. For instance, the amount of feedback, guidance, and tutoring to provide is roughly the inverse of student proficiency: too much for too long, and the student will have difficulty applying the knowledge; not enough, and learning will become inefficient. We think in terms of a VH tutor who may play any of a number of roles as the student progresses through lessons (Hubal, 2008b):

- Demonstrator. As the student is acquiring new knowledge or skills, the tutor can be most beneficial by demonstrating appropriate techniques and then virtually holding hands with the student to begin practice. The tutor demonstrates for the student best practices and good techniques, showing the sequence of steps of a task and what operations need to be done at each step.
- Trainer. Gradually, as the student gains proficiency, the tutor yields control. The tutor assists the student in progressing through learning material, providing content-relevant help. The student is largely in control of learning, though frequent assessments of knowledge can help keep learning on track.
- Coach. The tutor plays an active role in prompting or assisting the student through modules and exercises. For instance, the tutor can offer guidance in the form of suggested responses before each conversational turn in a mock interview and feedback after the turn. However, the student actually performs the steps of the task.
- Mentor. The tutor plays a less active role, offering help, remediation, or critique when necessary or when requested by the student. The tutor is available to answer questions posed by the student, and to interact with the student

via dialogs on specific steps of a process. While learning is proceeding, the SE is monitoring the student's actions to be able to provide context-sensitive assistance regarding the current state of the student's efforts. The tutor may intervene if the student makes a critical mistake.
- Observer. The tutor watches and records, noting the student's efforts at task performance but rarely interfering. After the task has been completed, the tutor conducts a dialog with the student about the student's efforts, and/or plays back portions of the interaction to the student so that the student may also observe and reflect on performance.

We are advocates for intelligent VH agents as tutors associated with an SE and their verbal dialogs. VH tutors can provide a more natural and realistic interface for training than pushing buttons to select video sequences or taking multiple-choice tests. VHs can step out of tutorial roles and into roles associated with the situation, such as a partner or observer, yet maintain awareness of the student's actions and intervene as or if needed. During skills acquisition and early practice, there may be no need for a second student to conduct the role play; in the second student's place, one or more VHs can play roles while a VH tutor simultaneously observes and records the interaction, and provides guidance and feedback when needed or requested. Observation and assessment become more robust but also easier to control when these roles are automated.

In the mentor role, the tutor is responsible for defining a structured training program for the student. This role involves two related efforts. First, the role demands selecting the appropriate sequence of situations for the student based on the student's background and history of performance during previous situations, known as outer-loop tailoring (Wray & Woods, 2013). Second, it means adjusting situational, context-specific parameters on the fly based on perceived student strengths and weaknesses to provide the most valuable learning experience, known as inner-loop tailoring.

Capture of Student Data

Interactive SEs provide opportunities to unobtrusively and continuously collect data on student behavior. Tutoring reports should provide guidance and feedback that students can use to adapt their practices within training and assessment sessions. The reports should be based on LOs required for performance success. A good tutor would have several key elements, including objective evidence of both expected and unexpected actions, processes for determining how and why the actions took place, and methods for determining how to repair what is unexpected or wrong and sustain what is expected or right.

LOs and performance measures are initially defined by an instructor or expert in terms of student actions that are detectable by the SE (Frank et al., 2004). For the tutor to issue Success and Non-Success assessments for an LO associated with a performance measure, there must be a log showing which particular student actions completed the requirements for a Success or triggered a Non-Success. These data help students determine why specific results were reported. We have identified several types of detectable patterns:

- Context errors occur when students perform actions that are not appropriate for the context (that is, the particular situation under which there are constraints on student activity).
- Errors of commission occur when students take actions that are to be avoided in the context. A student may receive a Non-Success but be allowed to continue to work the lesson.
- Errors of omission occur when students fail to complete required actions or sets of actions in a context.
- Dependency or sequencing errors occur when students perform context-appropriate actions in the wrong order (when there is a prescribed order).
- Timing violations occur when students exceed the time permitted for the task.
- System violations indicate mistakes by students so egregious that the lesson is immediately stopped. (These errors typically are associated with safety violations or indications of deviation so far from the required process that recovery is not possible in the test or assessment.)
- Impasses are points within the test or assessment where student actions indicate a mental hurdle to overcome, perhaps due to lack of knowledge or possibly due to misapplication of procedure.

Most of these types of errors can be assessed in SEs, by maintaining state variables to track students' activities (Hubal, 2008b), by calculating end-state measures (the final result of the test or assessment), by watching how and which production rules are triggered (Anderson & Corbett, 2014), or by applying data-driven methods (Koedinger et al., 2013).

A tutorial system could adapt to students based on their levels of learning, and present them with a variety of remediation or recommendation options (Frank et al., 2004). As examples, given the patterns identified (e.g., context errors vs. system violations) a tutor within an SE may encourage students to shift from a skill acquisition or practice mode lesson (focusing on procedural knowledge) to a lesson designed to obtain needed declarative knowledge; or it may back up, such as shifting from a practice lesson to an acquire lesson; or shift to analogous lessons (students having difficulty may shift from more realistic to more abstract lessons to reduce distraction, then transfer skills gained); or require repeating a practice or validate lesson resulting in a Non-Success, while helping students to determine where their errors occurred. The point is, additional information about students and their activities, along with links between actions and performance measures, enable the SE to better tailor and adapt its tutoring.

Development of Best Practices

These realizations can inform materials design and development. The designer should take into consideration the LOs, relevant situations to motivate students, available technology, and tutorial practices to create a desirable learning environment. Well-designed SE-based materials demonstrate many of these characteristics:

- They are modular. Different objects, characters and their behaviors, virtual worlds, multimedia, and other components can be inserted, combined, modified, or replaced to meet situation-specific LOs with minimal effect on other components.
- They are reusable. Effective reuse requires materials be developed with common standards. For example, a VH's behavior engine might employ social and emotional models that can be reused as training source material. Once constructed, these materials can be adapted and redeployed for different portrayed situations and conditions.
- They are reconfigurable. Each student has a unique set of learning needs. It benefits learning and student motivation when the environment, including materials, are tailored to the student. Within and across training modules, though, including in SEs, analogies, examples, and themes should remain as similar as possible.
- They are scalable. A key to reducing the cost of training materials is to enable materials to work across a variety of platforms, interaction techniques, and distribution methods. For example, an SE might be designed to work in a PC-based gaming environment but also accessible on a mobile device as an app or web-enabled service. A server sitting on the cloud can run the majority of an application, and, if the application is designed properly, only small changes and data need be sent to and from the client side, making distributed learning highly efficient over even small-bandwidth transmission systems.
- They are flexible. Practicing skills in a safe and supportive—virtual—environment allows the student to learn flexible approaches, meaning the student can learn multiple paths to success (thereby meeting LOs) and explore different techniques under different conditions. Flexibility is equally critical for hands-on interaction skills and for performing adequately under time- or resource-constrained, dangerous, information-poor, and other difficult conditions. The consistency that is gained by repeating this practice in SEs leads directly to good decisions in real situations. Practice also leads to increased confidence prior to the first real experience.
- They are self-contained. Open standards and open systems solutions present guidelines for the self-containment of reusable, reconfigurable training modules (Poltrack et al., 2012). Different situations portrayed by SEs should stand alone as presenting a unified set of LOs and performance measures, so that in

aggregate, across a sufficient range of situations, the student is able to acquire, practice, and demonstrate all of the relevant skills.
- They are cost-sensitive. The cost of developing SEs can be higher than the cost of developing, for example, lecture materials. However, costs associated with obtaining, maintaining, and retaining live systems far exceed costs associated with virtual acquisition and practice of skills on expensive, dangerous, or otherwise unavailable equipment. The cost of an SE—and especially the ability to fail safely in an SE—is much lower than in a live environment, so that as a whole the use of an SE for skills training may be cost-effective.

Presentation

Well-designed training SEs permit experiential learning on relevant material for a specific learner rather than following a hard-wired sequence of learning activities. The SE presents neither simple direct instruction nor complex high-end simulation, but instead pushes the student through a series of phases (Milrad et al., 2003). The first phase is presenting a real-life, applicable situation to motivate the student to explore the problem space. The second phase is to let the student attempt, and perhaps fail, at finding solutions; it is important to let the student create sub-problems and find mistakes in reasoning and perceived relationships, all in a low-risk environment. If successful, the student realizes a sense of disequilibrium that encourages a reconceptualization of the problem, pragmatically with feedback and guidance from a tutor. (There are many instructional concepts that underlie these ideas, chief among them the zone of proximal development that directs a learning system to constantly but carefully push the boundaries of what a student is capable [Vygotsky, 1978]). The third phase involves the student practicing and achieving proficiency in the SE in increasingly different situations (van Merriënboer et al., 2002). Iterations of this sustained exploration learning process lead to a cognitive flexibility that suits the student in analogous and, to some extent, unrelated situations.

To adapt the presentation of situations in an SE to support these three phases of the learning process requires technology to provide scaffolding and facilitation appropriate to each phase. Adaptation takes two forms, in presentation of information to the student, and to the individual requirements of the student.

The format in which a student encounters to-be-learned information affects how the student learns and what information the student gleans from it. Alternative representations research has shown that when identical information is displayed using different formats, resulting cognitive task performance varies (Day, 1988). For instance, charts and matrices provide dimensionally organized, indexed information but no sequential information. Graphs and pictures provide spatial cues and show visual patterns, but lack indexed cues into the material. Lists and outlines provide indices and sequential information but lack pattern and dimensionality. Generally, spatial visual representations assist performance more than non-spatial alternatives, on tasks including recall, comprehension, and motor skills. However, alternative representations differ in format used, and therefore differ in applicability to specific cognitive tasks, and affect acquisition of information. No one representation is necessarily superior to another; rather, the situation informs a good selection of format.

SEs use dynamic tailoring (Wray & Woods, 2013) to adapt and present instructional materials to the student. For instance, in a military setting, different representations are required at different echelons of command. Whereas a battalion commander needs to understand at an aggregate level such battlefield factors as terrain, logistics, readiness, and enemy information, a company commander needs much more specific and localized knowledge of those factors. As the LOs are defined differently so should the form of presentation change—from the symbols used to level of simulation of virtual entities (e.g., individuals vs. organizations).

Presentation is not solely display format. When it makes sense, an SE should support different students' desire for visual, auditory, haptic, spatial, or kinesthetic feedback and guidance. For instance, a tutor might use highlighting, voiceover, vibration, forced change in perspective, or some other mechanism to draw attention to a critical entity or aspect of the situation to the student (Frank et al., 2004). The same is true of the toolset provided to manipulate entities in the SE. For instance, there may be multiple methods to navigate the portrayed scene and manipulate objects (Hubal, 2005).

Historically, few systems have been adaptive to individuals considered as people with habits, interests, moods, and prior experience; few systems have dynamically changed the selection of the input materials, the nature of the interface, the construction of learning activities, or the tutoring based on a holistic profile of the student's preferences, prior experiences, and past performance. However, many current systems are using adaptive strategies by modeling the user's performance and behaviors (Brown & Guinn, 2014; Steichen et al., 2013; Woolf et al., 2009). Developers can use these models for incorporating student-specific information profiles. SE systems with this level of flexibility will optimize their potential.

Fidelity

SEs share many attributes with computer games and typically are built on top of game engines. Game designers have a broad view of fidelity that applies to SEs for training and assessment, in effect aiming to trigger willing suspension of disbelief on the part of the student using computationally efficient methods (typically maintaining a frame rate of 60 frames per second for most platforms). We and many others have explored different forms of fidelity (Parsons et al., 2012); what is discussed next has focused primarily on the virtual humans involved in simulations, though the concepts apply rather well to virtual objects, environments, and other aspects of the SE.

VHs can be simulated with variable degrees of fidelity, in this case, the degree to which they resemble people. Though there are no universal opinions about the nature, feasibility, and desirability of VH fidelity (Prendinger & Ishizuka, 2004), we have identified over a half-dozen types.

Appearance fidelity, the degree to which a VH looks or, in some cases, sounds, like a real human being, is important but potentially subject to the situation known as the uncanny valley, in which increasing realism eventually creates unrealistic expectations for the VH to exhibit intelligence (e.g., Burleigh et al., 2013; Reeves & Nass, 1996). By contrast, some developers rely on the power of artful low-fidelity animation to create strong user engagement with the VHs (Dukes et al., 2013; Lester et al., 1999).

VHs also have important dimensions of psychological fidelity, which may be an equally or more important factor in training efficacy. One dimension is the ability to improvise or exhibit a range of human-like intelligence (Hayes-Roth, 2004; Skorupski et al., 2012). Another dimension is ability to interact naturally, as with mixed-initiative natural language conversation, including degree of politeness, personalization, and tailoring of linguistic complexity (Hayes-Roth et al., 2009; Hubal et al., 2003b), and with appropriate gestures and overt behaviors (Cassell et al., 1999; Lhommet & Marsella, 2013). Yet another dimension is emotional realism exhibited by the VH during the interaction (Ferreira et al., 2012; Gratch & Marsella, 2001; Hubal et al., 2003b). Still another is comprehension of social and cultural roles and the degree to which VH behavior reflects and reinforces the relative social status as displayed during the interaction with the student (Hubal et al., 2008; Kistler et al., 2012; Maldonado & Hayes-Roth, 2003).

Levels of Interactivity

Given our suggestion that SEs can be supported by numerous platforms—from desktop PCs to mobile devices to VR and AR systems—it makes sense that there are different types of interaction with and within SEs. There is no one best path; the designer needs to consider how students will engage with the SE in what settings, and support those forms of engagement, but also allow for flexibility when possible. To be specific, a PC-based SE naturally lends itself mainly to traditional input mechanisms such as keyboards, mice, and game controllers, but also offers a high-resolution output display and high-quality sound. Immersion in the system comes from students focusing on the video and audio to the exclusion of the outside world, a state that game developers have long sought. The display and sound allow for some flexibility in what is presented to the student, such as scoring updates, ready links to help content, and alternative methods for the student to accomplish tasks. In contrast, a smartphone, even today's bigger ones, has a limited screen and very different input methods, from touch and swipe to shaking to voice input. It is part of the outside world, and as such might be incorporated more closely into the live environment. Meanwhile, donning an HMD separates the student from the world, in a sense, and encourages realistic activity within the confines of the situation that is presented. The same content may be contained in all versions of the SE, but the means of interaction and the modes of usage are necessarily different.

Measurement

Measurement in SEs involves a continuous data collection process aimed at understanding and improving student learning. It involves setting LOs, systematically gathering, analyzing, and interpreting evidence—including suggestive patterns such as errors of omission or commission—to determine how well performance meets those objectives, and using results to inform the tutorial process. Measurement at the front-end of training should identify and link measurable goals with critical accomplishments or best practices. These links will allow for later impact evaluation (described below) when the student attempts to use learned knowledge and skills.

A traditional measure of acceptable training held that students would be able to demonstrate their skills under certain conditions to set standards (Frank et al., 2007). This concept has evolved to an extent recently and a newer focus is now on outcomes—do students end up thinking and behaving adaptively to the situation presented (Riccio et al., 2010)? The use of SEs underlies some of this change of tack, since they allow students to explore better and worse paths and encourage reflection. Relatedly, the measure of educational productivity traditionally was schoolhouse-centric and mainly considered the effective use of instructor hours, classroom space, and other resources. The use of SEs strongly influences how productivity is measured, though. For example, SEs, along with other learning technologies, can increase student-to-teacher ratios and support asynchronous remote learning. Hence, the return on investment promised by SEs needs to take into account the cost shift from providing set instruction to delivering reusable, reconfigurable instructional materials.

Evaluation and Assessment Strategies

We use the terms assessment and evaluation carefully. In any learning context, students are assessed—formatively, to support improvement, and in a summative manner, to indicate level of mastery or understanding at the end of a training module. The learning context itself, though, is evaluated—formatively, to help instructional designers achieve intended goals and objectives, and in a summative manner, so as to be able to report the extent to which goals and objectives were attained. Evaluations often include student assessments, but also typically go beyond those assessments to include other factors such as cost, support requirements, and long-term benefits.

To obtain suitable measures of student learning and training cost-effectiveness, there is a need for evaluation at multiple levels. Here, five are described (adapted from Kirkpatrick & Kirkpatrick, 2005).

At Level I, reactions to the quality of training delivery itself are obtained. Training developers and instructors use these reactions as feedback on their efforts. Effective training is rated as specific, reliable, representative, and objective. We have consistently found SE-based training applications, when designed intelligently, to meet Level I criteria, meaning they are accepted by students who find them engaging. Gauging reactions is often done using surveys and observation of learning as it occurs, which can be built into the SE, but user sensing while the student is engaged in the SE and detailed analyses of actions taken within the SE can also inform reactions.

At Level II, actual learning by the student is measured. At this level, assessment comprises testing of knowledge and validation of (i.e., demonstrating of, in a cross-section of representative situations) skills. Students and instructors care most about results at this level. Given their ability to collect and analyze large amounts of performance data from students and use tutorial strategies to remediate or recommend next lessons, SEs are well-positioned for meeting Level II criteria.

At Level III, assessment is of the success or failure of transfer of knowledge and/or skills—the impact of training on real-world performance. Similar measures are used as at Level II, but under uncontrolled, out-of-routine, or analogous conditions rather than controlled, structured, already-encountered testing conditions, thus addressing outcomes-based testing and evaluation. Transfer is promoted by several principles for which SEs are helpful, including deliberate practice, distributed practice, variability of situations, and explicit outcome feedback (Hoffman et al., 2014). Instructors use performance measures to evaluate the value of training and the need for additional or restructured training, as well as sustainment of training as skills decay. For the same reasons as Level II, SEs are useful for satisfying Level III criteria.

At Level IV, organizational improvement as a result of training is evaluated. Management is concerned with whether or not skills are being applied effectively, whether those who are trained are more productive and efficient, and whether strategic missions, values, and goals are met. At Level V, societal impact is evaluated. Issues such as readiness and morale, ability to work with others (both inside and outside the organization), and perception of competence are important to strategists and decision-makers. For these levels, though SEs can support training, the measures are somewhat beyond scope.

Assessment Strategies

Assessment is the measure of LOs and skill competencies before, during, and after training. Performance is measured against set criteria, with outcomes in mind; therefore results focus training on what students need to know and when and where they need to know it, and provide links to prescriptive training. Assessment, including that done in an SE, can be used as a placement test, allowing for testing out of lessons, modules, or phases of training.

Performance Tests

A simple performance assessment, of course, has little to do with the SE. Instead, it is a means by which the student describes what processes would need to be performed, in what order, for a particular task, duty, or skill. These simple tests are useful for determining whether or not students have declarative knowledge of the skill, that is, they help us know whether the student understands and is able to state the requirements of the skill. These tests may also be useful for determining whether or not students have strategic knowledge, that is, if they understand the contexts and conditions in which the task or duty is to be performed or skill is to be demonstrated. If the questions are constructed well, errors that the students make will indicate areas in need of remediation.

A more complex performance assessment is usually needed, however, for students to actually demonstrate, not just describe, skills (Hubal, 2012). These tests are complex in part because they can be resource-intensive; an SE (perhaps with PTT), though a viable means to assess skills, must be developed and delivered. However, there are many reasons to view SE-based assessment as cost-effective. First, they are useful for determining whether or not students have procedural knowledge of the skill. Second, they are useful in that skills demonstrated in a range of situations portrayed by an SE typically transfer directly to real-world conditions. Third, the assessment can be integrated into the learning environment, making the transition back and forth between training and assessment seamless while keeping students engaged. Fourth, for SEs, the learning/assessment environment is portable to remote locations and to off-hour learning times, so that students can learn, test, re-learn, practice, and sustain training using distributed learning at their own schedules. Fifth, students who fail to be engaged in the standard knowledge learning such as takes place in a classroom will often become immersed in SEs. Sixth, because students demonstrate procedural knowledge, achievements that they show lead to directed forward recommendations while errors that they make directly indicate areas in need of remediation.

For many skills, students may need to understand the LO requirements and constraints, but they may not need to have achieved mastery of the skills. Assessment should reflect the need for each student, be it familiarity, competence, or mastery. More specifically, there may not be a need to validate students on all skills. Instead, there may be a need to validate students on some skills, have them practice to a lesser degree other skills, and let them become familiarized with still other skills. For instance, if a set of relatively non-critical tasks requires comparable skills, then performance on only a small subset of those tasks may need to be validated. For the remaining set, familiarization and acquisition should prove sufficient, so that the skills will successfully be applied to them. The identification up front of analogous skills is important for realizing cost-effectiveness from the use of SEs as part of the learning environment.

Links to Recommendation and Remediation

Feedback from knowledge test results, whether simple multiple-choice tests or complex adaptive tests, is used to link to training in specific areas that need to be remedied. Feedback from performance test results, such as are captured through SEs, is also used to link to training in specific areas that need to be remedied. The feedback is useful if two conditions are met. First, the tests themselves must be well constructed, for instance by using validated test items or well-defined LOs and outcome measures, so that a correct response can be assured of indicating areas of strength and an incorrect response those of weakness. Second, the training must be designed in modular fashion, so that remediation of specific learning areas can occur, without the need for the student to re-encounter areas that do not need to be remedied. The process is then iterative; students need complete only appropriate sections of the assessments.

In past work we have set out some rules for remediation and forward recommendation. For instance, if the student achieves an overall Success on a practice lesson, then consider what gains the student could make from either portraying a more complicated situation (using, as a framework for determining complexity, an LO hierarchy or a student model derived from a dynamic tailoring system) or by presenting new content to acquire. In contrast, if the student achieves an overall Non-Success, then consider re-introducing content to be gained or simplifying the situation.

Efficiency and Measuring Effectiveness

There are often effectiveness requirements of training. Students are expected to learn quickly, remember content over time, and apply their learning to analogous situations. To be effective, SE materials must emulate effective instructors and establish a motivating environment in which to learn. There are often efficiency requirements of training as well. There may be a need to put a certain number of students through training in a given period of time, a limit on organizational training dollars, or a limit on training time and associated costs. Additionally, there may be a need to distribute training and a consequent initiative to implement intelligent tutoring into the training environment.

Throughput, for instance, is traditionally limited by the availability of instructors and facilities and the real-life situations needed to validate skills. SEs are not live environments, and thus present some restrictions on how transferable successful demonstration of skills is to real-life situations, but they can be used to minimize the time needed within a live environment (Frank et al., 2000).

Further, by incorporating a PTT into the SE, trainers allow the practicing of hands-on skills, individualized tutoring with situations tailored to the given student, and, for high-fidelity trainers, validation of some skills. SEs, with facilitating intelligent VH agents, allow tutoring to take place as needed. SEs can also be used to train more students with fewer resources, as they can be designed for distributed usage at times most convenient to the students. Students can progress at their own pace, acquiring skills when they are prepared to do so and moving to practice facilities at staggered times. This staggering naturally increases throughput at no expense to learning. By obviating some live assessment and even minimizing travel expenditures to a schoolhouse or practice facility, SEs can reduce training costs. SEs are also available for sustainment training to address skills decay.

Skills Decay

The ability to perform a skill decays at different rates depending on the form and intensity of initial learning, ongoing use, and periodic sustainment training. A number of factors influence decay, including passage of time, lack of practice or repetition, fatigue, and situational characteristics (e.g., cognitive vs. hands-on tasks) (Hoffman et al., 2014). In general, SEs provide the opportunity to overcome decay. For instance, SEs allow for spacing of learning and presentation of a variety of situations, to avoid repetition over successive trials but also because one of the main determiners of successful performance after a delay is the similarity of conditions to those of the training. The skill can be practiced in an SE, with different virtual conditions easily inserted to adjust for individual student needs and application to analogous situations. Skills that are applied to increasingly different situations will generally be less prone to decay than those not applied at all or those not applied to contexts outside of the learning context. The student is able to form a more complex mental model of how the skill is to be performed, which in turn gets strengthened with each new application. In contrast, a student who applies a skill in only one context will become expert in a very narrow domain. SEs are easier and less costly to adapt than live equipment.

Spaced practice means that attempts at relearning occur at somewhat regular intervals, with each relearning session being short and goal-directed. Once knowledge is acquired or skills gained, spaced practice leads to better retention than brief, extremely intense bursts of relearning. An example session would consist of first rehearsal of the skill in a context similar to the original learning context, and then application of the skill under different contexts. In contrast, an example of a cramming session would be one where the skill must be applied immediately to an unfamiliar situation, requiring a stressful attempt at relearning without being allowed to rehearse what is remembered first. Relatedly, knowledge and skills are recalled best in an environment closest to the one originally learned. This does not contradict the requirement for generating a range of situations, but instead suggests that if the student is expected to master a skill, rather than become familiar or proficient with it, then initial training and later practice must become more intense. The more realistic the practice and validation settings, and the more able the student is to recreate that setting during sustainment training, the better performance will be, and the slower the skills decay.

At least three interrelated factors contribute to the decision of how frequently and how intensively to conduct sustainment training. The first factor is importance or criticality of the skill to be maintained. For critical skills, sustainment will generally require less intense training more frequently, whereas for less important items, sustainment will often require more intense training less frequently. The second factor is pre-established validation requirements. Some skills will require frequent validation (either because they are critical or because they are commonly needed), others only occasional. The third factor is intensity of retraining (i.e., amount of re-acquisition, practice, and validation needed). Less intensive sustainment training is required when students are already familiar with the skills and will likely be able to perform them. More intensive training is required when the skill is critical, difficult, or time-consuming, considerable time has elapsed since the original training, or the original program of instruction did not include intensive training for that skill. In all cases, SEs can be useful to support sustainment training of skills.

Example Applications

In this section we present some examples of our work with SEs for training and assessment. What is described is not only just an illustration of our work but also a small sample of the entirety of simulation systems used in medical, military, and education domains.

Virtual Human Patients for Training and Assessment

We have been engaged with research and development in two broad medical-related areas, healthcare provider training and decision support. Both areas use SEs, on the one hand to present an environment for students to acquire and practice basic skills and on the other hand for better acquiring health-related information.

In the first case, VH agents are used to create clinically relevant VH patients to apply to the training of clinicians, medical students, first responders, and other healthcare staff. VHs portray a patient with a clinical, medical, or physical condition and can interact with a healthcare provider in an effort to teach emergency response or interpersonal skills, or focus more on differential diagnosis and therapeutic intervention. The work reflects lessons learned over many years of research and development (Hubal et al., 2000, 2008; Parsons et al., 2008, 2009b).

SE technology has evolved to a point where there are now many applications that make use of VH patients. Figure 11.3 shows a few some readily accessible images from these SEs. Some applications include:

- Virtual standardized patients. The medical training world uses standardized patients (SPs)—specially trained actors who present as patients—for the acquisition, practice, and assessment of skills related to the physical examination, doctor–patient interaction, and diagnostic decision-making. Early on Hubal and colleagues realized VHs could be used as SPs for specialized skills (Hubal et al., 2000), including as patients who present with rare but serious cases such as exposure to bioterrorist agents (Kizakevich et al., 2003) as well as pediatric patients for whom it is very difficult to hire consistent, reliable actors (Hubal et al., 2003 Parsons et al., 2009). Parsons has used VHs as SPs for investigating training on topics such as structured interview procedures (Parsons et al., 2008), assessing bias (Parsons et al., 2009b), and post-traumatic stress disorder (Kenny et al., 2008).
- VHs for emergency response. First response to medical events is a combination of physical and cognitive skills. Hubal and colleagues have long been involved in developing SEs for emergency medical response training and assessment, beginning with the strategies needed for uncommon but critical

FIGURE 11.3 Virtual humans as patients and peers

trauma conditions like gunshot wounds and worksite explosions (Kizakevich et al., 1998) and progressing to specific procedures to follow in triage situations (Kizakevich et al., 2007). Others (e.g., Goolsby et al., 2014; Hsu et al., 2013) have investigated SE use for disaster preparedness and hands-on components of SEs for emergency response.

- SEs for clinical applications. Numerous studies, many conducted by Parsons, indicate that SEs are applicable to patients with neurodevelopmental or psychological disorders (Parsons et al., 2009). For instance, they may be especially enjoyable and motivating intervention platforms for persons with high functioning autism (Parsons & Mitchell, 2002). As they interact in virtual social situations, the consequences of patients' actions (positive or negative) can be carefully controlled by the clinician, the realism of social interactions can be varied, and the pace and complexity of exposure to social contexts controlled. The types of safe role-playing available in virtual social encounters may be especially vital as well for other neurodevelopmental disorders. For instance, SEs have been used during exposure therapy to emotionally engage anxious or phobic patients (e.g., with post-traumatic stress disorder) using gradual, controlled sensory stimuli (Parsons, 2015b; Parsons & Rizzo, 2008a).

In the second case, SEs and VH agents are used to augment a healthcare provider's ability to capture relevant or diagnostically important information from the patient. The SE presents a situation and the patient responds appropriately; data are then interpreted, summarized, and returned to the provider. Some applications include:

- Measures of social information processing (SIP). We have both—separately—developed systems for assessing SIP skills. Hubal developed an SE to help identify the underlying neurocognitive and emotional regulatory mechanisms in behavioral disorders that at-risk teens often present and to understand how these mechanisms influence treatment outcomes (Hubal et al., 2008; Paschall et al., 2005). Other colleagues have developed an SE focused on autistic-spectrum preteens (Russo-Ponsaran et al., 2015). These systems are an improvement over existing measures of social skill, given their standardized, SE-delivered form that reduces scoring time and increases comparability across populations, and their reliance on theory to pinpoint specific SIP deficits to guide intervention.
- Obtaining cognitive measures. Parsons has conducted a series of studies using SEs that focus on component cognitive processes, under the presumption that more engaging, ecologically valid environments will elicit better measures (Parsons, 2011b, 2015a; Parsons et al., 2015b; see also Hubal, 2012). The processes addressed include attention (Parsons et al., 2007; Parsons & Carlew, 2016), workload (Parsons et al., 2009a), spatial abilities (Parsons et al., 2004, 2013b), memory (Courtney et al., 2013; Parsons & Rizzo, 2008b), affective

processing (Macedonio et al., 2007; Wu et al., 2010a, 2010b, 2013), and executive functioning (Parsons et al., 2013a; Parsons & Courtney, 2014; Parsons & Carlew, 2016).

- VHs as neuropsychologists. We are currently engaged in a collaborative study to design, prototype, and test an SE that can be used by a clinician to administer neurocognitive assessments. The tool is intended to have a VH administer verbally based neuropsychological tasks including word-list learning, confrontation naming, and aural comprehension to the patient through a collaborative engagement that will yield data that are at least as comprehensive and accurate as those generated through patient interactions with a real clinician.

SEs for Warfare, Security, and Policing Environments

We make no attempt, in this section, to cover in any detail the extraordinarily large range of SEs used for military training and assessment. Instead, we outline five areas to give a taste of their use, most of which stress cognitive over physical skills. Figure 11.4 depicts some readily accessible images from these SEs.

- SEs for maintenance training. One area is the development of a line of virtual trainers for maintenance of United States Army ground tracked vehicles (Hubal, 2005). These SEs were mainly for hands-on skills training and were geared toward maintenance technicians and their need to learn to troubleshoot malfunctions in ground tracked vehicles. The SEs covered a number of vehicle variants and upgrades to equipment on the vehicles. Two conclusions, among

FIGURE 11.4 SEs portraying military and law enforcement operations

the many lessons learned from the development of these SEs, are particularly instructive (Hubal, 2009). First, the means of interaction within the SE should be flexible and to an extent customizable, so that students can choose from multiple modes to accomplish a task. Interaction includes navigation within the SE, manipulation of virtual objects using virtual tools, and communication with VHs. Second, the usefulness of an SE for maintenance training is tied closely with the entire training package, as is described above under the gain-practice-validate model. The acquisition of knowledge and basic procedures is cost-effectively accomplished in an SE, while for the practice and validation of skills a PTT and a realistic live environment are necessary.

- SEs for small unit training. Another area is SEs for practice of interactions with teammates, adversaries, and other noncombatants. VHs can provide features such as goal-directed, dynamic decision-making, non-determinism, and transparency (Stensrud et al., 2012). Under several projects a suite of VHs were created to engage students who were acting as squad leaders in small-unit training scenarios, including an intelligent enemy sniper capable of detecting and selecting friendly targets of opportunity, communicating with other insurgent support entities such as lookouts, and finding the appropriate escape path to avoid detection and capture; a fire team following the student; and noncombatant characters who engaged in normal patterns of life (Hubal et al., 2015a).
- SEs for stress training and therapy. A recent project focused on providing training to military personnel at risk for negative mental health outcomes due to combat and operational stress (Hourani et al., 2011). This training program was intended to prepare personnel for deployment by exposing them to a stressful environment (Hubal et al., 2010a), while simultaneously teaching coping skills and strategies that promote resiliency to stress. The program was designed to expose personnel to a simulated combat environment. This SE required personnel to manipulate joystick controllers in response to stimuli such as weapons, aircraft, and in general objects or events of potential concern (at their discretion) among snipers, explosions, flashes, objects, activities, and people. A separate project (Buckwalter et al., 2012; Rizzo et al., 2012); created a set of combat simulations as part of a multi-episode narrative experience. Personnel were immersed within "experiential" combat situations and interacted with VHs. The aim was to increase personnel thresholds for combat stressors.
- SEs for vigilance. Some homeland security operations require vigilance to potentially subtle events in the environment. An SE of airport security screening was developed to test issues such as detection of different classes of events (e.g., the presence of a gun in a bag vs. a particular individual entering a security line), individually or simultaneously, with varying time pressure, divided attention, and distraction (Hubal et al., 2010b). This work has been extended (e.g., Biggs et al., 2013) and is being used

to inform training of security personnel. Meanwhile, an SE-based cognitive performance assessment (Parsons et al., 2009a; Parsons, 2015a; Parsons et al., 2015b) is able to manipulate attention performance by varying stimulus complexity and intensity.
- SEs for managing explosive encounters. A final area involves SEs created to mimic difficult situations or those that might escalate into violence. One early example was an SE used for law enforcement officers to learn to manage encounters with the mentally ill (Frank et al., 2002). The student needed to learn appropriate verbal techniques to calm an angry and possibly psychotic VH. A more recent example involved "good stranger" skills that a deployed warfighter could use to manage the interaction with a foreign civilian sharing neither language nor culture (Hubal et al., 2015b).

Virtual School Hallways, Classrooms, and Street Scenes

Much of the previous work using SEs for assessment that focused on component cognitive processes were implemented into educational settings, with the purpose of teaching students (and assessing their progress) on very specific skills. Their effectiveness was made apparent through comparing the students' competencies within the area the SE was intended to teach before and after the students had been exposed to it. The SE used for much of this research, a virtual classroom (Parsons et al., 2007; Parsons, 2014), delivers a variety of continuous-performance tasks and attention-related tests in an ecologically valid, immersive setting. In other efforts students were presented with situations relevant to their backgrounds (e.g., inner-city male teens vs. suburban preteens) to assess their tendency towards risky behavior (Hubal et al., 2008; Russo-Ponsaran et al., 2015). In still other applications students were presented with street-level situations to gauge their ability to apply interaction and strategic skills to attend to multiple casualties or de-escalate a potentially explosive situation (Frank et al., 2002; Kizakevich et al., 2007). Figure 11.5 presents some images of these SEs.

Discussion

In this chapter we presented a number of considerations for education practitioners interested in using SEs for training and practice. Though we have been working with SEs for many years, and across many domains, the approach is still in its early stages, for at least two reasons. First, the technology upon which SEs are based is rapidly evolving. Our experience has largely been with PC-based SEs but, like many other researchers, we are moving to smaller, more mobile platforms with embedded sensors that were once less available and capable. These platforms and sensors present new affordances, and it will be important to determine how best to utilize them while adapting past processes and techniques. Second, SEs are not nearly so heavily used in education as they are in the military or medical fields

FIGURE 11.5 Virtual hallways, classroom, and street scene

for training and assessment. Though many researchers are developing interesting, novel, important applications, we believe the systematic approach we have taken to date will be critical to ensuring these applications are designed, developed, implemented, and measured appropriately to address future educational needs.

Impacts of Mobile and Wearable Technologies

As mobile and wearable devices decrease in size and cost, their usage for training and assessment will surely expand. Here we speculate how SEs might evolve as these emerging technologies become more capable and more commonplace.

One possibility is for tutoring to become tightly integrated into the use of the technology. Siri and Cortana are today's intelligent personal assistants with pedigrees stretching back to Apple's visionary 1987 knowledge navigator video, itself based on seminal artificial intelligence research (see Kay, 2013). They capture voice for basic speech recognition and can use built-in cameras to sense where the student is looking (Rozado et al., 2015). What they do not yet have, though, is an understanding of a particular student's needs, an ability to adapt to those needs, and a mechanism to track how that student has progressed through past training. We foresee the personalized assistants integrating components of dynamic tailoring and, through that enhancement, being able to better guide and provide feedback to students.

Another possibility is for location services to couple with the learning environment. Smartphones and -watches can capture GPS coordinates and potentially use other available sensors (e.g., gyroscope, accelerometer, or magnetometer) to gauge the student's physical movements; combined with augmented systems these data may be extremely valuable in tracking performance, as with PTTs or even stance and gestures during interactions. We envision sensing in SEs, indeed, to go beyond location into emotion and physiological state. For instance, components such as heart rate sensors or wireless heart rate variability monitors may be of interest for allowing the system to adapt to the student's current state, perhaps tailoring the learning experience to make it less or more difficult. A tool may adapt to the student based on some set of captured characteristics, including gender, age, vocal patterns, handedness (Wimmer & Boring, 2009), and gait (Iso & Yamazaki, 2006). So might near-future capabilities, from gauging emotional expression to assessing vocal affect (Sadat et al., 2014; Yang & Samuel, 2011), be used to influence what guidance and feedback is presented to the student and how it is portrayed. Even monitors of ambient temperature or environmental conditions could prove of interest to some training SEs, especially where they reflect realistic conditions of the live environment in which skills are applied.

A key to engaging the student on a mobile or wearable device is to enable "smart interaction," a means that is natural and intuitive to the student. It must be able to accept natural inputs across a variety of modalities and use those same natural modalities to communicate back. For example, speech is normal in most domains, and sketch overlays are often used when showing graphs, maps, diagrams, and other representational guides. We have conducted a number of studies using smart interaction to assist users in performing complicated tasks (Hubal et al., 2000; Guinn et al., 2004; Taylor et al., 2015). Smart interactive applications, as we view them, act as facilitators between the student and the system, interpreting student inputs in natural modes, translating these into commands to make sense of the environment, and then conversely translating sensed data from the environment into useful, relevant information for the student (Taylor et al., 2012).

Integration into the Science of Learning

In a comprehensive look at the state of the knowledge of how people learn (Bransford et al., 2000), a National Research Council (NRC) committee advocated for structured learning experiences, for taking into account cultural and social norms in how and where people learn, for the need for judicious guidance and feedback, and for taking continual advantage of the affordances of emerging technologies. The book was very influential when it was published almost two decades ago, and a new NRC committee is at present studying subsequent research that focuses on the study of learning in both formal and informal settings. We, then, are certainly not alone in practicing a systematic approach to learning. Nor are we unique in our promotion of synthetic learning environments. Researchers are studying how best to represent concepts in simulations, and help students establish relationships—both formally defined and intuitive patterns—among concepts. We are coming to see how and when different types of SEs can exploit a student's perceptual, spatial, verbal, and even kinesthetic abilities in environments that declarative or static presentations cannot. Because SEs simulate any situation, they can be valuable for dangerous, costly, rare, and even "impossible" (in the real world) situations, allowing students to explore, inquire, and interact as they desire. Cannon-Bowers and Bowers (2008), for instance, describe how simulations, virtual worlds, and games overlap but are all able to portray some sort of learning experience. They also present design considerations for SEs for learning much in line with many of our recommendations. Salas and colleagues (2012) argue for a "psychological" fidelity (i.e., the level of realism needed for gaining knowledge and acquiring skills to accomplish a task) in SE design, with the requisite measurement and tutoring. These and many other studies are showing why SEs work for training and assessment.

Summary

In this chapter we present a number of considerations for education practitioners interested in using synthetic environments for training and practice. Under development of these training environments we discuss learning objectives, the gain-practice-demonstrate model, part-task trainers, emerging technologies, and tutoring, and provide best practices. For presentation of SEs, we examine fidelity and levels of interactivity, leading to a discussion of measurement and its effectiveness and efficiency. We provide a host of examples from our work and others' to illustrate the many forms SEs for training and assessment can take and domains to which they have been applied. We see the content in this chapter as a framework to guide practitioners in their decisions of why and how to undertake their own SEs.

References

Anderson, J. R., & Corbett, A. T. (2014). Tutoring of cognitive skill. In J. R. Anderson (Ed.), *Rules of the mind* (Second Printing) (pp. 235–256). New York: Psychology Press.

Biggs, A. T., Cain, M. S., Clark, K., Darling, E. F., & Mitroff, S. R. (2013). Assessing visual search performance differences between Transportation Security Administration officers and nonprofessional visual searchers. *Visual Cognition, 21*(3), 330–352.

Bohil, C. J., Alicea, B., & Biocca, F. A. (2011). Virtual reality in neuroscience research and therapy. *Nature Reviews Neuroscience, 12*(12), 752–762.

Bowyer, M. W., Streete, K. A., Muniz, G. M., & Liu, A. V. (2008). Immersive virtual environments for medical training. *Seminars in Colon and Rectal Surgery, 19*(2), 90–97.

Bransford, J. D., Brown, A. L., & Cocking, R. R. (Eds.) (2000). *How people learn: Brain, mind, experience, and school.* Washington, DC: National Academies Press.

Brown, R., & Guinn, C. (2014). Developing game-playing agents that adapt to user strategies: A case study. In *Proceedings of the IEEE Symposium on Intelligent Agents* (pp. 51–56). IEEE.

Buckwalter, J. G., Rizzo, A., John, B., Newman, B., Williams, J., & Parsons, T. D. (2012). STRIVE: Stress Resilience in Virtual Environments. Proceedings of IEEE Virtual Reality Conference. Costa Mesa, CA, March 5, 2012.

Burleigh, T. J., Schoenherr, J. R., & Lacroix, G. L. (2013). Does the uncanny valley exist? An empirical test of the relationship between eeriness and the human likeness of digitally created faces. *Computers in Human Behavior, 29*(3), 759–771.

Cannon-Bowers, J. A., & Bowers, C. A. (2008). Synthetic learning environments. In J. M. Spector, M. D. Merrill, J. van Merrienboer, & M. P. Driscoll (Eds.), *Handbook of research on educational communications and technology* (3rd ed., pp. 317–327). New York, NY: Lawrence Erlbaum Associates.

Cassell, J., Bickmore, T., Campbell, L., Chang, K., Vilhjálmsson, H., & Yan, H. (1999). Requirements for an architecture for embodied conversational characters. In N. Magnenat-Thalmann & D. Thalmann (Eds.), *Computer animation and simulation* (pp. 109–122). Vienna, Austria: Springer-Verlag.

Caudell, T. P., & Mizell, D. W. (1992). Augmented reality: An application of heads-up display technology to manual manufacturing processes. *System Sciences, 2*, 659–669.

Courtney, C. G., Dawson, M. E., Rizzo, A. A., Arizmendi, B. J., & Parsons, T. D. (2013). Predicting navigation performance with psychophysiological responses to threat in a virtual environment. In R. Shumaker (Ed.), *Virtual augmented and mixed reality. Designing and developing augmented and virtual environments* (pp. 129–138). Heidelberg, Germany: Springer-Verlag.

Day, R. S. (1988). Alternative representations. In G. H. Bower (Ed.), *The psychology of learning and motivation* (pp. 261–305). New York: Academic Press.

Dukes, L. C., Pence, T. B., Hodges, L. F., Meehan, N., & Johnson, A. (2013). SIDNIE: Scaffolded interviews developed by nurses in education. In *Proceedings of the International Conference on Intelligent User Interfaces* (pp. 395–406). New York: ACM Press.

Ferreira, N., Mascarenhas, S., Paiva, A., Dignum, F., Mc Breen, J., Degens, N., & Hofstede, G. J. (2012). Generating norm-related emotions in virtual agents. In *Proceedings of the International Conference on Intelligent Virtual Agents* (pp. 97–104). Berlin, Germany: Springer-Verlag.

Frank, G. A., Helms, R. F., & Voor, D. (2000). Determining the right mix of live, virtual, and constructive training. In *Proceedings of the Interservice/Industry Training, Simulation and Education Conference* (pp. 1268–1277). Arlington, VA: NDIA.

Frank, G., Guinn, C., Hubal, R., Pope, P., Stanford, M., & Lamm-Weisel, D. (2002). JUST-TALK: An application of responsive virtual human technology. In *Proceedings of the Interservice/Industry Training, Simulation and Education Conference* (pp. 773–779). Arlington, VA: NDIA.

Frank, G., Hubal, R., & O'Bea, M. (2007). Using competency definitions to adapt training for mission success. In *Proceedings of the Interservice/Industry Training, Simulation and Education Conference* (pp. 1262–1270). Arlington, VA: NDIA.

Frank, G., Whiteford, B., Hubal, R., Sonker, P., Perkins, K., Arnold, P., Presley, T., Jones, R., & Meeds, H. (2004). Performance assessment for distributed learning using after action review reports generated by simulations. In *Proceedings of the Interservice/Industry Training, Simulation and Education Conference* (pp. 808–817). Arlington, VA: NDIA.

Gagné, R. M. (1962). Military training and principles of learning. *American Psychologist, 17*(2), 83–91.

Garris, R., Ahlers, R., & Driskell, J. E. (2002). Games, motivation, and learning: A research and practice model. *Simulation & Gaming, 33*(4), 44–467.

Goolsby, C., Vest, R., & Goodwin, T. (2014). New wide area virtual environment (WAVE) medical education. *Military Medicine, 179*(1), 38–41.

Gratch, J., & Marsella, S. (2001). Tears and fears: Modeling emotions and emotional behaviors in synthetic agents. In *Proceedings of the International Conference on Autonomous Agents* (pp. 278–285). New York: ACM Press.

Guinn, C., Hubal, R., Frank, G., Schwetzke, H., Zimmer, J., Backus, S., Deterding, R., Link, M., Armsby, P., Caspar, R., Flicker, L., Visscher, W., Meehan, A., & Zelon, H. (2004). Usability and acceptability studies of conversational virtual human technology. In *Proceedings of the SIGdial Workshop on Discourse and Dialog* (pp. 1–8). East Stroudsburg, PA: Association for Computational Linguistics.

Hale, K. S., & Stanney, K. M. (Eds.) (2015). *Handbook of virtual environments: Design, implementation, and applications (second edition)*. Boca Raton, FL: CRC Press.

Hayes-Roth, B. (2004). What makes characters seem life-like? In H. Prendinger & M. Ishizuka (Eds.), *Life-like characters: Tools, affective functions and applications* (pp. 447–462). Berlin, Germany: Springer-Verlag.

Hayes-Roth, B., Saker, R., & Amano, K. (2009). Using virtual patients to train clinical interviewing skills. In *Proceedings of the Workshop on Virtual Healthcare Interaction, AAAI Fall Symposium Series* (pp. 35–40). New York: ACM Press.

Hays, M. J., Campbell, J. C., Trimmer, M. A., Poore, J. C., Webb, A. K., & King, T. K. (2012). Can role-play with virtual humans teach interpersonal skills? In *Proceedings of the Interservice/Industry Training, Simulation and Education Conference* (pp. 279–290). Arlington, VA: NDIA.

Hoffman, R. R., Ward, P., Feltovich, P. J., DiBello, L., Fiore, S. M., & Andrews, D. H. (2014). *Accelerated expertise: Training for high proficiency in a complex world*. New York: Psychology Press.

Hourani, L. L., Kizakevich, P. N., Hubal, R., Spira, J., Strange, L. B., Holiday, D. B., Bryant, S., & McLean, A. N. (2011). Predeployment stress inoculation training for primary prevention of combat-related stress disorders. *Journal of CyberTherapy & Rehabilitation, 4*(1), 101–116.

Hsu, E. B., Li, Y., Bayram, J. D., Levinson, D., Yang, S., & Monahan, C. (2013). State of virtual reality based disaster preparedness and response training. *PLoS Currents, 5*.

Hubal, R. (2005). Design and usability of military maintenance skills simulation training systems. In *Proceedings of the Human Factors and Ergonomics Society Annual Meeting* (pp. 2110–2114). Santa Monica, CA: HFES.

Hubal, R. (2008a). Criteria for use of synthetic characters. In *Proceedings of the Interservice/Industry Training, Simulation and Education Conference* (pp. 1274–1283). Arlington, VA: NDIA.

Hubal, R. (2008b). Embodied tutors for interaction skills simulation training. *International Journal of Virtual Reality, 7*(1), 1–8.

Hubal, R. (2009). Between- and within-subjects experiences with desktop simulations. In *Proceedings of the Workshop on Users' Preferences Regarding Intelligent User Interfaces: Differences among Users and Changes over Time*. New York: ACM Press.

Hubal, R. (2012). The imperative for social competency prediction. In S. J. Yang, A. M. Greenberg, & M. Endsley (Eds.), *Proceedings of the International Conference on Social Computing, Behavioral-Cultural Modeling, & Prediction* (pp. 188–195). Heidelberg, Germany: Springer-Verlag.

Hubal, R. C., & Frank, G. A. (2001). Interactive training applications using responsive virtual human technology. In *Proceedings of the Interservice/Industry Training, Simulation and Education Conference* (pp. 1076–1086). Arlington, VA: NDIA.

Hubal, R., & Pina, J. (2012). Serious assessments in serious games. *International Journal of Gaming and Computer-Mediated Simulations (IJGCMS)*, 4(3), 49–64.

Hubal, R. C., Deterding, R. R., Frank, G. A., Schwetzke, H. F., & Kizakevich, P. N. (2003a). Lessons learned in modeling virtual pediatric patients. *Studies in Health Technology and Informatics*, 127–130.

Hubal, R. C., Fishbein, D. H., Sheppard, M. S, Paschall, M. J., Eldreth, D. L., & Hyde, C. T. (2008). How do varied populations interact with embodied conversational agents? Findings from inner-city adolescents and prisoners. *Computers in Human Behavior*, 24(3), 1104–1138.

Hubal, R., Folsom-Kovarik, J., Woods, A., Jones, R., & Carbone, J. (2015a). Patterns of life in the foreground and background: Practical approaches to enhancing simulation-based interaction skills training. In *Proceedings of the Behavior Representation in Modeling and Simulation Conference* (pp. 75–83). The BRIMS Society.

Hubal, R. C., Frank, G. A., & Guinn, C. I. (2003b). Lessons learned in modeling schizophrenic and depressed responsive virtual humans for training. In *Proceedings of the Intelligent User Interface Conference* (pp. 85–92). New York: ACM Press.

Hubal, R. C., Kizakevich, P. N., Guinn, C. I., Merino, K. D., & West, S. L. (2000). The virtual standardized patient: Simulated patient-practitioner dialogue for patient interview training. In J. D. Westwood, H. M. Hoffman, G. T. Mogel, R. A. Robb, & D. Stredney (Eds.), *Envisioning healing: Interactive technology and the patient-practitioner dialogue* (pp. 133–138). Amsterdam, The Netherlands: IOS Press.

Hubal, R., Kizakevich, P., & Furberg, R. (2007). Synthetic characters in health-related applications. In S. Vaidya, L. C. Jain, & H. Yoshida (Eds.), *Advanced computational intelligence paradigms in healthcare 2* (pp. 5–26). Heidelberg, Germany: Springer-Verlag.

Hubal, R., Kizakevich, P., McLean, A., & Hourani, L. (2010a). A multimedia environment for stressing warfighters before they deploy. In *Proceedings of the Interservice/Industry Training, Simulation and Education Conference* (pp. 1688–1696). Arlington, VA: NDIA.

Hubal, R., Mitroff, S. R., Cain, M. S., Scott, B., & DeWitt, R. (2010b). Simulating a vigilance task: Extensible technology for baggage security assessment and training. In *Proceedings of the IEEE Conference on Technologies for Homeland Security* (pp. 543–548). Los Alamitos, CA: IEEE.

Hubal, R., van Lent, M., Wender, J., Lande, B., Flanagan, S., & Quinn, S. (2015b). What does it take to train a good stranger? *Procedia Manufacturing*, 3, 3955–3962.

Iso, T., & Yamazaki, K. (2006). Gait analyzer based on a cell phone with a single three-axis accelerometer. In *Proceedings of the Conference on Human-Computer Interaction with Mobile Devices and Services* (pp. 141–144). New York, NY: ACM Press.

Jackson, S. L., Krajcik, J., & Soloway, E. (1998). The design of guided learner-adaptable scaffolding in interactive learning environments. In C. M. Karat, A. Lund, J. Coutaz, & J. Karat (Eds.), *Proceedings of the Conference on Human Factors in Computing Systems* (pp. 187–194). ACM Press.

Kay, A. (2013). *Afterword: What is a Dynabook?* Glendale, CA: Viewpoints Research Institute.

Kenny, P., & Parsons, T. D. (2011) Embodied conversational virtual human patients. In C. Perez-Marin & I. Pascual-Nieto (Eds.), *Conversational agents and natural language interaction: Techniques and effective practices* (pp. 254–281). Hershey, PA: IGI Global.

Kenny, P., Parsons, T. D., Pataki, C., Pato, M., St.-George, C., Sugar, J., & Rizzo, A. A. (2008). Virtual Justina: A PTSD virtual patient for clinical classroom training. *Annual Review of CyberTherapy and Telemedicine*, 6(1), 113–118.

Kirkpatrick, D. L., & Kirkpatrick, J. D. (2005). *Transferring learning to behavior: Using the four levels to improve performance*. San Francisco, CA: Berrett-Koehler Publishers, Inc.

Kistler, F., Endrass, B., Damian, I., Dang, C. T., & André, E. (2012). Natural interaction with culturally adaptive virtual characters. *Journal on Multimodal User Interfaces, 6*(1-2), 39–47.

Kizakevich, P. N., Culwell, A., Furberg, R., Gemeinhardt, D., Grantlin, S., Hubal, R., Stafford, A., & Dombroski, R. T. (2007). Virtual simulation-enhanced triage training for Iraqi medical personnel. In J. D. Westwood, R. S. Haluck, H. M. Hoffman, G. T. Mogel, R. Phillips, R. A. Robb, & K. G. Vosburgh (Eds.), *In vivo, in vitro, in silico: Designing the next in medicine* (pp. 223–228). Amsterdam, The Netherlands: IOS Press.

Kizakevich, P. N., Lux, L., Duncan, S., & Guinn, C. (2003). Virtual simulated patients for bioterrorism preparedness training. In J. D. Westwood, H. M. Hoffman, G. T. Mogel, R. Phillips, R. A. Robb, & D. Stredney (Eds.), *NextMed: Health horizon* (pp. 165–167). Amsterdam, The Netherlands: IOS Press.

Kizakevich, P. N., McCartney, M. L., Nissman, D. B., Starko, K., & Smith, N. T. (1998). Virtual medical trainer: Patient assessment and trauma care simulator. In J. D. Westwood, H. M. Hoffman, D. Stredney, & S. J. Weghorst (Eds.), *Art, science, technology: Healthcare (r)evolution* (pp. 309–315). Amsterdam, The Netherlands: IOS Press.

Koedinger, K. R., Brunskill, E., de Baker, R. S. J., McLaughlin, E. A., & Stamper, J. (2013). New potentials for data-driven intelligent tutoring system development and optimization. *AI Magazine, 34*(3), 27–41.

Lane, H. C., & Johnson, W. L. (2008). Intelligent tutoring and pedagogical experience manipulation in virtual learning environments. In J. Cohn, D. Nicholson, & D. Schmorrow (Eds.), *The PSI handbook of virtual environments for training and education* (pp. 393–406). Westport, CT: Praeger Security International.

Lester, J. C., Stone, B. A., & Stelling, G. D. (1999). Lifelike pedagogical agents for mixed-initiative problem solving in constructivist learning environments. *User Modeling and User-Adapted Interaction, 9*, 1–44.

Lhommet, M. & Marsella, S. C. (2013). Gesture with meaning. In R. Aylett, B. Krenn, C. Pelachaud, & H. Shimodaira (Eds.), *Proceedings of the International Conference on Intelligent Virtual Agents* (pp. 303–312). Berlin, Germany: Springer.

Macedonio, M., Parsons, T. D., & Rizzo, A. A. (2007). Immersiveness and physiological arousal within panoramic video-based virtual reality. *Cyberpsychology and Behavior, 10*, 508–516.

Maldonado, H., & Hayes-Roth, B. (2003). Cross-cultural believability in character design. In S. Payr & R. Trappl (Eds.), *Agent culture: Human-agent interaction in a multicultural world* (pp. 143–175). Mahwah, NJ: Lawrence Erlbaum Associates, Inc.

Mayer, R. E. (2009). Designing instruction for constructivist learning. In C. M. Reigeluth (Ed.), *Instructional-design theories and models: A new paradigm of instructional theory* (Volume II) (pp. 141–160). New York: Routledge.

McElhinney, B., Beard, A., Karthigasu, K., & Hart, R. (2012). Virtual reality simulation: A valuable adjunct to surgical training. In C. Eichenberg (Ed.), *Virtual reality in psychological, medical and pedagogical applications* (pp. 167–184). Rijeka, Croatia: InTech.

Milrad, M., Spector, J. M., & Davidsen, P. I. (2003). Model facilitated learning. In S. Naidu (Ed.), *Learning and teaching with technology: Principles and practices* (pp. 13–27). London, UK: Kogan Page.

Parsons, S., & Mitchell, P. (2002). The potential of virtual reality in social skills training for people with autistic spectrum disorders. *Journal of Intellectual Disability Research, 46*(5), 430–443.

Parsons, T. D. (2011a). Affect-sensitive virtual standardized patient interface system. In D. Surry, T. Stefurak, & R. Gray (Eds.), *Technology integration in higher education: Social and organizational aspects* (pp. 201–221). Hershey, PA: IGI Global.

Parsons, T. D. (2011b). Neuropsychological assessment using virtual environments: Enhanced assessment technology for improved ecological validity. In S. Brahnam & L. C. Jain (Eds.), *Advanced computational intelligence paradigms in healthcare 6: Virtual reality in psychotherapy, rehabilitation, and assessment* (pp. 271–289). Heidelberg, Germany: Springer-Verlag.

Parsons, T. D. (2014). Virtual teacher and classroom for assessment of neurodevelopmental disorders. In S. Brahnam & L. C. Jain, (Eds.), *Serious games, alternative realities, and play therapy* (pp. 121–137). Heidelberg, Germany: Springer-Verlag.

Parsons, T. D. (2015a). Virtual reality for enhanced ecological validity and experimental control in the clinical, affective, and social neurosciences. *Frontiers in Human Neuroscience*, 9, 1–19. doi.org/10.3389/fnhum.2015.00660

Parsons, T. D. (2015b). Virtual reality exposure therapy for anxiety and specific phobias. In M. Khosrow-Pour (Ed.), *Encyclopedia of information science and technology (third edition)* (pp. 288–296), Hershey, PA: IGI Global.

Parsons, T. D. (2016). Clinical neuropsychology and technology: What's new and how we can use it. New York: Springer Press.

Parsons, T. D., & Carlew, A. R. (2016). Bimodal virtual reality Stroop for assessing distractor inhibition in autism spectrum disorders. *Journal of Autism and Developmental Disorders*, 46, 1255–1267.

Parsons, T. D., & Courtney, C. (2014). An initial validation of the virtual reality paced auditory serial addition test in a college sample. *Journal of Neuroscience Methods*, 222, 15–23.

Parsons, T. D., & Phillips, A. (2016). Virtual reality for psychological assessment in clinical practice. *Practice Innovations*, 1, 197–217.

Parsons, T. D., & Rizzo, A. A. (2008a). Affective outcomes of virtual reality exposure therapy for anxiety and specific phobias: A meta-analysis. *Journal of Behavior Therapy and Experimental Psychiatry*, 39(3), 250–261.

Parsons, T. D., & Rizzo, A. A. (2008b). Initial validation of a virtual environment for assessment of memory functioning: Virtual reality cognitive Performance assessment test. *Cyberpsychology and Behavior*, 11, 17–25.

Parsons, T. D., Barnett, M., & Melugin, P. (2015a). Assessment of personality and absorption for mediated environments in a college sample. *Cyberpsychology, Behavior, and Social Networking*, 18, 752–756.

Parsons, T. D., Bowerly, T., Buckwalter, J. G., & Rizzo, A. A. (2007). A controlled clinical comparison of attention performance in children with ADHD in a virtual reality classroom compared to standard neuropsychological methods. *Child Neuropsychology*, 13(4), 363–381.

Parsons, T. D., Carlew, A. R., Magtoto, J., & Stonecipher, K. (2015b). The Potential of Function-Led Virtual Environments for Ecologically Valid Measures of Executive Function in Experimental and Clinical Neuropsychology. *Neuropsychological Rehabilitation*, 11, 1–13.

Parsons, T. D., Cosand, L., Courtney, C., Iyer, A., & Rizzo, A. A. (2009a). Neurocognitive workload assessment using the Virtual Reality Cognitive Performance Assessment Test. *Lecture Notes in Artificial Intelligence*, 5639, 243–252.

Parsons, T. D., Courtney, C., & Dawson, M. (2013a). Virtual reality Stroop task for assessment of supervisory attentional processing. *Journal of Clinical and Experimental Neuropsychology*, 35(8), 812–826.

Parsons, T. D., Courtney, C., Dawson, M., Rizzo, A., & Arizmendi, B. (2013b). Visuospatial processing and learning effects in virtual reality-based mental rotation and navigational tasks. *Lecture Notes in Artificial Intelligence*, 8019, 75–83.

Parsons, T. D., Kenny, P., Cosand, L., Iyer, A., Courtney, C., & Rizzo, A. A. (2009b). A virtual human agent for assessing bias in novice therapists. *Studies in Health Technology and Informatics, 142,* 253–258.

Parsons, T. D., Kenny, P., Ntuen, C., Pataki, C. S., Pato, M., Rizzo, A. A., St-George, C., & Sugar, J. (2008). Objective structured clinical interview training using a virtual human patient. *Studies in Health Technology and Informatics, 132,* 357–362.

Parsons, T. D., Larson, P., Kratz, K., Thiebaux, M., Bluestein, B., Buckwalter, J. G., & Rizzo, A. A. (2004). Sex differences in mental rotation and spatial rotation in a virtual environment. *Neuropsychologia, 42*(4), 555–562.

Parsons, T. D., Rizzo, A. A., Courtney, C., & Dawson, M. (2012). Psychophysiology to assess impact of varying levels of simulation fidelity in a threat environment. *Advances in Human-Computer Interaction, 5,* 1–9.

Parsons, T. D., Rizzo, A. A., Rogers, S. A., & York, P. (2009). Virtual reality in pediatric rehabilitation: A review. *Developmental Neurorehabilitation,* 12, 224–238.

Paschall, M. J., Fishbein, D. H., Hubal, R. C., & Eldreth, D. (2005). Psychometric properties of virtual reality vignette performance measures: A novel approach for assessing adolescents' social competency skills. *Health Education Research: Theory and Practice, 20*(1), 61–70.

Pataki, C., Pato, M., Sugar, J., Rizzo, A., St-George, C., Kenny, P., & Parsons, T. D. (2012). Virtual patients as a novel teaching tool in psychiatry. *Academic Psychiatry, 36,* 398–400.

Poltrack, J., Hruska, N., Johnson, A., & Haag, J. (2012). The next generation of SCORM: Innovation for the global force. In *Proceedings of the Interservice/Industry Training, Simulation and Education Conference* (pp. 703–711). Arlington, VA: NDIA.

Prendinger, H., & Ishizuka, M. (2004). *Life-like characters: Tools, affective functions and applications.* Berlin, Germany: Springer-Verlag.

Reeves, B. & Nass, C. (1996). *The media equation.* New York: Cambridge University Press.

Riccio, G., Diedrich, F., & Cortes, M. (Eds.) (2010). *An initiative in outcomes-based training and education: Implications for an integrated approach to values-based requirements.* Fort Meade, MD: U.S. Army Asymmetric Warfare Group.

Rizzo, A., Buckwalter, J., Williams, J., Parsons, T. D., & Kenny, P. (2012). Stress Resilience In Virtual Environments (STRIVE): A pre-deployment VR system for training combat relevant emotional coping skills and assessing stress response. *Studies in Health Technology and Informatics, 173,* 379–385.

Rozado, D., Moreno, T., Agustin, J. S., Rodriguez, F. B., & Varona, P. (2015). Controlling a smartphone using gaze gestures as the input mechanism. *Human–Computer Interaction, 30*(1), 34–63.

Russo-Ponsaran, N. M., McKown, C., Johnson, J. K., Allen, A. W., Evans-Smith, B., & Fogg, L. (2015). Social-emotional correlates of early stage social information processing skills in children with and without autism spectrum disorder. *Autism Research, 8*(5), 486–496.

Sadat, M., Bin Hossain, R., & Hasan, M. (2014). Recognizing human affection: Smartphone perspective. *Global Journal of Computer Science and Technology, 14*(6).

Salas, E., Tannenbaum, S. I., Kraiger, K., & Smith-Jentsch, K. A. (2012). The science of training and development in organizations: What matters in practice. *Psychological Science in the Public Interest, 13*(2), 74–101.

Schaffer, R., Cullen, S., Meas, P., & Dill, K. (2013). Mixed and augmented reality for Marine Corps training. In R. Shumaker (Ed.), *Virtual, augmented and mixed reality: systems and applications* (pp. 310–319). Heidelberg, Germany: Springer-Verlag.

Shapiro, D., McCoy, J., Grow, A., Samuel, B., Stern, A., Swanson, R., Treanor, M., & Mateas, M. (2015). Creating playable social experiences through whole-body interaction with virtual characters. In *Proceedings of the Conference on Artificial Intelligence and Interactive Digital Entertainment.* AAAI Digital Library.

Skorupski, J., McCoy, J., Zanbaka, C., Ryall, K., & Mateas, M. (2012). Three avatars walk into a bar: Defining and evaluating realism for virtual supporting characters. In *Proceedings of the International Conference on the Foundations of Digital Games.* New York: ACM Press.

Steichen, B., Carenini, G., & Conati, C. (2013). User-adaptive information visualization: Using eye gaze data to infer visualization tasks and user cognitive abilities. In *Proceedings of the International Conference on Intelligent User Interfaces* (pp. 317–328). New York: ACM.

Stensrud, B., Purcel, E., Fragomeni, G., Woods, A., Wintermute, S., & Garrity, P. (2012). No more zombies! High-fidelity character autonomy for virtual small-unit training. In *Proceedings of the Interservice/Industry Training, Simulation and Education Conference* (pp. 277–1287). Arlington, VA: NDIA.

Stone, R. (2001). Virtual reality for interactive training: An industrial practitioner's viewpoint. *International Journal of Human-Computer Studies, 55*(4), 699–711.

Taylor, G., Frederiksen, R., Crossman, J., Quist, M., & Theisen, P. (2012). A multi-modal intelligent user interface for supervisory control of unmanned platforms. In *Proceedings of the Conference on Collaboration Technologies and Systems* (pp. 117–124). IEEE Xplore Digital Library.

Taylor, G., Purman, B., Schermerhorn, P., Garcia-Sampedro, G., Hubal, R., Crabtree, K., Rowe, A., & Spriggs, S. (2015). Multi-modal interaction for UAS control. In *Proceedings of the Unmanned Systems Technology Conference, Symposium on SPIE Defense + Security,* 9468(1). Bellingham, WA: International Society for Optics and Photonics.

van Merriënboer, J. J. G., Clark, R. E., & de Croock, M. B. M. (2002). Blueprints for complex learning: The 4C/ID-model. *Educational Technology Research and Development, 50*(2), 39–61.

Vygotsky, L. (1978). *Mind in society: The development of higher mental processes.* Cambridge, MA: Harvard University Press.

Wimmer, R., & Boring, S. (2009). HandSense: Discriminating different ways of grasping and holding a tangible user interface. In *Proceedings of the International Conference on Tangible and Embedded Interaction* (pp. 359–362). New York: ACM Press.

Woolf, B., Burleson, W., Arroyo, I., Dragon, T., Cooper, D., & Picard, R. W. (2009). Affect-aware tutors: Recognizing and responding to student affect. *International Journal of Learning Technology, 4*(3/4), 129–163.

Wray, R. E., & Woods, A. (2013). A cognitive systems approach to tailoring learner practice. In *Proceedings of Annual Conference on Advances in Cognitive Systems* (pp. 21–38). Cognitive Systems Foundation.

Wu, D. D., Courtney, C. G., Lance, B. J., Narayanan, S. S., Dawson, M. E., Oie, K. S., & Parsons, T. D. (2010a). Optimal arousal identification and classification for affective computing using physiological signals: Virtual reality Stroop task. *IEEE Transactions on Affective Computing, 1*(2), 109–118.

Wu, D., Parsons, T. D., Mower, E., & Narayanan, S. (2010b). Speech emotion estimation in 3D space. *Proceedings of the IEEE International Conference on Multimedia & Expo,* Singapore, July 19-23, 2010.

Wu, D., Lance, B., & Parsons, T. D. (2013). Collaborative filtering for brain-computer interaction using transfer learning and active class selection. *PLOS ONE,* 1–18.

Yang, N., & Samuel, A. (2011). Context-rich detection of user's emotions using a smartphone. Microsoft Research Internship Report.

12
INSTRUCTIONAL DESIGN AND LEARNING DESIGN

Nancy Law

Introduction

The field of instructional design can be traced back to its beginnings at the start of the 20th century, and hence has a much longer history compared to learning design, which only emerged around the beginning of this millennium. There are many similarities between these two fields: both serve the same mission of supporting student learning and are influenced by developments in the learning sciences, and technology plays an important role in developments in both fields. On the other hand, there are also some major differences between these two fields. In fact, the term learning design has two different lineages and so can carry different meanings and emphasis depending on the specific community that is using the term.

This chapter provides a brief historical overview of developments in both fields and how these have been influenced by the learning sciences, and the role technology has played in these two fields. The final section will summarize the key similarities and differences between these two fields, and put forward possible scenarios of how these two fields may co-evolve in collaboration with the burgeoning field of Learning Analytics to launch the development of a design science for learning.

Instructional Design and Instructional Technology

A Brief Overview

Instructional Design and Instructional Technology are conceptually two different terms. However, as Reiser (2001) pointed out, the two have never existed without the other since their emergence in the first decade of the 20th century in the

US so that the field is generally referred to as Instruction Design and Technology (IDT for short). Implicit in the word *instruction* is the assumption that for learning to happen, a person needs to be instructed (or taught). The predominant theory of learning at the time the field came into being further included the ideas that the most important outcomes of learning are knowledge and skills, and that instructions are primarily conducted through presentations. Hence the most effective way to help people learn was to improve the quality of presentations, and the first instructional technologies were visual technologies: slide projectors, stereograph viewers, and films. Gagné and Merrill (1990) have emphasized the focus of instructional design on supporting the learner, and advocated a cognitive processing model to guide the design process. The instructional model (Gagné, 1992), while emphasizing the need to consider learning goals in a holistic manner, is very much grounded on a communication model in which instructional media plays a very important role. Each advance in instructional technology brings new instructional media, which is defined as the physical means through which instruction is presented to learners (Reiser & Gagné, 1983). Thus instructional media is often taken to be synonymous with instructional design and instructional technology, and the first IDT professional organization to emerge was the Department of Visual Instruction (DVI) of the National Education Association that was set up in 1923 (Reiser, 2001).

While the first implementations of IDT targeted schools and formal educational institutions, it gained wide initial attention to its potential impact through its contributions to military training, especially during WWII, when there was a great demand on trained military and affiliated personnel. There are claims that the effectiveness of the training videos was an important contributing factor that brought success to the US in World War II (Saettler, 1990). Subsequently, studies on how different audio-visual (AV) characteristics and features influence learning became an important area of IDT research. In particular, media comparison studies that compare the effectiveness of learning from AV resources with learning from live instructions became popular. It can be said that the idea of deploying communication technology to achieve the same instructional outcomes as the best live instructor has been a main driving force behind research and development in IDT. Hence, every major advance in communication technology (radio, film, video, television, computers, personal computers, the Internet, mobile technology, etc.) has inspired new developments and stimulated great optimism that the new technology will bring major breakthroughs in how people learn more effectively.

While there have been major changes in IDT during its century-long history, the adoption of IDT by the education community and its impact on mainstream educational practices have been rather limited throughout. McCluskey (1981) observed that the great commercial interest in visual instruction that spawned the AV industry did not bring about widespread adoption of AV in educational institutions. Computers promise to be most flexible and adaptive, but the scenario of lack of significant impact remains valid. Despite the increasing availability of computers and the Internet in schools, the actual use was still low (Anderson & Ronnkvist, 1999). Law, Pelgrum, and Plomp (2008) found that the reported use has increased, but the mode of use was largely traditional. On the other hand, the recent global interest and fast developments in MOOCs created strong demands for the service of instructional designers and provided a context and impetus for further advances in IDT. The remainder of this section will examine the core processes of IDT and its connections with research on learning, as well as the challenges and opportunities that learning in the 21st century poses for IDT.

IDT and Learning Research

According to Reiser (2001), IDT includes the analysis of learning and performance, as well as the provision of the entire set of processes and resources needed for their improvement in educational and workplace settings. The AECT (1994) definition of IDT includes five categories of activities: design, development, implementation, management, and evaluation, which encompass the entire process of instructional program development and evaluation (Seels & Richey, 1994). Since World War II, the instructional design process has been enriched by the research of psychologists and educators to take account of learners' characteristics and ability (Reiser, 2001). These include the use of screening tests to ensure that learners have the requisite ability to engage productively in the learning activities offered, and that instructions can be programmed in small chunks with frequent feedback and self-pacing support to cater for different learner needs. More recent descriptions of a model for ID development highlight the analysis of the learning needs and the requirements of the learning context as the first step in the design process, and the general approach taken is referred to as the ADDIE model (acronym for Analysis, Design, Development, Implementation, and Evaluation) (Molenda, 2003).

IDT also includes non-instructional designs such as the development of performance technology to address situations where the poor performance is non-training related. Performance technology involves changing the learning environment design to enhance learner performance through technology augmentation (i.e., the provision of appropriate tools) during the performance process, which could be in the form of just-in-time tutorials, advisement systems, etc.

Reiser and Ely (1997) provide a systematic overview of developments in the field of IDT in the US from the 1960s, and identify five trends that are also evident globally:

- Shifting from a focus on media and resources to a systems approach in the use of resources and associated processes
- Broadening the focus from utilization to include progressively design, evaluation, development, management, analysis and organization

- Increasing influence of cognitive and constructivist learning theories on the field
- Changing perception of the role of IDT in relation to the live instructor from being supplemental to being on equal footing
- Changing perception of the function of IDT from improving instruction to facilitating learning and improving performance

In recent years, there are strong voices within the IDT community to further strengthen the interactions between learning sciences research and IDT. Ertmer and Newby (2013) report that less than 2% of courses offered in university educational technology programs emphasize learning theory, and argue for the need to give greater importance to learning theories in IDT as effective designs for learning should be contextualized, personally relevant and collaborative. Sims (2015) goes even further to argue that the design of effective learning environments does not need to give explicit or initial reference to subject matter. Rather, the focus of instructional design should be on aligning learning outcomes with assessment, and the design of learning activities should be problem oriented. In this approach subject matter resources would be decided as necessary based on the pedagogical design.

Challenges and Opportunities for IDT in the 21st Century

There are two key forces that have shaped instructional design over the ages: developments in technology and developments in our understanding of learning (or theories about learning). This influence is not unidirectional, particularly the relationship between learning theory and instructional design. The instructional materials/courses developed through ID are in themselves an encapsulation of a theory about how people learn, albeit an implicit one. It thus provides an opportunity for the underpinning theories to be put to the test. A century of explorations and practice in IDT have shown that instructional design may pay much more attention to understanding learners and learning.

The most important technological changes impacting IDT development are the inventions of personal computers and the Internet. The instructional technologies available before the advent of computers offered increasingly powerful means to create and transmit instructional media (IM). However, there is little flexibility in how a particular piece of IM is used, and the transmission is unidirectional only, from the instructor to the learner. Computers bring much great flexibility to the design of IM due to the possibility of feedback and interactions with the learner. There is a possibility of adaptation based on learner performance and/or intervention. The Internet brings in the social dimension of learning, which was otherwise not possible in computer-mediated learning. In fact, advances in Internet technology open up whole new worlds in social interactions that would not have been possible through face-to-face interactions only. Starting only as asynchronous interactions, computer-mediated communication (CMC) advanced its capabilities to include synchronous interactions that can now include text, audio, video, and augmented or virtual reality. With the emergence of social media, the role of learners is no longer confined to that of a consumer of IM, but has expanded to include the creation of media. There are also many more ways of organizing and supporting interactions among learners, and among learners and teachers. The recent debut of Massively Open Online Courses (MOOCs), as well as the increasing public interest in innovative ways of organizing learning such as flipped classrooms, etc. have created strong demands on IDT professionals. At the same time, these new developments and technological possibilities also bring new challenges to the field of IDT, requiring advances in theories and tools for instructional design (Sims, 2015).

Another challenge to the field of IDT is the changing emphasis on what counts as important learning outcomes. With the rapid expansion in human knowledge, there is growing recognition that a lot of what we know or learn today will become obsolete in a few years, a phenomenon that Arbesman (2012) refers to as the half-life of facts. So education can no longer serve the role of preparing learners for life if the focus is only on learning important knowledge and skills. Generic cognitive and meta-cognitive competences such as critical thinking, problem solving, communication, creativity, knowledge building and digital literacy, as well as interpersonal and intrapersonal competences such as collaboration and reflection have become core candidates in the global discourse on what constitutes 21st century skills/competences (Griffin et al., 2012; Pellegrino & Hilton, 2013). Further, fostering and assessing these competences cannot be achieved through quality presentations, but learning designs that pay attention to learning environments and interactions during the *process* of learning rather than the products of learning.

Learning Design and Learning Technology

The term *learning design* only appeared around the beginning of this millennium, and hence has a much shorter history compared to IDT. Agostinho and colleagues (2011) describe learning design as:

> [R]esearch and development dedicated to the quest of equipping teachers with tools and strategies to aid their design of high-quality learning environment. (p. 97)

On the other hand, Mor, Ferguson and Wasson (2015) define learning design as:

> [T]he practice of devising effective learning experiences aimed at achieving defined educational objectives in a given context. (p. 221)

The differences in foci between these two descriptions captures well the two lines of development in learning design research and practice: the first is concerned with the representation of teaching practices for implementation and interoperability of learning activities on e-learning environments (Koper & Tattersall, 2005; Koper, 2006), and the second definition focuses on representation of teaching practices from a professional sharing, learning, and collaboration perspective (Hansen & Wasson, 2013; Emin-Martinez et al., 2014). Both lines of development involve working with teachers to *capture* the designs they use in their actual practice, and representational issues are core. However, the former is primarily concerned with machine-readable representations (Koper, 2006), and builds more on the theoretical and methodological traditions of the IDT community. The latter is more concerned with design practices and tools used by teachers, and human readable representations, building on the theoretical principles and methodologies in the Learning Sciences. The roles and importance of technology in LD also differ depending on the specific focus of LD adopted.

Another complexity in understanding learning design is that this term is often used interchangeably to represent three different ontological entities. It can refer to (1) the formal representational language (especially when the capitalized form *Learning Design* is used) in documenting and communicating learning designs, (2) the practice or act of engaging in the learning design process, or (3) the artifacts that are the outcomes of the design process. The remainder of this section will describe in turn the conceptualization, key concerns, and technology development in learning design under each of these two developmental foci and delineate how these relate to the three ontological meanings presented here.

Learning Design with a Focus on Technical Representation

This strand of development in learning design reflects primarily efforts and concerns of the IDT community to address the design challenges of representing and implementing innovative pedagogical designs in online learning environments to meet the needs of education in the 21st century. IDT is an established field, which serves directly the professional communities in educational technology and educational software/courseware development. The core issues considered by this community include interoperability, reusability, and cost-effectiveness. These communities have long been aware of the need for a representational language and a technical platform and tools to develop courseware and online courses that are interoperable. SCORM is a standard that was created for use by e-learning software companies, course designers, and other users in the development of courses so that these can be interoperable across different Learning Management Systems (LMS), authoring tools, and content providers. However, this standard was developed based on a single learner model, primarily focusing on content-focused sequences of learner activities targeting largely cognitive outcome goals. There is a need for a representational formalism to incorporate emerging innovative, social constructivist pedagogies such as role plays, simulations, and problem-based learning designs that typically involve complex multi-role interactions among students and between teachers and students (Koper & Olivier, 2004). Among the earliest and most influential efforts to develop such a formalism and tools began in the Open University of the Netherlands in 1997, which resulted in the development of the Educational Modelling Language (EML). This work was further developed with funding from the European Union through the UNFOLD project and in partnership with IMS, which is a consortium of global e-learning software companies and users (Koper & Tattersall, 2005). The outcome of this project was IMS-LD, which is a technical language and formalism that can be used to develop interoperable online courses. In this technical language, learning is conceptualized as *people in specific groups and roles engaging in activities using an environment with appropriate resources and services* (ibid., p. 4). This formalism comprises a conceptual model, information models, and XML schemas to serve as a middle layer that enables the representation of a full range of pedagogies. When used in this context, LD is always capitalized.

While IMS-LD provides a formalism that can be used to represent learning designs, it does not define how learning designs should be categorized and organized. Falconer, Finlay, and Fincher (2011) find that researchers prefer more generic, hierarchically structured organizations of LD, often referred to as design *patterns*, which connect some generic pedagogical problem to the core elements of the design solution, and linking these with example instantiations of these patterns in actual implementations in specific pedagogical contexts. Teachers, on the other hand, do not find these abstracted representations to be helpful and much prefer the contextualized examples. Hence, as De Vries, Tattersall, and Koper (2006) point out, one important concern for LD researchers is the nature of the intended/targeted users. Will teachers in general be involved in making use of LD tools and designs in LD repositories, or would it be just a novelty for the inquisitive teacher only? If specialist knowledge about LD were required for the bulk of its users, it would be difficult for its use to be popularized. Hence, even though IMS-LD is considered as powerful in its pedagogically expressiveness (McAndrew et al., 2006), its adoption has been limited due to the perceived complexity of the tools involved (Hermans et al., 2015).

Most of those engaged in LD research from the technical development perspective came from an IDT background, and designers of LD are often not the teachers, but instructional designers. On the other hand, with the pervasive use of online technology to support blended learning in on-campus course, and the ease of incorporating synchronous interactions in fully online courses, the pedagogical design challenges faced in different institutional contexts become much more complex and indeed more similar. In fact, there is a need in many institutions to develop a new strategy for the authoring and delivery of online courses and educational resources in order to provide a more integrated approach to course development and administration, as described by Hermans, Janssen, and Koper (2015) in the case of OUNL, to cater to different types of learners. Such developments inevitably bring a multitude of professional backgrounds and institutional roles to the fore as potential users of LD authoring tools and resources. Hermans et al. (ibid.) describe a new approach to the design of LD and course delivery systems that integrates IMS-LD authoring tools and the runtime Learning Management System (LMS) to provide flexible editing of courses in either authoring or runtime modes. The system also adopts a layered architecture for the LD authoring system such that authoring of the course and activity designs takes place via templates that do not require specialist technical knowledge or complex terminology. The system was implemented starting in May 2011 and an analysis of the course activities recorded on the system until February 2014 found that 59% have been either modified or created during runtime. As runtime modification is normally carried out by the teachers concerned, this is evidence that teachers without specialist LD knowledge would be able to make use of the LD authoring system.

Learning Design to Improve Pedagogical Theory and Practice

In addition to technical representations such as the IMS-LD discussed above, there are also representations that are developed to support learning design as a collaborative professional activity. Some of these focus on the the pedagogical approaches adopted in the design, and are concerned with the rationale underpinning pedagogical decisions at a more generic level based on an analysis of the problem context and pedagogical goals targeted. Design patterns and pattern languages are typical of this type of representation.

At the other end of the spectrum are representations that provide a step-by-step description of the learning activities and their connections to the associated conditions and resources. These are usually in the form of flow diagrams, such as LAMS (www.lamsinternational.com/) or CompendiumLD (compendiumld. open.ac.uk/), and these representations are much closer to the way the designs are enacted. While these two types of representation can co-exist, these serve different priorities. This section gives a brief introduction to these two types of representations.

Pedagogical Design Patterns and Pattern Languages

One prominent line of work focusing on educational representations of learning design is the work on design patterns and pattern languages (Goodyear & Retalis, 2010b), which is very much influenced by the work of the architect Christopher Alexander (1979). It is underpinned by the idea that learning cannot be directly designed as there is no direct connection between design intentions and the actual learning process or outcome (Goodyear, 2000). According to Goodyear and Retalis (2010a), design patterns are problem solution pairs set within a particular context and include a rationale for why the solution is chosen, which could be theoretically or empirically based. The solution in this case is not meant to be a specific sequence of concrete steps, but an approach to solving a recurrent problem. A sequence of patterns is known as a pattern language. Design patterns and pattern languages can be used together to support and align the decision-making process from micro-level design (e.g., a small learning task) to the macro level (e.g., an entire course). The value of design patterns and pattern languages lies in the ability to identify recurrent problems and in their refinement and sharing. Such an approach to learning design is expected to advance both research and development on educational practice.

On the other hand, design patterns and pattern languages are abstract descriptions, and hence cannot be directly translated into pedagogical practices for teachers. This level of design representation is naturally more distant from teachers or TEL designers. Perhaps this is the reason why Goodyear and Retalis (2010a) assumed the TEL R&D community but not teachers or TEL designers to be a natural audience for their edited volume. Some chapters in this volume report work that engaged a variety of education professionals, including teachers and TEL designers. In these cases, the researchers elicited the design patterns from the practitioners. It is not clear in these reported cases how far the practitioners were able to make use of the design patterns without mediation from the researchers.

Learning Design to Support Teacher Inquiry

Mor, Ferguson, and Wasson (2015) define learning design as "the practice of devising effective learning experiences aimed at achieving defined educational objectives in a given context" (p. 221). This definition focuses on learning design not as an artifact (such as a plan) or a method (such as a design pattern), but as a process for teacher inquiry and professional learning. Learning design becomes one component within a three-step process: design, inquiry, and analytics. Here, the representational focus for learning design is not in looking for a solution to a recurrent problem, but in providing a basis for constructing the inquiry questions to be explored through analysis of the data collected from learners and the learning process. The design focus is not the content to be studied, but the learning experiences of learners. Learning design serves as a critical link within the iterative learning process so that the analytics can address the teachers' inquiry on the efficacy of their own practice, as advocated by the teacher as reflective practitioner literature (e.g., Schön, 1992). The goal is to improve teachers' professional practice through supporting inquiry and reflection on their own practice, so that teachers play the triple role of designer, developer, and evaluator.

There is a strong interest emerging both from the community interested in learning design as teacher-led inquiry and from the learning analytics community to connect these two areas of research to complement development in the two areas (Lockyer & Dawson, 2012). The Society for Learning Analytics Research (SoLAR) (https://solaresearch.org/) refers to learning analytics as "the measurement, collection, analysis and reporting of data about learners and their contexts, for purposes of understanding and optimizing learning and the environments in which it occurs." As this definition indicates, this field is very much focused on the learner in its orientation. However, for learning in formal institutional settings, the learners' experiences are very much influenced by the learning designs. Connecting learning design with learning analytics thus closes the loop such that the former provides the framework to guide the specification of questions that the latter should address, while outcomes of the latter provide feedback on the efficacy of the learning design and its implementation.

If learning design were to closely couple with learning analytics to support teachers' inquiry of student learning, what kind of representational formalism would suffice? Teaching is a complex practice. The efficacy of a teaching practice depends not only on the multiple layers of design (Gibbons, 2010) it encompasses, but also the pragmatics of the implementation. A design pattern as a representational form would not be specific enough to serve the crucial role of specifying the analytics needed to evaluate the efficacy of a design *and* how that is implemented. Learning design as specifications of sequences of learning activities and associated conditions and resources would provide the granularity needed to link the operational description of the design with the relevant data about the learners, their learning behavior, and outcomes. On the other hand, such micro-level design specifications miss the underpinning higher level design assumptions and conceptualizations, which is critical for teachers to achieve deep understanding and improvement in learning design.

Teaching as a Design Science: Representational Issues and Tools

Laurillard (2012) argues that teachers should be design professionals and teaching should be a design science. Teaching, like architecture and engineering, has formally specifiable goals and teaching professionals should have a disciplined approach towards improving practice. Teaching should be a design science as put forward by Simon (1996), building on design principles and heuristics of practice. Learning design, or the design of learning experiences, lies at the core of a teacher's practice, as we now know that deep learning occurs through students' construction of understanding via personally meaningful and engaging experiences. Just as the natural sciences advance through knowledge co-construction by the scientific community rather than individual efforts alone, teaching as a design science can only advance through collaborative inquiry and learning design should be a participatory activity.

If co-participation in learning design and teacher-led inquiry of student learning are expected of all teachers as a core professional activity, we need a representation of learning that is easy to understand, not burdened with technical jargon and yet powerful enough to allow teachers to formulate inquiry questions at different layers and granularity of the design. The representation needs to be strict enough for the learning design to be implemented on an online learning support platform, and for the teachers' inquiry questions to be translated into operationalizable queries and visualization requirements for a coupled learning analytics engine to execute.

Mor, Ferguson, and Wasson (2015) go a step further to advocate that this design science activity should go beyond improvement of practice as an individual or small group inquiry to a community-wide, citizen science type of endeavor. This is an exciting vision and aspiration, which if realized, has the potential to revolutionize the entire teaching profession to become a much more evidence-based practice grounded on the cumulative knowledge of researchers and professionals. For this to happen, there needs to be a common design language at the level of professional and machine communications to ensure that there can be a common protocol for communication and sharing of learning designs and learning analytics results. This also implies that the representation of learning designs needs to be multimodal and multilevel. We need representational tools that can (1) connect conceptual designs such as design patterns and pattern languages to operationalizable activity sequences, which can be interpreted by machines to online implementations, and (2) support the specification of inquiry questions at particular level(s) and granularity(ies) of a learning design and linked to a taxonomy of the learning outcomes targeted.

Persico and Pozzi (2015) provide a wide-ranging review of the tools that have been developed to support learning design. Some tools are text-based and provide narrative descriptions of designs that make explicit the context, assumptions, and important features in the implementation. These tools are good at preserving the richness of the design thinking, but are difficult to operationalize into TEL implementations. Some design tools are developed for specific pedagogical approaches and serve as a helpful design tool and a collaborative platform for those interested in specific pedagogies but would not be able to cater for a wider range of learning designs. There are some pedagogically neutral learning design tools that provide spaces for users to share the pedagogical rationale behind the design. There is a tradeoff between the level of customized support in the relevant design details captured and the specificity of pedagogical orientation that the tool caters for.

One valuable resource for anyone interested in learning about or collaborating with others on learning design is the Design Principles Database (www.edu-design-principles.org/dp/designHome.php). It is a well-developed repository of learning designs that are well curated and indexed with links to the pedagogical principles involved as well as to the relevant examples and learning resources for each design. The learning design principles, designs, and patterns in this database resulted from bottom-up collation and categorizations of research-based design ideas from TEL technology software innovations. It has a design vocabulary and a well-defined database structure, and has built-in features to support participation and collaboration. Unfortunately, database development ended in 2008.

While a learning design system that can link up with learning analytics tools is yet to emerge, there are some learning design tools that support multimodal and multilevel representations of learning design that offer some insight to what possible future systems could look like and which further developments are necessary. For example the Pedagogical Pattern Collector (http://web.lkldev.ioe.ac.uk/PPC/live/ODC.html) developed by Ljubojevic & Laurillard (2011) is a tool that was designed to capture both the design pattern as a solution to an abstracted problem context, as well as instances of the same pattern in different learning contexts. It allows users to start from concrete designs towards an abstract pattern or to work in the reverse direction, adapting a design pattern for a specific learning context. The tool provides a textual view and a visual presentation of the activity sequences, as well as a graphical display of the proportions of time a student is expected to spend on different kinds of learning activities for the design as a whole. Laurillard et al. (2013) developed further features in a prototype Learning Designer that serves primarily as a manipulable microworld for teachers to explore the pedagogical features of a learning design, how the different activities in the design may or may not contribute to the targeted learning outcomes, and possible adaptations. This form of representation, as the authors argue, is not pedagogically neutral in the way that the IMS-LD representation is. On the other hand, the current form of Learning Designer does not communicate with a LMS to provide a runtime version of the resulting designs, thus limiting what it can contribute as a vehicle for teacher inquiry.

Another interesting system is the CompendiumLD (http://compendiumld.open.ac.uk/) learning design software developed by Open University (UK). It provides a set of icons and three different graphical representations for users to create and share designs: (1) a learning outcomes view that highlights the targeted learning outcomes to be achieved, a high-level description of the learning activities (such as applying theory to practice) selected to help students to achieve the outcomes, and the underpinning pedagogical principles for the activities selected; (2) a sequence map view of the detailed sequence of activities at a micro level, such as reading, writing an essay, and discussing with peers that comprise each of the high-level activity descriptions, as well as the learning outputs, resources, and support needed for each activity at this level; and (3) a task times view to record the times that the student and the tutor are expected to spend on each of the micro-level learning activities specified in the sequence map. Again, like the Learning Designer, CompendiumLD serves as a tool for the creation, sharing, and editing of learning designs for individual teachers and TEL designers, as well as a platform for pedagogical collaboration and community building for teachers, TEL designers, and researchers. It does not support the direct operationalization of designs into runtime TEL implementations.

It is clear from the above review that despite the many exciting research and developments in learning design over the past two decades, we still do not have the necessary design language or tools to realize the vision of connecting learning design to learning analytics to establish a citizen design science of learning. We need accepted "standards" with regard to the learning design vocabulary, the mapping of the concepts in the vocabulary to necessary elements in operationalizing the implementation of the design in a TEL environment, and an ontology to map the relationships among intended learning outcomes, learning and teaching activities, learner behavior to be tracked, and assessment tasks.

The Future of Instructional Design and Learning Design, and the Role of Technology

In this chapter, we provided a brief review of the fields of instructional design and learning design, which have different histories. Instructional design is a well-established field that has developed for over a century. It has established professional societies, academic journals and conferences, and has given rise to a recognized profession (the members of which are sometimes referred to as educational technologists). There are many universities that offer programs and qualifications catering for those aspiring to enter into the profession. Developments in the field of instructional design have always co-evolved with advances in instructional technology, which are closely linked to advances in media and communications technology. Recent developments in Open Educational Resources (OER) and open learning (e.g. Massively Open Online Courses or MOOCs in short), and blended modes of educational provisions (such as flipped classrooms) have created even bigger demands for instructional designers and educational technologists to support the development of TEL implementation, online learning resources, and course offerings. On the other hand, the knowledge and expertise traditionally expected of the ID profession focuses on delivering instructional materials to achieve primarily cognitive outcome goals. The demand now is for TEL implementations that foster the development of 21st century skills such as problem solving, critical thinking, collaboration, and communication. To design learning activities that are effective in fostering these outcomes requires a much deeper knowledge of how people learn, and the focus of the design has to be the learners' experiences rather than the instructional media. From the literature on IDT reviewed in this chapter, there is every indication that the IDT field is aware of these challenges and embraces the need for ID to take account of underpinning pedagogical design assumptions (Sims, 2015).

Learning design has a much shorter history of less than two decades. While there are books, journal papers, and tools devoted to learning design, it has not yet fully developed into a distinct academic or professional field. The emergence of learning design as a field of inquiry and professional practice reflects the wide recognition in the field of education that it is learning that matters, and instruction is only one of the pedagogical approaches that can be used to support learning. There have been two broad approaches to learning design. One approach focuses on the technical representation of learning activities to convert representations of designs into TEL implementations on LMSs, and its contributors usually have an instructional design or engineering background. One important outcome from this line of work is the development of IMS-LD, which has become an accepted standard for the representation of learning design for TEL implementation by professionals and tool developers.

Another approach to learning design focuses on promoting and supporting a shift in the professional role of teachers from instructors and evaluators to designers of learning experiences. Contributors to this approach are often researchers in the learning sciences, particularly those involved in TEL design, development, and/or implementation, and those involved in supporting learning for technology-enhanced pedagogical innovation. While technology also plays a role in this approach to learning design, the primary focus is on the pedagogical design rationale and associated representation of the design ideas at various levels of scale (e.g., a learning activity, a lesson, a course, or a program) and granularity (e.g., from the broad specification of the learning spaces and environment to specific resources and tools for a given learning activity). There are as yet no commonly accepted standards for learning design representation at any level though there are many shared concepts and objectives that are embraced by the community, such as the desirability of coupling learning design with learning analytics to support teacher inquiry of student learning as a collaborative professional practice and a mechanism for teacher learning. We do not yet see the emergence of a new profession labeled as learning designers in the way we see with instructional designers. In fact, learning design is not yet a practice, and most of the work involved in the elicitation, analysis, representation, manipulation, and dissemination of learning designs has been done by researchers. The vision for those engaged in learning design research and development from this perspective is not to create a new learning design profession, but to transform teachers into seeing their primary role as learning designers.

Reflecting on the development of these two closely related fields, it is clear that despite differences in focus and emphasis, and perhaps differences in disciplinary background for those involved in ID and learning design, there is much potential for synergy and collaboration across these two areas. One exciting future that both communities could embrace and contribute to through interdisciplinary and inter-professional collaboration is to join hands with researchers in the area of learning analytics to build the theoretical, social, and technological infrastructure for developing the design science of learning.

Acknowledgment

This paper relates to the project "An Open Learning Design, Data Analytics and Visualization Framework for E-Learning" funded by the Innovative Technology Fund of the Innovation and Technology Commission of the HKSAR Government, grant number ITS/306/15FP.

References

AECT (Association for Educational Communications and Technology) (1977). *Educational technology: Definition and glossary of terms.* Washington, DC: AECT.

Agostinho, S., Bennett, S., Lockyer, L., & Harper, B. (2011). The future of learning design. *Learning, Media and Technology, 36*(2), 97–99.

Alexander, C. (1979). *The timeless way of building* (Vol. 1). New York: Oxford University Press.

Anderson, R. E., & Ronnkvist, A. (1999). *The presence of computers in American schools. Teaching, learning, and computing: 1998 national survey. Report No. 2.* Irvine, CA.: Center for Research on Information Technology and Organizations and Minneapolis: Minnesota University.

Arbesman, S. (2012). *The half-life of facts: Why everything we know has an expiration date.* New York: Penguin.

De Vries, F., Tattersall, C., & Koper, R. (2006). Future developments of IMS Learning Design Tooling. *Educational Technology & Society, 9*(1), 9–12.

Emin-Martinez, V., Hansen, C., Rodriguez Triana, M. J., Wasson, B., Mor, Y., Dascalu, M., Ferguson, R., & Pernin, J.-P. (2014). Towards teacher-led design inquiry of learning. *eLearning Papers* (36). Milton Keynes: Open University UK.

Ertmer, P. A., & Newby, T. J. (2013). Behaviorism, cognitivism, constructivism: Comparing critical features from an instructional design perspective. *Performance Improvement Quarterly, 26*(2), 43–71.

Falconer, I., Finlay, J., & Fincher, S. (2011). Representing practice: practice models, patterns, bundles.... *Learning, Media and Technology, 36*(2), 101–127.

Gagné, R. M. (1992). The Events of instruction. In R. M. Gagné, L. J. Briggs, & W. W. Wager (Eds.), *Principles of instructional design* (4th ed., pp. 185–204). New York: Harcourt Brace Jovanovich College Publishers.

Gagné, R. M., & Merrill, M. D. (1990). Integrative goals for instructional design. *Educational Technology Research and Development, 38*(1), 23–30.

Gibbons, A. S. (2010). A contextual framework for identifying instructional design patterns. In P. Goodyear & S. Retalis (Eds.), *Technology-enhanced learning: Design patterns and pattern languages.* (pp. 29–47). Rotterdam: Sense Publishers.

Goodyear, P. (2000). Environments for lifelong learning: Ergonomics, architecture and educational design. In J. M. Spector & T. Anderson (Eds.), *Integrated and holistic perspectives on learning, instruction & technology: Understanding Complexity* (pp. 1–18). Dordrecht: Kluwer Academic Publishers.

Goodyear, P., & Retalis, S. (2010a). Learning, technology and design. In P. Goodyear & S. Retalis (Eds.), *Technology-enhanced learning: Design patterns and pattern languages* (pp. 1–28). Rotterdam: Sense Publishers.

Goodyear, P., & Retalis, S. (2010b). *Technology-enhanced learning: Design patterns and pattern languages.* Rotterdam: Sense Publishers.

Griffin, P., McGaw, B., & Care, E. (2012). *Assessment and teaching of 21st century skills.* Dordrecht: Springer.

Hansen, C., & Wasson, B. (2013). Teacher inquiry into student learning: The TISL heart model and method for use in teachers' professional development. *Nordic Journal of Digital Literacy, 11*(1), 24–49.

Hermans, H., Janssen, J., & Koper, R. (2015). Flexible authoring and delivery of online courses using IMS Learning Design. *Interactive Learning Environments, 24*(6), 1265–1279.

Koper, R. (2006). Editorial: Current research in learning design. *Journal of Educational Technology & Society, 9*(1), 13–22.

Koper, R., & Olivier, B. (2004). Representing the learning design of units of learning. *Journal of Educational Technology & Society, 7*(3), 97–111.

Koper, R., & Tattersall, C. (2005). Preface to learning design: A handbook on modelling and delivering networked education and training. *Journal of Interactive Media in Education, 18*, 1–7.

Laurillard, D. (2012). *Teaching as a design science: Building pedagogical patterns for learning and technology.* New York: Routledge.

Laurillard, D., Charlton, P., Craft, B., Dimakopoulos, D., Ljubojevic, D., Magoulas, G. et al (2011). A constructionist learning environment for teachers to model learning designs. *Journal of Computer Assisted Learning, 29*(1), 15–30.

Laurillard, D., Charlton, P., Craft, B., Dimakopoulos, D., Ljubojevic, D., Magoulas, G., . . . Whittlestone, K. (2013). A constructionist learning environment for teachers to model learning designs. *Journal of Computer Assisted Learning, 29*(1), 15–30.

Law, N., Pelgrum, W. J., & Plomp, T. (Eds.). (2008). *Pedagogy and ICT in schools around the world: Findings from the SITES 2006 study.* Hong Kong: CERC and Springer.

Ljubojevic, D., & Laurillard, D. (2011). *Pedagogical Pattern Collector software tool.* Paper presented at the Art and Science of Learning Design Conference, London Knowledge Lab, London.

Lockyer, L., & Dawson, S. (2012). Where learning analytics meets learning design. In *Proceedings of the 2nd International Conference on Learning Analytics and Knowledge* (pp. 14–15). ACM.

McAndrew, P., Goodyear, P., & Dalziel, J. (2006). Patterns, designs and activities: Unifying descriptions of learning structures. *International Journal of Learning Technology, 2*(2–3), 216–242.

McClusky, F. D. (1981). DVI, DAVI, AECT: A long view. In J.W. Brown & S. N. Brown (Eds.), *Educational media yearbook: 1981.* Littleton, CO: Libraries Unlimited.

Molenda, M. (2003). In search of the elusive ADDIE model. *Performance Improvement, 42*(5), 34–36.

Mor, Y., Ferguson, R., & Wasson, B. (2015). Editorial: Learning design, teacher inquiry into student learning and learning analytics: A call for action. *British Journal of Educational Technology, 46*(2), 221–229.

Pellegrino, J. W., & Hilton, M. L. (2013). *Education for life and work: Developing transferable knowledge and skills in the 21st century.* Washington, DC: National Academies Press.

Persico, D., & Pozzi, F. (2015). Informing learning design with learning analytics to improve teacher inquiry. *British Journal of Educational Technology, 46*(2), 230–248.

Reiser, R. A. (2001). A history of instructional design and technology: Part I: A history of instructional media. *Educational Technology Research and Development, 49*(1), 53–64.

Reiser, R. A., & Ely, D. P. (1997). The field of educational technology as reflected through its definitions. *Educational Technology Research and Development, 45*(3), 63–72.

Reiser, R.A., & Gagné R.M. (1983). *Selecting media for instruction.* Englewood Cliffs, NJ: Educational Technology.

Saettler, P. (1990). *The evolution of American Educational Technology.* Englewood, CO: Libraries Unlimited.

Schön, D.A. (1992). The theory of inquiry: Dewey's legacy to education. *Curriculum Inquiry, 22*(2), 119–139.

Seels, B. A., & Richey, R. C. (1994). *Instructional technology: The definitions and domains of the field.* Washington DC: Association for Educational Communication & Technology.

Simon, H.A. (1996). *The sciences of the artificial* (2nd ed.). Cambridge, MA: The MIT Press.

Sims, R. (2015). Revisiting "Beyond Instructional Design." *Journal of Learning Design, 8*(3), 29–41.

13
LEARNING ANALYTICS DESIGN

Dirk Ifenthaler

Introduction

The next frontier in educational research is a synergistic relationship between instructional design and learning analytics. Instructional designers use learning analytics information to evaluate designs of learning environments, learning materials, and tasks, and adjust difficulty levels, as well as measure the impact of interventions and feedback. This sophisticated information about learners, learning processes, and complex interactions within the learning environment provides educators (i.e., teachers, designers) valuable insights for educational planning and curricular decision-making.

Accordingly, learning analytics employ educational data to provide summative, real-time (formative), or predictive insights about the effect and effectiveness of various elements and features of learning environments (Martin & Whitmer, 2016). This newly available educational information requires different perspectives on instructional data processing and analysis including advanced theories, methods, and tools for supporting learning design processes (Ifenthaler & Erlandson, 2016).

Integrating real-time educational data and analysis into the design of learning environments, herein referred to as learning analytics design (LAD), seems to be a promising approach. Valid pedagogical recommendations may be suggested on the fly as learning analytics methodologies and visualizations evolve and as reliable tools become available and ready for classroom practice (Ifenthaler et al., 2014; Kevan & Ryan, 2016).

This chapter aims to offer an overview on design and analytics of learning environments before reviewing opportunities of learning analytics design for optimizing learning environments in near real time.

Design and Analytics of Learning Environments

Design for Learning

The design of formal learning environments includes three simple questions: What shall be learned? How shall it be learned? How shall it be assessed? However, there is no simple recipe for designing a learning environment (Bransford et al., 2000). The design of a learning environment will always change in alignment with the alteration of educational goals and the learning-dependent progression of cognitive structure (Ifenthaler & Seel, 2005). Yet, the design of a learning environment is not simply asking the above-stated three questions. Goodyear and Dimitriadis (2013) further point out that design needs to be accepted as the integral component of educational practice.

The approach of instructional design (ID) encompasses systematic and analytical procedures for optimizing learning and performance, such as analysis, planning, development, implementation, and evaluation (Branch, 2009; Dick, 1987; Gagné, 1965, 1985; Gustafson & Tillman, 1991). The analysis phase includes needs analysis, subject matter content analysis, and job or task analysis. The design phase includes the planning for the arrangement of the content of the learning environment. The development phase results in the tasks and materials that are ready for the learning environment. The implementation phase includes the scheduling of learning as well as preparing teachers, timetables, and evaluation parts. The evaluation phase includes various forms of formative and summative assessments focusing on learning environments, courses, lessons, or learning activities (Ifenthaler, 2012a). Further, evaluation needs to be distinguished from assessments which focus on learning outcomes (Boud, 2000). Instructional design models have been especially successful for improving large instructional programs. However, instructional design is often criticized for being too narrow and inflexible (Dijkstra & Leemkuil, 2008) and difficult to apply to small-scale educational settings (Conole, 2013).

Bransford and colleagues (2000) differentiate four perspectives for the design of learning environments: (a) learner-centered, (b) knowledge-centered, (c) assessment-centered, and (d) community-centered learning environments. The design of learner-centered learning environments needs to take notice of learner's knowledge, skills, attitudes, beliefs, and cultural practices as well as including instructors and/or virtual tutors who are aware of the learners' characteristics (see Bransford et al., 2000). The design of knowledge-centered learning environments highlights the prior knowledge of learners. Accordingly, learners' preconceptions about a specific phenomenon in question are vitally important. Additionally, the design of knowledge-centered learning environments includes authentic problem situations for learners. The design of assessment-centered learning environments aims at combining assessment of content knowledge and necessary skills for specific tasks or problems. Providing feedback is the main objective for designing assessment-centered learning environments (Scardamalia et al., 2011).

Feedback could be any type of information provided to learners that is intended to engage learners or support learning activities and processes (Narciss, 2008). Moreover, feedback is considered a fundamental component for supporting and regulating learning processes. The nature of feedback plays a critical role in learning and instruction especially in technology-based and self-regulated learning environments (Ifenthaler, 2012b). The design of community-centered learning environments combines several aspects of community, including classrooms, schools, universities, workplaces, homes, cities, states, countries, and the virtual world. Hence, the sense of community is involved in the design of community-centered learning environments where instructors and learners share their understanding of norms and values (Brown & Wyatt, 2010).

Instructional design evolved further from focusing on authentic tasks (Gagné & Merrill, 1990; Merrill, 2002, 2007) to emphasizing the aspects of learners (Jonassen, 2000, 2006; Luckin et al., 2014), also referred to as learning design (LD). The concept of learning design, however, has been primarily used in Europe and Australia, emphasizing the learner-centered and technology-enhanced perspective of learning environments and advancing the quality of learning environments (Koper & Manderveld, 2004; Persico & Pozzi, 2015). Further, learning design emphasizes the reusability of learning artifacts, materials, and designs across educational contexts (Lockyer et al., 2013). These efforts are supported by online repositories where designers, teachers, or facilitators share their designs for learning (Conole & Culver, 2010; Dalziel, 2015). Common elements for documenting learning designs include (a) resources, (b) tasks, and (c) support mechanisms (Lockyer et al., 2013).

Goodyear and Retalis (2010) emphasize that good design is the missing link between the learning sciences and the learning environments needed for success in the 21st century, also referred to as educational design. Design patterns may offer a way of capturing design experience including (1) connecting recognizable problems with tested solutions, (2) relating design problems at any scale level (micro, meso, macro, etc.), and connecting design solutions across scale levels, (3) supplementing design with research-based evidence, (4) balancing guidance with creativity, (5) having a wide application of designs but being customizable to meet specific needs, and (6) improving design performance while also educating the designer (Goodyear & Retalis, 2010).

Another example of design for learning is the MAPLET (Matching Aims, Processes, Learner Expertise and Technologies) Framework which was developed to map and link teaching aims, learning processes, learner expertise, and technologies (Ifenthaler & Gosper, 2014). Drawing on cognitive theory, MAPLET provides an approach to the design of learning environments that supports the development of expertise in a particular knowledge domain. Its characteristic features are that it makes explicit the relationships between the learner and their existing levels of expertise in the domain; the knowledge and skills for development; and the teaching and learning process. The application of MAPLET to the design of learning involves a six-step process (Ifenthaler & Gosper, 2014): *Step 1* identifies aims and outcomes and situates them in the appropriate phase of acquisition. *Step 2* identifies the knowledge and competencies to be developed and the learning processes involved. *Step 3* identifies the level of expertise of students. *Step 4* identifies the teaching methods, learning activities, and recourses. *Step 5* identifies assessment strategies. *Step 6* checks for alignment to see if all the different elements are aligned and that there are appropriate supports in place to enable students to move between phases (Ifenthaler & Gosper, 2014).

To sum up, instructional design as well as learning design aim to provide a description of optimal designs for learning environments, however, they do not offer real-time insights into how students are engaged and learn (Lockyer et al., 2013). Therefore, linking design for learning with learning analytics provides helpful information for optimizing learning environments in real time.

Learning Analytics

Learning analytics (LA) use static and dynamic information about learners and learning environments—assessing, eliciting, and analyzing them—for real-time modeling, prediction, and optimization of learning processes, learning environments, and educational decision-making (Ifenthaler, 2015). Learning analytics applications, such as dashboards and reporting engines, are being developed which use learner-generated data and other relevant information in order to personalize and continuously adapt the learning environment (Long & Siemens, 2011). Learning analytics are expected to provide the pedagogical and technological background for producing real-time interventions at all times during the learning process (Gibson & de Freitas, 2016; Mah, 2016).

Various data sources are collected for real-time analysis and visualization including sociodemographic information, personal preferences and interests, responses to standardized inventories (e.g., learning strategies, achievement motivation, personality), skills and competencies (e.g., computer literacy), and prior knowledge and academic performance, as well as institutional transcript data (e.g., pass rates, enrollment, dropout status, special needs). Further, rich behavioral data is available from learners' activities in an online learning environment (i.e., a learning management system, a personal learning environment, a learning blog, etc.). These mostly numeric data refer to logging on and off, viewing and/or posting discussions, navigation patterns, learning paths, content retrieval (i.e., learner-produced data trails), results on assessment tasks, and responses to ratings and surveys. More importantly, rich semantic and context-specific information is available from discussion forums as well as from complex learning tasks (e.g., essays, wikis, blogs). Another data source is curricular information, which includes metadata of the learning environment. These data reflect the learning design (e.g., sequencing of materials, tasks, and assessments) and learning objectives as well as expected learning outcomes. Formative and summative evaluation data are directly linked to specific curricula, facilitators, and/or student cohorts (Ifenthaler, 2015).

Students benefit from learning analytics through optimized learning pathways, personalized interventions and real-time scaffolds (Gašević et al., 2015). Learning analytics provide instructors detailed analysis and monitoring on the individual student level, allowing identification of particularly instable factors, like motivation or attention losses, before they occur (Gašević et al., 2016). Instructional designers use learning analytics information to evaluate learning materials, adjust difficulty levels, and measure the impact of interventions (Lockyer et al., 2013). Learning analytics further facilitate decision-making on an institutional level and help to analyze churn and identify gaps in curricular planning (Ifenthaler & Widanapathirana, 2014).

Learning Analytics Design

Currently, the design of learning environments offers an optimal description for supporting learning processes and high engagement as well as reaching desired learning outcomes. However, learning design does not offer real-time insights into how students are engaged and learn. Therefore, learning analytics design involves the idea of using available information from various educational sources including learner characteristics, learner behavior, learner performance, as well as detailed information of the learning design (e.g., sequencing of events, task difficulty) for supporting pedagogical interventions and redesigns of learning environments (Berland et al., 2014). Three perspectives of learning analytics design provide summative, real-time, and predictive insights (Ifenthaler, 2015):

1. The summative perspective (at the end of a course) of learning analytics design may reveal the impact of interventions for individual students and how they support the learning progress toward a specific learning outcome. Different pedagogical models may be identified and further developed through alignment or misalignment of planned interventions and actual learning behavior. A curricular perspective may help to increase the quality of a study program and identify gaps or redundancies in such (Lockyer et al., 2013).
2. The real-time perspective (while a course is running) of learning analytics design may help to provide learners with resources, help, or scaffolds for supporting their ongoing learning processes. The availability and use of learning materials and tasks could be monitored and adjusted to the learners' needs. Individual and group characteristics may guide difficulty levels and required resources for better learning outcomes (Ifenthaler & Widanapathirana, 2014).
3. The predictive perspective (future course) of learning analytics design may help to model different pathways of learning. Given specific learner characteristics and behavior, algorithms can provide optimal sequences of learning events to better cater to individual needs and preferences of the learner. Critical events

during learning may be predicted and specific interventions may be provided to avoid course failure and dropouts (Mah, 2016).

Learning analytics design will generate valuable insights for planning and optimizing learning environments. Educators may specify benchmarks which help to identify alignment or misalignment towards learning outcomes. In addition, detailed insights into learning processes may facilitate micro interventions whenever the learner needs it.

Lockyer et al. (2013) identify social network analysis as a valuable tool to gain insights into teacher and learner online communication patterns. One example is SNAPP (Social Network Adapting Pedagogical Practice) which is a visualization tool embedded in a learning management system for helping to understand user interactions (Dawson et al., 2011). Given specific patterns of discussions, for example a teacher-centered discussion, may guide further pedagogical interventions to actively involve students in the ongoing conversations. A further development of interaction patterns using semantic analysis may help to identify misconceptions of learners and to provide further personalized scaffolds (Clariana, 2010; Spector, 2010). AKOVIA (Automated Knowledge Visualization and Assessment) is a web-based diagnostic toolset for the analysis of natural language (e.g., written essays, discussion forum posts) and graphical knowledge representations such as knowledge maps (Ifenthaler, 2014a; Pirnay-Dummer et al., 2010). A number of research studies have already used AKOVIA or parts of its functionalities for the automated assessment of knowledge representations. Cross-validation studies have been conducted in order to test the reliability and validity of the automated assessment algorithm (Al-Diban & Ifenthaler, 2011; Eseryel et al., 2013; Kim, 2012). These studies confirmed the high reliability and validity of AKOVIA using well-established outside criterion in multiple domains and acceptable robustness of the automatically generated results (Al-Diban & Ifenthaler, 2011; Ifenthaler, 2014b; Kim, 2012; McKeown, 2009).

Currently, LeAP (Learning Analytics Application; http://wipaed.bwl.uni-mannheim.de/LeAP) is being developed, which includes a holistic learning analytics engine for producing benefits for learners, teachers, and designers. LeAP is a mobile learning tool for tablets which uses multiple data sources from learners, teachers, learning environments, and the predefined learning designs. LeAP provides all stakeholders insights into learning processes in near real time. The dashboard for learning designers shows interaction patterns of learners, use of learning materials, results of performance assessments, and learner satisfaction. Alignment and misalignment of learning processes can be identified and predicted toward future events. Additional functionalities are being implemented and empirical investigations regarding the reliability and validity of LeAP are underway.

To sum up, learning analytics design offers an opportunity to better understand learning processes and the effectiveness of learning designs. However, the interpretation of analysis results requires an in-depth understanding of pedagogical theories and contextual idiosyncrasies of learning environments.

Conclusion

In view of the unfulfilled promises of artificial intelligence (AI) in the 1980s and 1990s, however, one would be well advised to remain skeptical with regard to what learning analytics design may offer for educators. Nevertheless, the integration of real-time data into the design of learning environments is a promising approach. Learning design may offer the right set of theoretical foundations for planning optimal learning environments. Learning analytics in turn offer detailed insights into learning processes and validating assumptions about the effects of learning designs in various contexts. Accordingly, the synergistic relationship between learning design and learning analytics, i.e., learning analytics design, opens up a bright future for personalized and adaptive learning environments. It is up to educators to make the links between learning design and learning analytics operational and use learning analytics design to further advance the educational arena.

References

Al-Diban, S., & Ifenthaler, D. (2011). Comparison of two analysis approaches for measuring externalized mental models: Implications for diagnostics and applications. *Journal of Educational Technology & Society, 14*(2), 16–30.

Berland, M., Baker, R. S. J. D., & Bilkstein, P. (2014). Educational data mining and learning analytics: Applications to constructionist research. *Technology, Knowledge and Learning, 19*(1–2), 205–220. doi:10.1007/s10758-014-9223-7

Boud, D. (2000). Sustainable assessment: Rethinking assessment for the learning society. *Studies in Continuing Education, 22*(2), 151–167. doi:10.1080/713695728

Branch, R. M. (2009). *Instructional design: The ADDIE approach*. New York, NY: Springer.

Bransford, J. D., Brown, A. L., & Cocking, R. R. (Eds.). (2000). *How people learn: Brain, mind, experience, and school*. Washington, DC: National Academy Press.

Brown, T., & Wyatt, J. (2010). Design thinking for social innovation. *Stanford Social Innovation Review, 8*(1), 31–35.

Clariana, R. B. (2010). Deriving individual and group knowledge structure from network diagrams and from essays. In D. Ifenthaler, P. Pirnay-Dummer, & N. M. Seel (Eds.), *Computer-based diagnostics and systematic analysis of knowledge* (pp. 117–130). New York: Springer.

Conole, G. (2013). *Designing for learning in an open world*. New York, NY: Springer.

Conole, G., & Culver, J. (2010). The design of Cloudworks: Applying social networking practice to foster the exchange of learning and teaching ideas and designs. *Computers & Education, 54*(3), 679–692. doi:10.1016/j.compedu.2009.09.013

Dalziel, J. (2015). Reflections on the art and science of learning design and the Larnaca declaration. In M. Maina, B. Craft, & Y. Mor (Eds.), *The art & science of learning design* (pp. 3–14). Rotterdam: Sense Publishers.

Dawson, S., Tan, J. P. L., & McWilliam, E. (2011). Measuring creative potential: Using social network analysis to monitor a learners' creative capacity. *Australasian Journal of Educational Technology, 27*(6), 924–942.

Dick, W. (1987). A history of instructional design and its impact on educational psychology. In J. A. Glover & R. R. Ronning (Eds.), *Historical foundations of educational psychology* (pp. 183–202). New York, NY: Springer.

Dijkstra, S., & Leemkuil, H. (2008). Developments in the design of instruction. From simple models to complex electronic learning environments. In D. Ifenthaler, P. Pirnay-Dummer, & J. M. Spector (Eds.), *Understanding models for learning and instruction. Essays in honor of Norbert M. Seel* (pp. 189–210). New York: Springer.

Eseryel, D., Ifenthaler, D., & Ge, X. (2013). Validation study of a method for assessing complex ill-structured problem solving by using causal representations. *Educational Technology Research and Development, 61*(3), 443–463. doi:10.1007/s11423-013-9297-2

Gagné, R. M. (1965). *The conditions of learning*. New York, NY: Holt, Rinehart, and Winston.

Gagné, R. M. (1985). *The conditions of learning* (4th ed.). New York, NY: Holt, Rinehart, and Winston.

Gagné, R. M., & Merrill, M. D. (1990). Integrative goals for instructional design. *Educational Technology Research and Development, 38*(1), 23–30. doi:10.1007/BF02298245

Gašević, D., Dawson, S., & Siemens, G. (2015). Let's not forget: Learning analytics are about learning. *TechTrends, 59*(1), 64–71. doi:10.1007/s11528-014-0822-x

Gašević, D., Dawson, S., Rogers, T., & Gašević, D. (2016). Learning analytics should not promote one size fits all: The effects of instructional conditions in predicting academic success *Internet and Higher Education, 28*, 68–84.

Gibson, D. C., & de Freitas, S. (2016). Exploratory analysis in learning analytics. *Technology, Knowledge and Learning, 21*(1), 5–19. doi:10.1007/s10758-015-9249-5

Goodyear, P., & Dimitriadis, Y. (2013). In medias res: Reframing design for learning. *Research in Learning Technology, 21*, 19909. doi:10.3402/rlt.v21i0.19909

Goodyear, P., & Retalis, S. (Eds.). (2010). *Technology-enhanced learning: Design patterns and pattern languages*. Rotterdam: Sense Publishers.

Gustafson, K. L., & Tillman, M. H. (1991). Introduction. In L. J. Briggs, K. L. Gustafson, & M. H. Tillman (Eds.), *Instructional design: Principles and applications* (2nd ed., pp. 3–8). Englewood Cliffs: Educational Technology Publishers.

Ifenthaler, D. (2012a). Design of learning environments. In N. M. Seel (Ed.), *Encyclopedia of the sciences of learning* (Vol. 4, pp. 929–931). New York: Springer.

Ifenthaler, D. (2012b). Determining the effectiveness of prompts for self-regulated learning in problem-solving scenarios. *Journal of Educational Technology & Society, 15*(1), 38–52.

Ifenthaler, D. (2014a). AKOVIA: Automated Knowledge Visualization and Assessment. *Technology, Knowledge and Learning, 19*(1–2), 241–248. doi:10.1007/s10758-014-9224-6

Ifenthaler, D. (2014b). Toward automated computer-based visualization and assessment of team-based performance. *Journal of Educational Psychology, 106*(3), 651–665. doi:10.1037/a0035505

Ifenthaler, D. (2015). Learning analytics. In J. M. Spector (Ed.), *The SAGE encyclopedia of educational technology* (Vol. 2, pp. 447–451). Thousand Oaks, CA: Sage.

Ifenthaler, D., & Erlandson, B. E. (2016). Learning with data: Visualization to support teaching, learning, and assessment. *Technology, Knowledge and Learning, 21*(1), 1–3. doi:10.1007/s10758-015-9273-5

Ifenthaler, D., & Gosper, M. (2014). Guiding the design of lessons by using the MAPLET Framework: Matching aims, processes, learner expertise and technologies. *Instructional Science, 42*(4), 561–578. doi:10.1007/s11251-013-9301-6

Ifenthaler, D., & Seel, N. M. (2005). The measurement of change: Learning-dependent progression of mental models. *Technology, Instruction, Cognition and Learning, 2*(4), 317–336.

Ifenthaler, D., & Widanapathirana, C. (2014). Development and validation of a learning analytics framework: Two case studies using support vector machines. *Technology, Knowledge and Learning, 19*(1–2), 221–240. doi:10.1007/s10758-014-9226-4

Ifenthaler, D., Adcock, A. B., Erlandson, B. E., Gosper, M., Greiff, S., & Pirnay-Dummer, P. (2014). Challenges for education in a connected world: Digital learning, data rich environments, and computer-based assessment – Introduction to the inaugural special issue of technology, knowledge and learning. *Technology, Knowledge and Learning, 19*(1–2), 121–126. doi:10.1007/s10758-014-9228-2

Jonassen, D. H. (2000). Toward a design theory of problem solving. *Educational Technology Research & Development, 48*(4), 63–85. doi:10.1007/BF02300500

Jonassen, D. H. (2006). On the role of concepts in learning and instructional design. *Educational Technology Research and Development, 54*(2), 177–196.

Kevan, J. M., & Ryan, P. R. (2016). Experience API: Flexible, decentralized and activity-centric data collection. *Technology, Knowledge and Learning, 21*(1), 143–149. doi:10.1007/s10758-015-9260-x

Kim, M. K. (2012). Cross-validation study of methods and technologies to assess mental models in a complex problem solving situation. *Computers in Human Behavior, 28*(2), 703–717. doi:10.1016/j.chb.2011.11.018

Koper, R., & Manderveld, J. (2004). Educational modelling language: modelling reusable, interoperable, rich and personalised units of learning. *British Journal of Educational Technology, 35*(5), 537–551.

Lockyer, L., Heathcote, E., & Dawson, S. (2013). Informing pedagogical action: Aligning learning analytics with learning design. *American Behavioral Scientist, 57*(10), 1439–1459. doi:10.1177/0002764213479367

Long, P. D., & Siemens, G. (2011). Penetrating the fog: Analytics in learning and education. *EDUCAUSE Review, 46*(5), 31–40.

Luckin, R., Puntambekar, S., Goodyear, P., Grabowski, B. L., Underwood, J., & Winters, N. (Eds.). (2014). *Handbook of design in educational technology*. New York, NY: Routledge.

Mah, D.-K. (2016). Learning analytics and digital badges: Potential impact on student retention in higher education. *Technology, Knowledge and Learning*. doi:10.1007/s10758-016-9286-8

Martin, F., & Whitmer, J. C. (2016). Applying learning analytics to investigate timed release in online learning. *Technology, Knowledge and Learning, 21*(1), 59–74. doi:10.1007/s10758-015-9261-9

McKeown, J. O. (2009). *Using annotated concept map assessments as predictors of performance and understanding of complex problems for teacher technology integration*. Tallahassee, FL: Florida State University.

Merrill, M. D. (2002). First principles of instruction. *Educational Technology Research and Development, 50*(3), 43–59.

Merrill, M. D. (2007). The future of instructional design: The proper study of instructional design. In R. A. Reiser & J. V. Dempsey (Eds.), *Trends and Issues in Instructional Design and Technology* (pp. 336–341). Upper Saddle River, NJ: Pearson Education, Inc.

Narciss, S. (2008). Feedback strategies for interactive learning tasks. In J. M. Spector, M. D. Merrill, J. J. G. van Merriënboer, & M. P. Driscoll (Eds.), *Handbook of research on educational communications and technology* (pp. 125–143). New York, NY: Taylor & Francis Group.

Persico, D., & Pozzi, F. (2015). Informing learning design with learning analytics to improve teacher inquiry. *British Journal of Educational Psychology, 46*(2). doi:10.1111/bjet.12207

Pirnay-Dummer, P., Ifenthaler, D., & Spector, J. M. (2010). Highly integrated model assessment technology and tools. *Educational Technology Research and Development, 58*(1), 3–18. doi:10.1007/s11423-009-9119-8

Scardamalia, M., Bransford, J. D., Kozma, B., & Quellmalz, E. (2011). New assessments and environments for knowledge building. In P. Griffin, B. MacGaw, & E. Care (Eds.), *Assessment and teaching of 21st century skills* (pp. 231–300). New York, NY: Springer.

Spector, J. M. (2010). Mental representations and their analysis: An epestimological perspective. In D. Ifenthaler, P. Pirnay-Dummer, & N. M. Seel (Eds.), *Computer-based diagnostics and systematic analysis of knowledge* (pp. 27–40). New York: Springer.

14
CONTINUING THE DISCOURSE

Lin Lin and J. Michael Spector

Introduction

The authors in this book have presented diverse and constructive perspectives on the relationships and on creating constructive dialogues between the learning sciences (LS) and instructional design and technology (IDT) communities. In this volume, some authors focused on learning and teaching, the core interest of both communities (e.g., Pirnay-Dummer & Seel, Chapter 2) while others discussed the commonalities and differences between the two communities and suggested alignments and the middle ground for collaborations (e.g., Kirschner & Lund, Chapter 3; Reeves & Oh, Chapter 4; Foshay & Roschelle, Chapter 5; Elen, Chapter 6; Gibbons & Williams, Chapter 7). Some authors discussed their own design, teaching, and professional development experiences integrating principles of both LS and IDT communities (e.g., Lajoie, Chapter 8; Yuen, Chapter 9; Meier, Chapter 10; Hubal & Parsons, Chapter 11); and others advocated for incorporating learning analytics in IDT to improve learning in real time (e.g., Law, Chapter 12; Ifenthaler, Chapter 13). In this chapter, we will highlight several key concepts and issues raised by the authors in the book, and project ways to continue the discourse in the constructive articulation between the two communities.

Focus on Learning and Far Transfer of Learning

By providing a comprehensive and retrospective history of the sciences of learning, Pirnay-Dummer and Seel focused on the core interest of both the LS and IDT communities, which is learning, and its counterpart, teaching. The chapter started with a historical overview, added insights into contemporary learning research, and discussed the cognitive architecture of learning including details of schema-based learning and model-based learning. The authors began as far back as the early 1800s with reference to Herbart (1806) and Willmann (1889) and their definitions of teaching as the making of learning, and the documented evidence that scholars were attempting to define the relationship between teaching and learning long ago. They continued to Skinner (1954) discussing the *science of learning and the art of teaching* and to Bransford and colleagues' (2000) argument that one must know how people learn if one wants to teach people. The authors concluded their chapter with a discussion of the need for all teachers (and designers) to have an in-depth knowledge of both the history and specifics of teaching and learning. They stressed the need to better understand how teaching and learning take place, how they can be influenced, on what they depend, how goals are reached, and how changes take place within and between the individuals who are learning and teaching. They highlighted the need for technology to adapt to the core processes of learning and teaching and not make learning and teaching adapt to the technology, which happens all too often.

Along this line, Foshay and Roschelle discussed the concept of *far transfer*, an important element of learning. Foshay and Roschelle defined far transfer as the ability to use what is learned well beyond the learning environment and in circumstances that differ in significant ways from the learning environment. They noted that it is still quite rare in school contexts for assessment efficacy to extend to anything but the initial learning experience. They noted that there does not appear to be a robust causal model that describes what far transfer is and how it occurs. Based on the research of Schwartz and Martin (2004), Foshay and Roschelle hypothesized that transfer will no longer be thought of merely as what one learns at time one in order to perform at time two, but will become transfer in terms of preparation for future learning. They suggest that research in far transfer of learning can greatly benefit from collaborative approaches by scholars from both the LS and IDT communities.

The concept of learning and transfer of learning, including what is to be learned and how it is to be learned, will continue to evolve. The concept of transfer has been discussed in recent technology-based learning and neuroscience studies. Advocates of games such as those found at the Lumosity website (see www.lumosity.com/) claim that they help people obtain learning strategies, but in many cases, games have proven to help people become better only at the games they play rather than transferring the newly acquired knowledge or skill to a different context. In addition, the artificial intelligence, virtual, and augmented reality technologies have blurred the boundaries between human learning and machine learning, a topic to be further discussed in the chapter.

Cherishing the Middle Ground: Similarities and Differences between LS and IDT Communities

Elen started his chapter by stating the common interest of the LS and IDT communities, which is the interest in learning and support for learning. While acknowledging common issues shared by both communities, and that individuals may belong to both communities, Elen observed that LS members or sub-communities are more interested in understanding learning and the theoretical relevance to learning, but that IDT members or sub-communities are more interested in applicability, scalability, and goal-directed interventions.

Foshay and Roschelle argued that LS and IDT are cousins, but not twins—both are focused on application of theory to the design of learning environments, but they have important differences in goals and perspectives, which make their contributions complementary and not competitive. The authors pointed to the fact that there is a qualitative difference in the two: the defining focus of LS is the process of research in designed settings, while the focus of ID is the process of design itself. LS emerged from the cognitive science revolution of the 1980s. Cognitive science has had a major impact on how we talk about learning and think about learning processes; for example, we now recognize the importance of misconceptions and can articulate a nuanced view of why they are instructionally complex. Yet, more recently metacognition and self-regulation are being addressed by both LS and IDT. Foshay and Roschelle argued that collaborative insights from both fields are needed to advance the state of the art for challenges such as domain knowledge, assessment, and scalability. Foshay and Roschelle believe that the guidance on how to select disciplinary core concepts provided by the Next Generation Science Standards (NGSS) may be the key to organizing a discipline. The NGSS documents provide tools for solving complex problems and tools to relate to the interests and life experiences of students. The NGSS documents are influenced by both LS and ID fields, and will be improved over time with increasing depth.

The commonalities and differences between the LS and IDT communities discussed by Elen as well as Foshay and Roschelle are supported by Reeves and Oh's review of research articles published between 2009 and 2014 in two journals, namely, the *Journal of the Learning Sciences* (JLS) and the *Educational Technology Research and Development* (ETR&D), the former being more aligned with the LS communities and the latter with IDT communities. Reeves and Oh found several major differences in the goals and methodologies between the papers published in the two journals. For instance, more exploratory/hypothesis-testing papers were published in ERT&D (68%) than in JLS (28%). More descriptive/interpretive and design/development researchers were published in JLS (over 53%) than in ETR&D (21%). Over half (52%) of the papers in ETR&D used quantitative methods exclusively while only 16% in JLS used these methods alone. Neither journal, however, published any critical theory research studies during the six years.

That is, there were no articles using deconstruction of textual content, no discussion of hidden (learning) agendas, nor any synopsis of marginalized minorities. The authors spoke to this and offered recommendations for improvements in the future. The findings led to several conclusions and recommendations for encouraging cross-pollination in research design. For a more detailed analysis of what is being published and by whom, see Gloria Natividad's (2016) recent dissertation entitled "An analysis of educational technology publications: Who, what and where in the last 20 years."

A good example in practice is Meier's chapter, which highlighted ongoing research to unite the learning sciences and educational technology. Meier cited Pasteur's Quadrant to illuminate the possible synergies between fundamental research understanding through pure research and research that is undertaken with a consideration of use and for developing learning theories. She pointed to the various differences between research done in the past by Bohr (pure research with no concern about application or practice), versus research performed by Pasteur that considers how the theories might be put into practical use in the future, or research similar to Edison's which is categorized as strictly applied research. The author made the point that adoption of technology in classrooms since the 1990s has oftentimes had the effect of only "digitizing the status quo" of education and that this represents a missed opportunity for scaffolding intellectual collaboration.

Meier discussed the Innovation Instruction model created at the Center for Technology and School Change (CTSC) established in 1996, which has evolved to include three major components: (1) design, (2) situate, and (3) lead new learning and instructional efforts. Meier made the case for incorporating new forms of professional development for teachers including ongoing learning and development fashioned to keep pace with emerging technologies while suggesting more research on problem-based learning where the schools are effectively used as learning labs for educational theory and practical educational and organizational reform. Meier further underscored an important distinction that the learning sciences have evolved to the design point that knowledge must be thought of as *constructed* or *created* versus *discovered* as previously proposed or held by some epistemologists (Scardamalia & Bereiter, 2014). This translates to the role that technology must play as the means to help create new forms of interactive inquiry and problem solving. Meier highlighted the issue of equity as it applied to the application of technology resources as the two possible bridges of professional development and design-based research were used to create innovative, interactive, theory-based learning designs seasoned by the practical needs of today's stress-filled schools and the resultant administrative agendas. Educators and researchers must continue to situate themselves in realistic research settings that seem to be routinely squeezed by federal, state, and school district requirements and legislation.

Systems Thinking

Systems thinking has been advocated as a necessary element for more effective organizations (Senge, 1990). It is obvious that almost all the authors agree that there is a seminal approach transforming education and the educational sciences, namely a dramatic and rapid move towards *systems thinking*. Several authors cited Gagné's seminal work (1965, 1992; Gagné & Merrill, 1990) that started the move towards large programmatic training systems where assessment was an integral part of the design intended to build in quality control through more formal reproducible and repeatable means. This formalization could only occur in the larger efforts where both the means and willingness were available to fund this more scientific and systematic approach, since training failure had such serious consequences in military and medical contexts. Today, with different-sized efforts moving forward—from mobile learning apps, to online learning and knowledge management systems, and to large government and corporate training efforts, we know that evaluation and assessment need to be designed up front or otherwise learning and teaching designs are not likely to succeed.

In this book, Kirschner and Lund, as well as Gibbons and Williams, discussed the historical underpinnings of a systems approach, steeped in the teaching of a number of systems thinkers with a background in cybernetics such as George Klir (1972) and Ernst von Glasersfeld (1995). The authors used different terms, for instance, a systematic or systemic approach, especially as design becomes inextricably intertwined with evaluation and assessment (see also Davidsen & Spector, 2015).

Gibbons and Williams situated the dynamic relationships between LS and IDT in their discussions of the relationships between instructional design and educational evaluation. They argued that the separation between instructional design and educational evaluation has contributed to a lack of progress of theory and practice in both areas. The authors identified four approaches to describing design: design as a process, design as a cybernetic activity, design as a logical exercise, and design beyond logic. According to the authors, the common goal of LS (applied scientists) and IDT (designers and developers, a.k.a. engineers) is the study of the properties of systems. The systems being studied by scientists and engineers (designers) are the same, but they are solving different problems with respect to the systems. Scientists hold certain system quantities fixed while allowing others to vary so that unknown relationships within the system can be studied (e.g., independent variables are controlled to determine their relationships to dependent variables.) In design, what would be for the scientist the dependent variables—the outcomes—become fixed, and the designer's job is to determine what relationships among the scientist's independent variables can be manipulated to achieve the desired outcomes (see Reigeluth, 1983). Making decisions based on judgment, followed by the evaluation of the decisions by trial, lies at the heart of both LS and IDT processes. This systems perspective not only shows the closeness of the design–evaluation relationship, but also unifies concepts of science and design.

Technology advances have generally lessened the negative impact of span of control of any one person even though interlocking systems and networks have become extremely complex. As we discuss how to better improve the creative articulation between LS and ID, we must consider scale in our need for speed to enrich the dialogue and condense the design efforts. In this respect, Yuen reviewed the development and implementation of information and communication technology (ICT) in education in the Asian (Hong Kong and Singapore) context, and characterized the differences in the orientation, thinking, and approach between the fields of IDT and LS. His discussions provided a lens to understand the beliefs and experiences of stakeholders involved with the ICT development and implementation on a national level, focusing on four aspects: policy-driven development, the focus of learning, understanding ICT in education, and research and practice. He demonstrated what can be accomplished within a given time frame when there is alignment in the learning sciences, emerging technologies, design and development, and the will of progressive government policy.

Yuen's chapter brings up a number of interesting aspects. In a number of management and military texts the concept of span of control states that there exists some maximum or optimum number of connections that one person can manage effectively, otherwise the system bogs down or fails completely. Since our learning designs, learning organizations, and learning policies are all governed by human systems, span of control needs to be taken into account. Until machines autonomously create learning designs without human intervention, span of control, network theory, and system saturation need to be discussed as system limits.

We can see that this is directly related to the issue of scalability of design. Several authors tackled the issues of scalability and non-scalability pointing out that what works in certain environments does not always work in others. They specifically discussed what causes collapse when trying to take something to scale (i.e., to work effectively in larger and different contexts). Surprisingly, this is not always related directly to the cost of the development, but is often just as easily related to the environment or the learning objectives. Foshay and Roschelle discussed the issues of scalability of learning designs highlighting the many variables that can positively or negatively impact trying to take a design to scale. The authors detailed their experience and lessons learned from successful instances, and discussed the critical attributes to be incorporated into a robust design.

Systems Science, in particular, the area of requirements engineering, has often pointed to the need to define the requirements for learning systems and, by extrapolation, synthetic environments as discussed in Hubal and Parsons' chapter, well up front, before the software code is written. In software design and development, if the requirements are not adequately defined well in advance, by the time software development gets to the point of actually coding the software being developed, the software coder, lacking any clearer direction, will make a decision (Gause and Weinberg, 1989). This software code decision may not be based on the best system solution, or on the best learning sciences approach, or on the best instructional design approach. Given these coding decisions, one can easily see why a collaborative approach and early definition of the right requirements needed for the learning sciences and instructional design technology is so important.

Fit for Purpose: Alignments of Assessment, Evaluation, and Learning

Another key trend within these chapters is the call for the necessary alignment of assessment and evaluation throughout all levels of the instructional and learning design process. The chapter by Kirschner and Lund took a stand against scientific paradigms being turned into *paradogmas*. The authors described some of the main paradigms used to study education such as behaviorism, cognitivism, and constructivism, and argued that each of them is best adapted to examining different types of problems and issues. They pointed out that educational processes take place within an ecology of education and an educational system made up of learners, educators, technologies, media, and the larger environment. They further argued that given the systemic nature of this ecology, research should integrate different theoretical and methodological perspectives into the objective of improving the quality of education. They introduced the notion of constructive research alignment where the research question studied, the empirical method employed, the analytical techniques used, and the conclusions drawn should all be aligned in a coherent way. They suggested conceptualizing the whole of research in education as being a set of local coherently aligned research methods and processes that allow different paradigms to coexist with each other. In this way, researchers can use each paradigm in its most useful way and collectively work toward solving the main problems and issues in education.

Foshay and Roschelle outlined the concept of educational blueprints, which may include things such as knowledge structures, learning progressions, assessment frameworks, and analyses of learner characteristics or profiles. These are important because, taken together, the blueprints clarify and specify the key structural elements of the design. Both LS and ID hold that learning happens when learners enact activities with the given inputs that lead to desired outcomes. Hence the quality of enactment (i.e., the quality of the implementation and subsequent learning involvement) can significantly mediate the learning process and outcomes. Everything that precedes the outcomes should be coherent with the intended learning gains. Together, the blueprints, learning activities, and planned outcomes are called a *logic model*, because the strength of the logic connecting each element is essential to the quality of the design (see also, Spector, 2016).

Law's chapter contained a historical synopsis on the development of IDT. She included important global trends that showed the trajectory of the research as seen below:

- Shifting from a focus on media and resources to a systems approach in the use of resources and associated processes
- Broadening the focus from utilization to include progressive design, evaluation, development, management, analysis, and organization
- Increasing influence of cognitive and constructivist learning theories on the field
- Changing perception of the role of IDT in relation to the live instructor from being supplemental to being on equal footing
- Changing perception of the function of IDT from improving instruction to facilitating learning and improving performance

Law echoed what others have also stated in their chapters that "the focus of instructional design should be on aligning learning outcomes with assessments, and the design of learning activities should be problem oriented. In this approach subject matter resources would be decided as necessary, based on the pedagogical design." Critical is the reference she makes to Arbesman's "the half-life of facts" (2012), as she points to the importance of understanding the learning process versus going after more specific learning products. She makes a great case for the study of metacognition as it applies to the future of the learning sciences. She argues for the emerging importance of processes such as critical thinking, problem solving, communication, creativity, knowledge building, and digital literacy.

Scaffolding and Cognitive Apprenticeship

According to Pirnay-Dummer and Seel, scaffolding and how it is accomplished, especially as it relates to the efficacy of the learning design, is a key area of overlap between the learning sciences and instructional design. Whether the learning design encourages the layering and construction of schemas, or it is the scaffolding encouraged by a virtual agent, learning designs do not succeed unless this aspect is well defined and thought through. Whether it is completion of a task or creative problem solving, the scaffolding methodology must be well constructed and integrated with assessment and user-driven feedback.

While many of the chapters in this book spoke of scaffolding, it is Hubal and Parsons' chapter on synthetic environments that went into great detail about how the scaffolding works, or how it is internally performed. Hubal and Parsons discussed in great detail how the synthetic environments do a train-up in skills with ever-increasing ambiguity, increasing complexity, and increasing uncertainty and volatility. All this scaffolds as they work to shape a synthetic environment that moves from familiarization and orientation to more sophisticated forms of learner inquiry. After some time in the synthetic environment a student becomes capable of policy formation, develops rules and his/her own heuristics to perform successfully with a given problem type, and eventually learns to generalize to new types of problems. These forms of synthetic environments give both direct and intrinsic support as they can be seen as types of tutoring and highlighting, and they contain numerous help functions. Hubal and Parsons' chapter covered changes to the educational landscape, including implications for human safety, training for dangerous and rare events, critical medical education for life-threatening events, and training for things like medical triage that cannot be captured in any other realistic, humanistic way.

Lajoie discussed an interdisciplinary approach to medical training and education that included among others the use of anthropologists and ethnographers. Lajoie pointed out that when designing specific learning environments, great consideration in the manner in which specific types of knowledge can be scaffolded is critical to that learning context and the larger medical domain. She illustrated this point by discussing a specific blood test result for bilirubin and discusses what the learner must do next based on the outcome of the test. Lajoie discussed some key observations in the area of expertise acquisition for learners in the medical domain and notes that the competence trajectory vector has highlighted superior performers' reliance on domain-specific knowledge and memory and their affinity for self-regulation.

Lajoie talked about the need for "cognitive apprenticeship" in the medical domain and stresses its importance over traditional apprenticeship. She talked about the importance of teaching, mentoring, and being present when the learner reaches an impasse. She discussed the need for the learner to be able to verbalize what was going on so that the mentor/teacher could help scaffold the learning in the moment of confusion. Finally, she discussed the fact that cognitive apprenticeships situate the learning experience in the context of meaningful, realistic tasks where students can experience a situation that might mimic a community of practice where learners work together to accomplish a critical health care task. She discussed a learning environment for clinical reasoning using the cognitive apprenticeship model and some early successes she has had implementing these models in a safe environment to help guide medical decision-making. She introduced the concept of BioWorld and talked about the successes that she has witnessed in this area of medical learning. She introduced us to some very interesting software (FaceReader 6.0 by Noldus) that is used in the medical profession to read emotions to help with possible diagnosis and how it is being used to better understand human behavior and human response.

Evolving Learning Environments and Learning Analytics

New technologies appear to be converging as we approach the much talked about singularity (Kurzweil, 2005; Vinge, 1993) or the moment of convergence of informatics, artificial intelligence, machine learning, knowledge engineering, cognitive computing, robot learning, natural language processing, intelligent tutorial systems, data mining, search algorithms, and face-reading software, among others. We see possible converging technologies as pointing to an even greater need to define the areas of overlap between the learning sciences and instructional design and technologies.

Hubal and Parsons' chapter highlighted the types of decisions and scaffolding that must go on inside the learning sciences in order for the design of virtual learning environments to succeed. According to Hubal and Parsons, synthetic environments not only offer great potential for students to train and practice the physical and cognitive components of social interaction skills in a safe, diverse, and controllable context, they also serve to highly motivate students to explore their virtual environments and demonstrate desirable behaviors they should demonstrate in a real situation. All of this may lead to better retention of the content while performing realistic tasks and taking advantage of the dynamic feedback of the system and virtual agents.

Historically, synthetic environments have been used for training of skills or contexts that tend to be logistically complex or dangerous. While synthetic environments have continued to hold that historic ground, the newer synthetic environments are moving ahead rapidly to pioneer a landscape where use of the intelligent virtual human (VH) is trending towards both social and interactive skills training. These artificially intelligent characters can express themselves both verbally and non-verbally. It is no wonder, therefore, that synthetic environments are very adept at controlling both the *pace* of the instruction, and the *complexity* of the exposure to the learning contexts. These capabilities are then combined with the ability to "feed" the learner more or less data or information based on the system's assessment of the feedback going from the student to the virtual human. This implies that great care and forethought have been given to the number of possible student responses, and that the logical and dialogic clues for the learners' possible responses have been thought through for a series of tripwires or tipping points to have been set up in advance, helping to assess the learners' scaffolding of interlocking knowledge concepts.

The synergistic relationship between instructional design and learning analytics has the potential for improving learning environments in real time. An example of this happens in the designs of mobile applications with embedded GPS tracking, interactive modelling, and social networking assessments. The approach of instructional design includes procedures for planning optimized learning environments. Learning analytics use educational data to provide insights about the effects and effectiveness of various elements and features of learning environments. Ifenthaler offered an overview on the design and analytics of learning environments and reviewed opportunities of learning analytics design which generates valuable insights for planning and optimizing learning environments using educational data in real time. As we move towards the use of Big Data and the

Internet of Things (IoT), we can understand the wisdom of this approach. All of our newer designs interactively capture assessments automatically for the purpose of near real-time feedback and evaluation triangulation.

Similarly, Law commented on the emerging importance of the Society of Learning Analytics Research (SoLAR) and the efforts to incorporate learning analytics into the design process. Law's discussion of the seeming paradox between what learning design researchers are trying to accomplish versus what teachers need to accomplish as they try to shoulder the three-part roles of designer, developer, and evaluator as discussed by Schön (1992) helps us to better understand why these two fields have not yet merged successfully and more importantly, the profound responsibilities, tasks, and goals that each role carries.

Law also differentiated learning designs and their intended purposes in terms of whether the learning design will be readable by a human being (such as a teacher in a learning presentation), or readable by a machine or computer as a preamble and used by other machines or to feed Artificial Intelligence software (Koper, 2006). As we consider whether our designs are going to be readable by a human or only by machines and computers, we have different decisions to make within the designs. A number of other chapter authors link learning design to cybernetics and we can now project that the issue of who or what will read the learning design in the future may end up being quite important in terms of usability of existing designs.

Channels to Continue the Discourse: The Roles of Stakeholders in LS and IDT Communities

The chapter by Reeves and Oh and the chapter by Elen discussed the roles different stakeholders could play to facilitate collaborations between the LS and IDT communities. There are a number of overlapping communities relevant to learning sciences, instructional design and development, and educational technology. The act of going between different communities allows the opportunity for dialogue and collaboration. However, when a scholar goes from one community to another, they may experience a sense of disconnect or a feeling of being an imposter, regardless of their expertise in their familiar community. In addition, the growing globalization and the diversity of global communities are beneficial in the sense that they allow new information and foster new conversations; yet, they also add complexity to the dialogue and make it more difficult to gather and synthesize the proper information, and propel the work forward.

Reeves and Oh hypothesized that the lack of more and better coordination and collaboration among research in the learning sciences and educational technology research was due to the structure of the (faculty researcher) tenure (track), promotion, and award systems currently in place in the US and aboard. Reeves and Oh noted that researchers are generally promoted and awarded within the tenure track based on fierce (research) independence as well as publishing research articles in just the right publications to elicit the most citations and prestigious funding lines. It is easy to see how the pressure to publish swiftly and often flies in the face of the obvious need to collaborate, be more socially responsible in research design, and encourage the greatest positive system impacts for improved design for practitioners. Staying in one community allows one a better chance to rise to leadership rather than moving to different communities. The limited time forces a scholar to stay focused and to choose a limited number of community circles as his or her base. Reeves and Oh recommended that representatives of both communities come together to discuss differences and identify steps towards a more robust shared research agenda that benefit the field of education.

There are some important gaps that need to be bridged as we move to improve our learning research and designs. During their literature review of JLS and ETRD journal articles, Reeves and Oh pointed to the lack of critical theory reviews and analysis. While it is always more difficult to notice something that is "not present" versus seeing something that is present but imperfect, we must make more concerted efforts to do a better job when being critical of our own designs. Reeves and Oh made realistic recommendations about ways and opportunities to correct these oversights, such as using the AERA annual conference venue as an opportunity to convene great minds around specific issues to address the lack of critical theory reviews in a forum where researchers routinely converge and present such ideas. This may be the basis of an action plan needed to correct such gaps. We might also recommend creating a live online discussion forum to capture researchers emerging thoughts and insights (specifically on gap recognition) so that we can effectively compress the time required to resolve such oversights.

Elen considered implications of three roles assumed by members of both communities: that of being a teacher, researcher, and editor. As a teacher, one needs to be critical of one's own epistemological assumptions. As a researcher, there needs to be collaboration between communities. As an editor, one needs to embrace complexity.

Concluding Remarks

Different communities enrich one another and the field. Embracing complexity implies the need to dig deeper, to look for underlying structures and to reveal the underlying mechanisms. This suggests more precision in the formulation of research questions as well as formulating better descriptive frameworks. More importantly, it points to the need to acknowledge the limits of one's own contributions, which then points to the inherent need for more collaboration, complementary approaches, processes, and insights. Researchers and practitioners in both LS and IDT should adopt a decision that helps to recursively depict their sense of overarching values about what is most important as these two fields come together. To what extent are we in need of speaking from exactly the same base, and in which cases should we intentionally preserve the nuances of the variations in order to elicit deeper understanding of the diversity of that which we intend to unite? We close with these questions with the hope that answers will be collaboratively pursued.

References

Arbesman, S. (2012). *The half-life of facts: Why everything we know has an expiration date*. New York: Penguin.

Bransford, J. D., Brown, A. L., & Cocking, R. R. (Eds.) (2000). *How people learn: Brain, mind, experience, and school*. Washington, DC: National Academy of Sciences.

Davidsen, P. I., & Spector, J. M. (2015). Critical reflections: Symposium on system dynamics. *Simulation & Gaming, 46*(3–), 430–444.

Gagné, R. M. (1965). *The conditions of learning*. New York: Holt, Rinehart and Winston.

Gagné, R. M. (1992). The events of instruction. In R. M. Gagné, L. J. Briggs, & W. W. Wager (Eds.), *Principles of instructional design* (4th ed., pp. 185–204). New York: Harcourt Brace Jovanovich College Publishers

Gagné, R. M., & Merrill, M. D. (1990). Integrative goals for instructional design. *Educational Technology Research and Development, 38*(1), 23–30.

Gause, D. C. & Weinberg, G. M. (1989). *Exploring requirements: Quality before design*. New York: Dorset House Publishing.

Herbart, J. F. (1806). *Allgemeine Pädagogik aus dem Zweck der Erziehung abgeleitet* [Common pedagogy derived from the purpose of education]. Göttingen: Röwer.

Klir, G. J. (1972). *An approach to general systems theory*. New York: Van Nostrand Reinhold.

Koper, R. (2006). Editorial: Current research in learning design. *Journal of Educational Technology & Society, 9*(1), 13–22.

Kurzweil, R. (2005). *The singularity is near: When humans transcend biology*. New York: Viking Press.

Natividad, G. B. d. R. (2016). *An analysis of educational technology publications: Who, what and where in the last 20 years* (Doctoral dissertation). University of North Texas, Department of Learning Technologies, Denton, TX.

Reigeluth, C. M. (1983). *Instructional-design theories and models: An overview of their current status*. Hillsdale, NJ: Erlbaum.

Scardamalia, M. & Bereiter, C. (2014). Knowledge building and knowledge creation. In R. K. Sawyer (Ed.), *The Cambridge handbook of the learning sciences* (2nd ed., pp. 397–417). Cambridge, UK: Cambridge University Press.

Schön, D. A. (1992). The theory of inquiry: Dewey's legacy to education. *Curriculum Inquiry, 22*(2), 119–139.

Schwartz, D. L. & Martin, T. (2004). Inventing to prepare for future learning: The hidden efficiency of encouraging original student production in statistics instruction. *Cognition and Instruction, 22*(2), 129–184.

Senge, P. (1990). *The fifth discipline: The art and practice of the learning organization*. New York: Currency Doubleday.

Skinner, B. F. (1954). The science of learning and the art of teaching. *The Harvard Educational Review, 24* (2), 86–97.

Spector, J. M. (2016). Program evaluation. In J. M. Spector, B. B. Lockee, & M. D. Childress (Eds.), *Learning, design and technology: An international compendium of theory, research, practice and policy*. New York: Springer.

Vinge, V. (1993). The coming technology singularity: How to survive in the post-human era. *NASA Vision 21 Symposium paper: Interdisciplinary science and engineering in the era of cyberspace* (pp. 11–22). San Diego, CA.

von Glasersfeld, E. (1995). *Radical constructivism: A way of knowing and learning.* Studies in Mathematics Education Series: 6. Bristol, PA: Falmer Press.

Willmann, O. (1889). *Didaktik als Bildungslehre nach ihren Beziehungen zur Socialforschung und zur Geschichte der Bildung* [Didactics as educational teachings after its relation to social research and the history of education], Vol 2. Braunschweig: Vieweg.

CONTRIBUTORS

Dr. Jan Elen is Full Professor of Educational Technology and Teacher Education at KU Leuven, Belgium. His dissertation (under the supervision of Joost Lowyck at the KU Leuven) pertained to the issue of the transition from description to prescription in instructional design. His main research interests relate to the design of blended learning for vulnerable learners, the use of tools in digital learning environments, and supporting the development of critical thinking. He teaches in the domains of educational technology and teacher education. He is one of the founders of the special interest group on instructional design in the European Association for Research on Learning and Instruction (EARLI). He is editor of *Instructional Science* and has been co-editor of the *Handbook of Research for Educational Communications and Technology* (fourth edition).

Dr. Wellesley R. (Rob) Foshay consults on e-learning and education technology product strategy and design for the K-12 and training markets. He advises Ph.D. students in the field for the University of North Texas at Denton, and for Walden University. He is also a Practice Leader for The Institute for Performance Improvement (TIfPI). His experience includes management of educational research, product strategy, and design for Texas Instruments Education Technology Group, PLATO Learning, Inc., and Applied Learning, Inc. He is a founding Certified Performance Technologist. He has published and presented frequently on Instructional Design, Learning Science, technology and education, and Human Performance Technology.

Dr. Andrew S. Gibbons holds a faculty emeritus position at Brigham Young University in the Department of Instructional Psychology and Technology.

His current research focuses on the architecture of instructional designs. His latest book, *An Architectural Approach to Instructional Design* (Routledge, 2014), brings together the concepts of design layers, design languages, and modularity. Gibbons has published a domain theory of Model-Centered Instruction, and is currently studying the use of layers, languages, and modularity as tools for creating instructional systems that are adaptive, generative, and scalable.

Dr. Robert Hubal is at the University of North Carolina Eshelman School of Pharmacy, where he is involved in research focusing on using technology intelligently to better train and assess knowledge and skills. He has conducted basic and applied research in decision-making, mental modeling, vigilance, intelligent tutoring, linguistic analyses, patterns of life, scientific visualization, codability, and usability. He has applied these research results to everyday and specialized domains such as clinical assessment of social and interpersonal skills, improved patient communications, law enforcement interactions, warfighter/civilian sociocultural engagement, survey non-response, and driving skills assessment.

Dr. Dirk Ifenthaler is Chair and Professor for Learning, Design and Technology at the University of Mannheim, Germany, Adjunct Professor at Curtin University, Australia, and Affiliate Research Scholar at the University of Oklahoma, USA. His previous roles include Professor and Director, Centre for Research in Digital Learning at Deakin University, Australia, Manager of Applied Research and Learning Analytics at Open Universities, Australia, and Professor for Applied Teaching and Learning Research at the University of Potsdam, Germany. He was a 2012 Fulbright Scholar-in-Residence at the Jeannine Rainbolt College of Education at the University of Oklahoma, USA. Dirk Ifenthaler's research focuses on the intersection of cognitive psychology, educational technology, learning science, data analytics, and computer science. His research outcomes include numerous co-authored books, book series, book chapters, journal articles, and international conference papers, as well as successful grant funding in Australia, Germany, and the USA—see Dirk's website for a full list of scholarly outcomes at www.ifenthaler.info. He is editor-in-chief of the Springer journal *Technology, Knowledge and Learning*.

Dr. Paul A. Kirschner is University Distinguished Professor at the Open University of the Netherlands. He is also a Visiting Professor of Education with a special emphasis on Learning and Interaction in Teacher Education at the University of Oulu, Finland. He is an internationally recognized expert in his field. He is a past President (2010–2011) of the International Society for the Learning Sciences and a former member of the Dutch Educational Council and, as such, was advisor to the Minister of Education (2000–2004). He is also a member of the Scientific Technical Council of the Foundation for University Computing Facilities (SURF WTR), chief editor of *Journal of Computer Assisted Learning* and associate editor of *Computers in Human Behavior*. As for books, he is co-author of the recently released book *Urban Myths about Learning and Education* as well as of the highly successful book *Ten Steps to Complex Learning*, and editor of two other books (*Visualizing Argumentation* and *What We Know about CSCL*).

Dr. Susanne P. Lajoie is Professor and Canadian Research Chair Tier 1 in Advanced Technologies for Learning in Authentic Settings in the Department of Educational and Counselling Psychology at McGill University and a member of the Centre for Medical Education. She is a Fellow of the American Psychological Association and the American Educational Research Association. Dr. Lajoie explores how theories of learning and affect can be used to guide the design of advanced technology-rich learning environments in different domains, i.e., medicine, mathematics, history, etc.

Dr. Nancy Law is a professor in the Division of Information Technology in Education, Faculty of Education at the University of Hong Kong. She served as the Founding Director of the Centre for Information Technology in Education (CITE) for 15 years from 1998. She has served on a number of policy advisory boards/working groups related to ICT in education for the University of Hong Kong, the Hong Kong SAR Government, and other community groups. She was a core member of the International Study Centre for the IEA SITES 2006 Study, served on the Editorial and Publication Committee of the IEA, the Technology Working Group of the Cisco-Intel-Microsoft Project on Assessment and Teaching of 21st Century Skills, and the Board of Directors of the International Society of the Learning Sciences (ISLS) and the Society for Learning Analytics and Research (SoLAR). She is currently an Executive Editor of the *International Journal of Computer-Supported Collaborative Learning*. She has provided expert input/consultancy to national and international agencies such as the European Commission, UNESCO, and OECD on various aspects of technology-enhanced learning. Her interests include learning design, technology-enhanced learning innovations, models of ICT integration and change leadership, CSCL, and the use of expressive and exploratory computer-based learning environments.

Dr. Lin Lin is Associate Professor of Learning Technologies at the University of North Texas. She received her doctoral degree in Communication, Media, and Learning Technologies Design from Teachers College, Columbia University. Lin's research interest lies at the intersections of new media and technologies, cognitive psychology, and education. In the past years, she has published studies on media multitasking, online learning, and game-based learning in a wide range of journals such as the *Proceedings of the National Academy of Sciences, Computers and Education, Journal of Educational Computing Research, Computers in the Schools, Learning, Media, and Technology, and Educational Technology Research and Development*. Lin is Associate Editor of the *International Journal of Smart Technology and Learning* (IJSmartTL). Lin has held leadership positions in AECT, AERA and SITE and remains active in those professional associations.

Dr. Kristine Lund is CNRS Senior Research Engineer in the ICAR laboratory at the University of Lyon and served as the deputy director of ICAR for 4 years (2007–2010). She is head of an ICAR research team focusing on cognition in collaborative settings, Chief Scientific Officer at the www.Cognik.net company, and one of its three co-founders. She is a member of the Board of Directors of the Society of the Learning Sciences (ISLS). Dr. Lund earned her Ph.D. in Cognitive Science from the University of Grenoble, a master's degree in Artificial Intelligence from the University of Paris, and a bachelor of arts degree in Computer Science from Gustavus Adolphus College in Minnesota. Her interdisciplinary background led her to focus her research program on better understanding the factors that influence how small groups build knowledge together. She is co-editor of *Productive Multivocality in the Analysis of Group Interactions.*

Dr. Ellen B. Meier is Director of the Center for Technology and School Change, and Associate Professor of Practice, Computing, and Education at Teachers College, Columbia University. She also coordinates the Technology Specialist Certification Program for the Department of Math, Science and Technology. Her research is focused on the emerging role of technology in creating engaging, authentic learning environments, particularly for urban students. The Center has worked teachers and administrators to identify the factors that influence effective use of technology. The resulting model, *Innovating Instruction,* is currently being refined with support from the National Science Foundation. Meier has also worked with educators in Ghana, Bulgaria, Mexico, Chile, China, and Korea. She is Co-Chair for the University of the State of New York's Technology Policy and Practice Council, which advises the New York Board of Regents on technology issues, and serves on the New York Online Advisory Council. She is a Co-Editor for the CITE Journal, *Contemporary Issues in Teachers and Teacher Education.*

Dr. Eunjung Grace Oh is Assistant Professor in the Human Resource Development Division of the Department of Education Policy, Organization and Leadership at the University of Illinois at Urbana-Champaign. She has diverse professional experience in higher education and corporate training as an HRD specialist, instructional designer, instructor, and consultant in Korea and the United States. Prior to teaching at UIUC, she taught at the University of Georgia and the Georgia College and State University. Her research interests include (1) innovating and understanding teaching and learning experiences in technology-enhanced learning environments, with a particular focus on the design of and support for learning in online and blended learning environments, (2) understanding different generational groups of workforce and their use of and perspectives on technology and ethics in digital world, and (3) conducting design-based research as a methodological approach. Her Ph.D. is in Learning, Design and Technology, earned at the University of Georgia.

Dr. Thomas D. Parsons is a Clinical Neuropsychologist and Associate Professor of Psychology at the University of North Texas. His work integrates neuropsychology and simulation technologies for novel assessment, modeling, and training of neurocognitive and affective processes. In addition to his patents for the eHarmony.com Matching System, he has invented and validated virtual reality-based assessments of attention, spatial abilities, memory, and executive functions. He uses neural networks and machine learning to model mechanisms underlying reinforcement learning, decision making, working memory, and inhibitory control. He has over 100 publications in peer reviewed journals and book chapters. His contributions to neuropsychology were recognized when he received the 2013 National Academy of Neuropsychology Early Career Achievement award. In 2014, he was awarded Fellow status in the National Academy of Neuropsychology.

Dr. Pablo N. Pirnay-Dummer is Associate Professor for Research Methods in Psychology at the Brandenburg Medical School Theodor Fontane and head of the privately funded ParaDocks® Research Labs. He graduated from the University of Freiburg, Germany in 2006. His research and publications are located in the area of language, cognition, learning, expertise, and technology with a particular interest on the use of language in learning processes. Also, some of his applied work is on model-based knowledge management and organizational learning. He developed computer-linguistic language-oriented knowledge assessment methodologies that are built to assess, analyze, and compare individual and group models of expertise. Among other research interests, he also developed the web-based training framework L-MoSim (Learner Model Simulation), including new approaches to automated tasks synthesis for complex problem solving.

Dr. Thomas C. Reeves is Professor Emeritus of Learning, Design, and Technology in the College of Education at the University of Georgia. He earned his Ph.D. in the Division of Instructional Design, Development, and Evaluation at Syracuse University with a concentration in program evaluation. He is a former Fulbright Lecturer in Peru and has been an invited speaker in the USA and more than 30 other countries. From 1997–2000, he was the editor of the *Journal of Interactive Learning Research*. In 2003, he received the AACE Fellowship Award from the Association for the Advancement of Computing in Education, in 2010 he was made a Fellow of the Australasian Society for Computers in Learning in Tertiary Education (ASCILITE), and in 2013 he received the Lifetime Award from the International Association for Development of the Information Society (IADIS) as well as the David H. Jonassen Excellence in Research Award by the Association for Educational Communications and Technology (AECT). His books include *Interactive Learning Systems Evaluation* (with John Hedberg), *A Guide to Authentic E-Learning* (with Jan Herrington and Ron Oliver), *Conducting Educational Design Research* (with Susan McKenney), and *MOOCs and Open Education around the World* (with Curt Bonk, Mimi Lee, and Tom Reynolds).

Contributors **231**

Dr. Jeremy Roschelle directs the Center for Technology in Learning at SRI International, a nonprofit research organization. He also leads the Center for Innovative Research in Cyberlearning, which hosts the community for the advanced learning technology projects funded by the National Science Foundation. His research investigates potential improvements to mathematics learning and assessment that build on learning science principles and have the potential to serve low-income students at scale. His projects build on a range of rigorous methods, including Evidence-Centered Design, randomized controlled trials, and design-based research.

Dr. Norbert M. Seel, professor emeritus, graduated from Saarland University in 1975. From 1998 to 2012 he was a distinguished professor in the field of education with a focus on research on learning and instruction. Until September 2012 he was the chair of the Department of Educational Science at the Albert Ludwig University in Freiburg, Germany. From 1992 to 1998 he was Professor at the Technical University of Dresden where he also was the Dean of the School of Education. Currently, he is affiliated with the National Research University: Higher School of Economics in Moscow, Russia. His research interests include model-based learning and thinking, inductive reasoning and complex problem solving, and the investigation of exploratory learning, creativity, and processes of decision making in instructional design. Dr. Seel has published or edited more than 20 books as well as more than 200 refereed journal articles and book chapters in the area of cognitive psychology, research on learning and instruction. He is the editor of the *Encyclopedia of the Sciences of Learning*.

Dr. J. Michael Spector is Professor and former Chair of Learning Technologies at the University of North Texas. He was previously Professor of Educational Psychology and Instructional Technology at the University of Georgia and Professor of Instructional Systems at Florida State University. He served as Chair of Instructional Design, Development and Evaluation at Syracuse University and Director of the Educational Information Science and Technology Research Program at the University of Bergen. He earned a Ph.D. in Philosophy from the University of Texas at Austin. His research focuses on intelligent support for instructional design, assessing learning in complex domains, and technology integration in education. Dr. Spector is a Past President of the Association for Educational and Communications Technology. He is editor of *Educational Technology Research & Development* and serves on numerous other editorial boards. He edited the third and fourth editions of the *Handbook of Research on Educational Communications and Technology*, as well as the *Encyclopedia of Educational Technology*, and has more than 150 publications to his credit.

Dr. David D. Williams is a professor emeritus from the Instructional Psychology and Technology Department at Brigham Young University, specializing in evaluation. He conducts and studies evaluations of teaching and learning in different settings. His research interest is the interaction among stakeholders as they use values to shape criteria and standards for evaluating learning environments. In recent work, he has been conducting interviews with the leaders in the field of evaluation to study their formal and informal evaluation lives and how they use evaluation to enhance their learning.

Dr. Allan H. K. Yuen is currently an Associate Professor in Information and Technology Studies and Director of the Centre for Information Technology in Education (CITE), Faculty of Education at the University of Hong Kong. His primary research interests focus on technology adoption and educational change, evaluation of e-learning and pedagogical innovations, social and cultural aspects of ICT use, and the digital divide in education. Dr. Yuen is the Editor of the *Journal of Communication and Education*, and has more than 110 publications including journal articles, book chapters, and books. He has served as Vice Chairman of the Hong Kong Educational Research Association (HKERA), and President of the Hong Kong Association for Educational Communications and Technology (HKAECT).

INDEX

Page numbers with f and t refer to figures and tables.

academic turf wars 64
analytic access 27
apprenticeships 72, 110–3, 116, 219–20
artificial intelligence (AI) 17–8, 176, 208, 213, 221–2
artificial learning 17–8
Asian perspective 119–28
assessments: alignments of 218–9; of instructional design 72–3, 218–9; of learning environments 203–4; in learning medicine 113–6; of learning objectives 159–70; of learning sciences 72–3, 218–9; of skills training 159–70; strategies for 165–70; in synthetic environments 165–70; *see also* evaluations
association, laws of 13
associative psychology 13–4
augmented reality (AR) environments 157, 164–5, 213

behaviorism 9, 14, 37–8, 98, 218
best practices 138, 158, 161–2, 165, 178

Center for Technology and School Change (CTSC) 140–8, 143t, 215
cognitive apprenticeships 72, 110–3, 116, 219–20
cognitive load theory 23–4

cognitive psychology 2–4, 16–7, 24, 28, 37–8, 132
cognitive science 2, 25, 65–7, 108–9, 214
cognitive system of learning 19–21
cognitive theories 16–9, 70, 204
cognitivism 37–40, 218
coherence epistemology 25
collaboration challenges 4–7
collaboration imperative 131–48
collaboration implications 134–5
collaboration opportunities 139–46
Common Core State Standards (CCSS) 136–9, 145–6
conflict and puzzlement principle 27
connectionism 13–4, 40
connectivism 40
constructionism 40
constructive research alignment 45–6, 45f; *see also* research
constructivism 16, 38–9, 82, 218
contemporary research 18–9
cybernetic activity 94, 99; *see also* instructional design

de-contextualization 27
design-based research 139–40; *see also* research
design patterns 192–7, 204
design science 53–4, 69, 186, 195–9
diagnostic access 27
dialectical perspective 127–8

digital tools 42, 131–43, 146; *see also* technology
diversity: of experience 64; of global communities 222–4; of perspectives 83–4, 127–8; of surfaces 27
domain knowledge 69–73, 110–2, 116, 214

e-learning technologies 65–6, 125–6, 191–2; *see also* technology
editors 85–6
education: collaboration imperative 131–48; collaboration implications 134–5; ecology of 41–5, 42f; educators and 41; environments for 42–3, 152–78; goals of 43–5; high-stakes testing 73, 93, 138; improving 135–9; interventions 138–9; journals about 53–5; learners and 41; media and 42; research on 18–9, 43–7; standards for 136–9, 145–6; technology and 42; *see also* learning environments; learning sciences
education policies 120–4, 120t
educational materials 153–78; *see also* instructional design
educational technology: collaboration imperative 131–48; collaboration implications 134–5; definitions of 132–3; digital tools 42, 131–43, 146; fields of 51–2, 59–60, 147, 186–91, 198–9, 217; journals about 53–5; Pasteur's Quadrant and 65, 134–6, 135f, 147, 215; *see also* instructional design and technology
educational technology researchers: comparing 56–61, 56t, 57t; goals of 52–3; implications of 60–1; methodologies of 52–3
engaged learning 147, 152–3, 153f, 167, 205–7; *see also* learning
epistemic access 27
essentialism 40
evaluations: alignments of 218–9; analyzing 88–104; descriptions of 91–2; emphasis on 91; escalation of 90; factors in 90, 96, 100–2, 101f; as formal practice 88–9; instructional design and 88–104; of learning objectives 159–70; stagnation of 92; superficiality of 91–2; symmetry of 89–90; in synthetic environments 165–70; theory development in 91; for unifying theories 89; *see also* assessments

false dichotomies 40–1, 40t
"far transfer" concept 71–3, 213
frame creation 96–8
functionalism 13

gain-practice-demonstrate framework 155–6, 155f
goals: of education 43–5; of instructional design 1–7; for learning environments 65, 154–62; of learning sciences 1–7; of learning scientists 52–3; multiplicity of 27; of researchers 52–3

hands-on skills 153, 156–7, 173
high-stakes testing 73, 93, 138; *see also* testing
Human Performance Improvement (HPI) 64–5, 72, 99
hypothesis testing 52, 57–60, 214; *see also* testing

idealism 40
inductive testing 21, 27; *see also* testing
informatics 17, 45, 221
information and communication technology (ICT): access to 73–4; in education policies 120–4, 120t; role of 73–4, 119–20, 123–8, 148, 217; stakeholder experiences in 120, 217; *see also* educational technology
Innovating Instruction model 142–6, 143t
inquiry-based learning 134; *see also* learning
instructional design (ID): analyzing 88–104; assessment of 72–3, 218–9; challenges of 64–77; as cybernetic activity 94, 99; definitions of 92–100; domain knowledge and 69–73, 110–2, 116, 214; editors and 85–6; evaluations and 88–104; goals of 1–7; implications of 79–87, 80f, 95–9; journals about 2–4, 85–6; knowledge structures for 71–2; learning analytics design and 202–8; learning design and 186–99; learning sciences and 64–77, 212–24; learning trajectories for 71–2; as logical exercise 95–9; mental models for 71–2; middle ground of 79–87, 80f, 214–5; new literature on 92; optimizing 202–3; as process 92–3; researchers and 55, 84–7, 102, 222–4; scalability of 73–6, 217; teachers and 82–6

Index **235**

instructional design and technology (IDT): analytics on 202–8; Asian perspective on 119–28; background on 1–6; challenges for 4–7, 189–90; collaboration challenges 4–7; differences and 214–5; evaluation of 88–104; fields of 40, 45, 51–2, 59–60, 82–3, 115–6, 119–21, 128, 147, 186–91, 198–9, 217; goals of 1–7; introduction to 1–6; journals about 2–4; learning design and 186–99; learning technology and 127, 165, 190–1; middle ground of 79–87, 80f, 214–5; opportunities for 189–90; overview of 3–7, 186–8; reconsidering 88–104; research and 188–9; similarities and 214–5; solutions for 64–77; stakeholder roles in 222–3; systems thinking approach to 122–3, 188–9, 216–9; technical representation of 191–3; terminology of 1–7
instructional media (IM) 127, 187–90, 198
intelligence: artificial intelligence 17–8, 176, 208, 213, 221–2; capabilities of 9–11, 10f; characteristics of 9–10
Internet of Things (IoT) 221–2
interpretation network 19
interventions 138–9

journals 2–4, 6, 53–5, 85–6, 223

knowledge: domain knowledge 69–73, 110–2, 116, 214; knowledge-centered environment 203–4; learning trajectories for 71–2; mental models of 71–2; structures of 71–2; testing 167–8; types of 66–7, 70–2, 108–12, 116, 220
knowledge tests 167–8; *see also* testing

language and learning 28–30, 29f
laws of association 13
LeAP tool 207
learning: apprenticeships for 72, 110–3, 116, 219–20; architecture of 19–21, 20f; art of 8; assessments of 218–9; cognitive system of 19–21; concept of 8–12, 71–3, 212–3; contemporary research on 18–9; diagnostic access to 27; ecology of 41–5, 42f; educators and 41; engaged learning 147, 152–3, 153f, 167, 205–7; "far transfer" concept of 212–3; focus of 39, 119–24, 217; historical review of 11–8; inquiry-based learning 134; language and 28–30, 29f; mechanisms for promoting 109–10; model-based learning 20f, 24–8, 213; pillars of 122–4; problem-based learning 55, 192, 215; project-based learning 141–6; reasoning and 10–1; research-based learning 139; schema-based learning 20f, 21–4, 213; teaching and 18, 31; technology-based learning 213; transfer of 71–3, 212–3; trial-and-error learning 13–4; *see also* education
learning analytics design: artificial intelligence and 208, 221–2; evolving analytics 220–2; field of 186; instructional design and 202–8; introduction to 202; LeAP tool for 207; learning environments and 203–8, 220–2; MAPLET Framework for 204–5; opportunities for 202, 207–8, 221–2; perspectives of 206–9; predictive perspective of 206–7; real-time perspective of 206; summative perspective of 206
learning design: concept of 204; design patterns 192–7, 204; fields of 186–91; instructional design and 186–99; learning technology and 190–1; pedagogical theory and 193–7; teaching and 195–8; technical representation of 191–3
learning environments: analytics on 203–8, 220–2; assessment-centered environment 203–4; community-centered environment 203–4; creating 147, 202–3; design patterns for 192–7, 204; designing 65, 82–5, 108–13, 147; educational system and 42–3; engaging 108; evolving strategies for 220–2; goals for 65, 154–62; improving 202–7, 221; knowledge-centered environment 203–4; learner-centered environment 203–4; learning analytics design for 202–8; logic models in 66–9, 67f, 218; for medical students 108–12, 116; model-based environments 24–7, 213; objectives for 65, 153–78; optimizing 202–7, 221; perspectives for 203–4; self-regulated environment 114, 204; for skills training 152–78; student-centered environments 111, 123–4, 127–8; synthetic environments 152–78; technology-based environments 204,

213; technology-rich environments 112, 116; types of 203–4; *see also* learning sciences
learning management system (LMS) 71, 191–3, 197–9, 205–7, 216
learning objectives (LOs): achieving 154–5; assessment of 159–70; best practices for 158, 161–2, 165, 178; defining 154; evaluation of 159–70; gain-practice-demonstrate framework for 155–6, 155f; for learning environments 65, 154–62; part-task trainers 156–7, 167; performance measures for 155, 159–68; performance tests for 167–8; requirements for 159–68; for student needs 154–5; for synthetic environments 153–78
Learning Sciences Lab (LSL) 125–6
learning sciences (LS): applications for medicine 108–16; approach to 108–9; Asian perspective on 119–28; assessment of 72–3, 218–9; background on 1–6; challenges of 4–7, 64–77; collaboration challenges 4–7; collaboration imperatives 131–48; collaboration implications 134–5; continuing discourse on 212–24; definitions of 132–4; differences and 214–5; domain knowledge and 69–73, 110–2, 116, 214; editors and 85–6; evolving strategies for 126, 220–2; fields of 17, 40, 45, 51–2, 59–60, 82–3, 115–6, 119–21, 128, 131–3, 147, 198–9, 217; goals of 1–7; historical review of 11–8; implications of 79–87, 80f; instructional design and 64–77, 212–24; introduction to 1–6, 8–11; journals about 2–4, 6, 53–5, 85–6, 223; knowledge structures for 71–2; learning trajectories for 71–2; medicine and 108–16; mental models for 71–2; middle ground of 79–87, 80f, 214–5; overview of 2–4, 8–31; Pasteur's Quadrant and 65, 134–6, 135f, 147, 215; practice environments for 152–78; researchers and 69, 84–7, 102, 108, 135, 139, 147, 223–4; roots of 133–4; similarities and 214–5; skills training for 152–78; solutions for 64–77; stakeholder roles in 222–3; synthetic environments and 152–78; systems thinking approach to 122–3, 188–9, 216–9; teachers and 82–6; terminology of 1–7; training

environments for 152–78; *see also* learning environments
learning scientists: comparing 56–61, 56t, 57t; goals of 52–3; methodologies of 52–3
learning technology 127, 165, 190–1; *see also* technology
logic models 66–9, 67f, 218
logical implications 95–9

machine learning 17–8, 213, 221
MAPLET Framework 204–5
math wars 36
medicine: apprenticeships in 110–3, 116; evidence of learning in 113–6; instructional methods in 112–5; knowledge types for 108–12, 116; learning assessments in 113–6; learning environments for 108–12, 116; learning sciences and 108–16; research in 108–16
middle ground: cherishing 79–87; finding 36–47; implications of 79–87; instructional design and 79–87, 80f, 214–5; learning sciences and 79–87, 80f, 214–5
model-based learning 20f, 24–8, 213; *see also* learning

National Institute of Education (NIE) 125–7
naturalism 40
No Child Left Behind (NCLB) 136, 138

objectivism 82, 85
operant conditioning model 14
outcomes-based testing 166; *see also* testing

paradigm wars 36
paradogmas 36, 47, 218
part-task trainers (PTTs) 156–7, 167
Pasteur's Quadrant 65, 134–6, 135f, 147, 215
pedagogical design patterns 193–7
performance measures 27, 73, 155, 159–68
performance tests 167–8; *see also* testing
practice environments 152–78
pragmatism 40
problem-based learning 55, 192, 215; *see also* learning

professional development (PD) 5, 75, 136–48, 215
project-based learning 141–6; *see also* learning

reasoning 10–1
remediation 158, 160, 167–8
research: carrying out 43–5; constructive alignment of 45–6, 45f; contemporary research 11, 18–9, 213; design-based research 139–40; implications of 60–1; instructional design and technology 188–9; methods of 46–7
research-based learning 139; *see also* learning
researchers: educational technology researchers 52–61, 56t, 57t; instructional design and 55, 84–7, 102, 222–4; learning sciences and 69, 84–7, 102, 108, 135, 139, 147, 223–4

scaffolding concepts 67–8, 109–16, 137–46, 154–62, 215, 219–20
scalability 73–6, 217
schema-based learning 20f, 21–4, 213; *see also* learning
school change 140–8, 143t, 215
simulation systems 157–8, 170; *see also* synthetic environments
skills training: assessments for 159–70; educational materials for 153–78; effectiveness requirements for 168–9; examples of 170–8; learning environments for 152–78; performance measures for 155, 159–68; performance tests for 167–8; skills decay 169–70; synthetic environments for 152–78, 217–21
social information processing (SIP) 172
social interaction skills 152, 156, 221
stakeholder experiences 120, 217
stakeholder roles 222–3
standardized testing 91, 136–8; *see also* testing
student data, capturing 159–60
synthetic environments (SEs): assessments in 165–70; best practices for 158, 161–2, 165, 178; computer game design and 152, 156–8, 163–5; educational materials for 153–78; effectiveness requirements for 168–9; evaluations in 165–70; examples of 170–8; gain-practice-demonstrate framework for 155–6, 155f; health-related examples of 170–3, 171f; interactivity in 164–5; law enforcement examples of 173–5, 173f; learning objectives for 153–78; learning sciences and 152–78; measurement in 165–70; military examples of 173–5, 173f; overview of 152–3; part-task trainers 156–7, 167; performance measures for 155, 159–68; performance tests for 167–8; presentation of materials for 162–5; simulation systems and 157–8, 170; skills decay 169–70; for skills training 152–78, 217–21; student control in 158–9; student data for 159–60; technologies and 152–78; tutorial roles in 158–61; virtual humans in 153, 156–64, 169–76, 171f, 173f, 176f, 213, 221; virtual school examples of 175–6, 176f
systems thinking approach 122–3, 188–9, 216–9

teaching: art of 8, 213; defining 8; as design science 195–9; educators and 41; instructional design and 82–6; learning and 18, 31; learning design and 195–8; learning sciences and 82–6; professional development for 5, 75, 136–48, 215
technology: digital tools 42, 131–43, 146; e-learning technologies 65–6, 125–6, 191–2; education and 42, 51–2, 59–60; fields of 51–2, 59–60, 147, 198–9; learning design and 190–1; learning technology 127, 165, 190–1; media and 42; role of 198–9, 217; school change and 140–8, 143t, 215; synthetic environments and 152–78; technology-based learning 213; *see also* instructional design and technology
technology researchers: comparing 56–61, 56t, 57t; goals of 52–3; implications of 60–1; methodologies of 52–3; *see also* research
technology-rich environment (TRE) 112, 116
testing: factors in 101–2, 101f; high-stakes testing 73, 93, 138; hypothesis testing 52, 57–60, 214; inductive testing 21, 27; judging and 100, 101f; knowledge tests 167–8; outcomes-based testing 166;

performance tests 167–8; standardized testing 91, 136–8
TOTE (test-operate-test-exit) 99–100
training environments 152–78; *see also* learning environments
trial-and-error learning 13–4
turf wars 64

tutorial roles 158–61
tutorial systems 17, 160–6, 188, 221

virtual humans (VHs) 153, 156–64, 169–76, 171f, 173f, 176f, 213, 221
virtual reality (VR) environments 157–8, 164–5